Specially Designed Instruction

SPECIAL EDUCATION LAW, POLICY, AND PRACTICE

Series Editors
Mitchell L. Yell, PhD, University of South Carolina
David F. Bateman, PhD, American Institutes for Research

The *Special Education Law, Policy, and Practice* series highlights current trends and legal issues in the education of students with disabilities. The books in this series link legal requirements, evidence-based instruction, and practical applications for working with students with disabilities. The titles are designed to be textbooks for general education and special education preservice education programs and also for practicing teachers, administrators, principals, school counselors, school psychologists, parents, and others interested in improving the lives of students. The series is committed to research-based practices to provide appropriate and meaningful educational programming for students with disabilities and their families.

Titles in Series

Sexuality Education for Students with Disabilities by T. C. Gibbon, E. A. Harkins Monaco, and D. F. Bateman

The Essentials of Special Education Law by A. M. Markelz and D. F. Bateman

Developing Educationally Meaningful and Legally Sound IEPs by M. L. Yell, D. F. Bateman, and J. G. Shriner

Creating Positive Elementary Classrooms: Preventing Behavior Challenges to Promote Learning by S. Smith and M. L. Yell

Service Animals in Schools: Legal, Educational, Administrative, and Strategic Handling Aspects by A. O. Papalia, K. B. Ewoldt, and D. F. Bateman

Evidence-Based Practices for Supporting Individuals with Autism Spectrum Disorder edited by L. C. Chezan, K. Wolfe, and E. Drasgow

Special Education Law Annual Review 2021 by D. F. Bateman, M. L Yell, and K. P. Brady

Dispute Resolution Under the IDEA: Understanding, Avoiding, and Managing Special Education Disputes by D.F. Bateman, M. L. Yell, and J. S Dorego

Advocating for the Common Good: People, Politics, Process, and Policy on Capitol Hill by J. E. West

Related Services in Special Education: Working Together as a Team by L. Goran and D. F. Bateman

The Essentials of Special Education Advocacy by A. M. Markelz, S. A. Nagro, K. Monnin, and D. F. Bateman

Disability and Motor Behavior: A Handbook of Research by A. S. Brian and P. S. Haibach-Beach

Supporting and Accommodating Students with Special Health Care Needs by A. D. S. Angelov and M. Rattermann

You're Hired! Practical Strategies for Guiding Individuals with Autism Spectrum Disorder to Competitive Employment by P. S. Arter, T. B. H. Brown, and J. Barna

Unraveling Dyslexia: A Guide for Teachers and Families by K. L. Sayeski

Disability, Intersectionality, and Belonging in Special Education: Socioculturally Sustaining Practices by E. A. Harkins Monaco, L. L. Stansberry Brusnahan, M. C. Fuller, and M. Odima Jr.

The Educator's Guide to Action Research: Practical Connections for Implementation of Data-Driven Decision-Making by M. E. Little, D. D. Slanda, and E. Cramer

The Essentials of Special Education Research by A. M. Markelz and B. Riden

The Classroom Teacher's Guide to Special Education: Essential Knowledge, Skills, and Mindsets by D. D. Slanda, L. Pike, and M. E. Little

Specially Designed Instruction: The Definitive Guide by M. P. Weiss, M. N. Faggella-Luby, L. Goran, and D. F. Bateman

For a full list of books in this series, visit https://www.bloomsbury.com/us/series/special-education-law-policy-and-practice/

Specially Designed Instruction

The Definitive Guide

Margaret P. Weiss
Michael N. Faggella-Luby
Lisa Goran
David F. Bateman

BLOOMSBURY ACADEMIC
NEW YORK • LONDON • OXFORD • NEW DELHI • SYDNEY

BLOOMSBURY ACADEMIC

Bloomsbury Publishing Inc, 1359 Broadway, New York, NY 10018, USA
Bloomsbury Publishing Plc, 50 Bedford Square, London, WC1B 3DP, UK
Bloomsbury Publishing Ireland, 29 Earlsfort Terrace, Dublin 2, D02 AY28, Ireland

BLOOMSBURY, BLOOMSBURY ACADEMIC and the Diana logo are trademarks of Bloomsbury Publishing Plc

First published in the United States of America 2025

Copyright © Bloomsbury Publishing, 2025

Cover image © iStock.com/hatchakorn Srisook

All rights reserved. No part of this publication may be: i) reproduced or transmitted in any form, electronic or mechanical, including photocopying, recording or by means of any information storage or retrieval system without prior permission in writing from the publishers; or ii) used or reproduced in any way for the training, development or operation of artificial intelligence (AI) technologies, including generative AI technologies. The rights holders expressly reserve this publication from the text and data mining exception as per Article 4(3) of the Digital Single Market Directive (EU) 2019/790.

Bloomsbury Publishing Inc does not have any control over, or responsibility for, any third-party websites referred to or in this book. All internet addresses given in this book were correct at the time of going to press. The author and publisher regret any inconvenience caused if addresses have changed or sites have ceased to exist, but can accept no responsibility for any such changes.

A catalog record for this book is available from the Library of Congress.

ISBN: HB: 978-1-5381-9947-3
PB: 978-1-5381-9948-0
ePDF: 979-8-8818-5992-3
eBook: 978-1-5381-9949-7

Typeset by Deanta Global Publishing Services, Chennai, India

For product safety related questions contact productsafety@bloomsbury.com.

To find out more about our authors and books visit www.bloomsbury.com and sign up for our newsletters.

Contents

Figures ix
Tables and Textboxes x

1   **Read Me First!** 1

2   **Introduction to Specially Designed Instruction** 17

3   **Development of the IEP for Guiding Specially Designed Instruction** 35

4   **Steps for Determining Specially Designed Instruction** 51

5   **Specially Designed Instruction in the Classroom: Evidence-Based Instructional Strategies and Interventions** 71

6   **Classroom and Individual Assessment to Inform Specially Designed Instruction** 99

7   **Integrating Specially Designed Instruction within a School-Wide Assessment Framework** 133

8 **System-Wide Collaboration and Specially Designed Instruction** 159

9 **System-Wide Problem-Solving: Overcoming Challenges to Implementing Specially Designed Instruction** 181

10 **Future Directions and Emerging Trends in Specially Designed Instruction** 197

Index 217
About the Authors 220

Figures

1.1 SDI as part of a school-wide system. 1
1.2 How SDI and whole group instruction are similar and different. 13
2.1 Specially Designed Instruction (SDI). 17
3.1 Specially Designed Instruction (SDI). 35
3.2 Internal consistency ("Golden Thread") of the IEP. 45
4.1 Specially Designed Instruction (SDI). 51
4.2 The two-step test for determining SDI. 54
4.3 Three areas and examples of SDI. 64
5.1 Specially Designed Instruction (SDI) + Classroom Instruction and Assessment System. 71
5.2 SDI problem-solving mindset. 80
5.3 Continuum of evidence. 88
6.1 Specially Designed Instruction (SDI) + Classroom Instruction and Assessment System. 100
6.2 The alignment of learning objectives and assessments to guide classroom and individual assessment. 103
6.3 Methods of instruction as pedagogical bridge between learning objectives and aligned learning assessments. 109
6.4 The hierarchical relationship of different types of formative assessment with examples. 113
7.1 Specially Designed Instruction (SDI) + School-Wide Instruction and Assessment System. 134
8.1 Collaboration within and across systems. 159
8.2 Three-element model of co-teaching. 173
9.1 SDI as part of a school-wide system. 181
10.1 SDI as part of a school-wide system. 197

Tables and Textboxes

Tables

3.1 Example Standards and Related IEP Goals 41
4.1 Consolidated Data Sheet (Example with Ernesto) 58
5.1 Differences in Sample Dialogue between Tiers during Instruction of the Self-Questioning Strategy 83
5.2 Characteristics of Scientifically Based Research 87
5.3 Sample Resources for Finding Evidence-Based Practices 91
6.1 Example Curriculum-Based Measures (CBMs) for Reading and Common Grade Levels 118
7.1 Example Academic and Behavioral Assessments 145
8.1 Who Is Collaborating? 164
8.2 Sample Problem-Solving Process 167

Textboxes

6.1 Common Standardized and Norm-Referenced Diagnostic Measures 106
6.2 Procedural Checklist for Ensuring SDI Alignment with Classroom Assessments 120
6.3 Key Suggestions for Analyzing Classroom Assessments Related to SDI 126
7.1 Establishing Data-Informed Collaboration among Teams 149
7.2 Questions to Help Guide Reviews of School-Wide Assessment Protocols 156
8.1 Collaborating in an IEP meeting 170

1
Read Me First!

Chapter Outline

Clarify	3
Simplify	12
Integrate	12

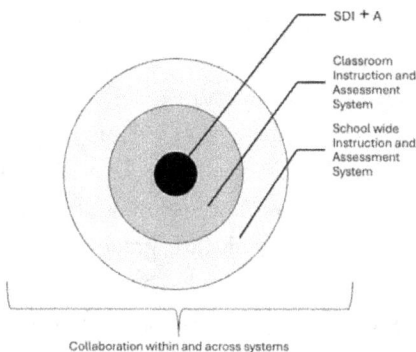

Figure 1.1 SDI as part of a school-wide system.

Chapter Objectives:

- Define specially designed instruction (SDI).
- Clarify how SDI is related to but different from differentiation, universal design for learning (UDL), culturally responsive practices, and other terms used in schools.
- Integrate SDI into what we already know about effective instruction.
- Describe how this book examines SDI as part of the system of schools.

> It's no use of talking unless people understand what you say.
> —Zora Neale Hurston

Reflection questions:

- What is SDI and why is it important?
- How is SDI different from all the current education initiatives I hear about? How do they all fit together?
- What are my responsibilities for SDI? How will I know?

Mr. Dixon sighed, leaned back, and ran his hand through his hair. Ms. Welsch looked at him with tired eyes and said, "I'm sorry. I thought we did everything to make it so Jada could access this material. We used small groups, graphic organizers, and guided notes. We let students choose their final projects for the unit. And you read the *Midsummer Night's Dream* test aloud to Jada. Everything we could think of to differentiate her experience. But she still failed it and so did several other students in the class. I thought this SDI thing would work." Mr. Dixon took a deep breath and said, "I need to learn more."

Mr. Dixon, a special educator, and Ms. Welsch, an elementary school English/language arts teacher, are again working overtime to meet the wide range of needs in their co-taught classroom. They have students from many cultural backgrounds, students who speak multiple languages, and students with disabilities, all together in their fifth-grade language arts class. Add in a challenging curriculum and multiple "new" administrator and district initiatives, and they are feeling exhausted, overwhelmed, and ineffective. They came to teaching because they wanted to be catalysts for student learning and to bring excitement about new things. A year ago, they jumped at the opportunity to co-teach so that they could put their expertise together to better meet student needs. They have been to the required professional development sessions and have read multiple articles about differentiated instruction, universal design for learning (UDL), culturally informed instruction, and SDI. And yet they feel like they are failing students like Jada, a young woman who is eager to learn but who has a learning disability that impacts her reading comprehension.

Unfortunately, Mr. Dixon and Ms. Welsch are not alone. As the number of academically diverse students continues to increase (National Center for Education Statistics, 2019) and more students with disabilities spend most of their time in general education classrooms (US Department of Education, 2024), these classrooms include students with a much broader range of abilities, needs, and background knowledge than ever before. Teachers and co-teachers are tasked with meeting the needs of these students as they teach increasingly challenging curriculum standards and are evaluated by student performance on state-mandated standardized tests (Pressley et al., 2024). Multiple instructional initiatives, such as multi-tiered systems of support (MTSS), UDL (CAST, 2024), differentiated instruction (Tomlinson, 2017) to name a few, have attempted to help teachers meet these diverse needs but there is tremendous confusion about terms, ideas, and implementation.

What if educators could work smarter, not harder? What if there was a way to untangle terms and better understand how initiatives might integrate instead of separate? What if instead of having to do one more thing, their efforts were aligned to federal law and initiatives from the start? As experienced educators, administrators, and parents, we know there are only so many hours in a day, multiple people to report to, and a seemingly unlimited number of mandates for action. We also understand that we all entered the field of education to have a positive impact on students. So, the purpose of this book is to *clarify*, *simplify*, and *integrate* federally mandated SDI with many of the other initiatives and demands that occur in schools so that educators can feel more in control and successful in their work. The education field is filled with jargon, acronyms, and over-used and over-generalized terminology, often leading to miscommunication, misunderstanding, and lackluster outcomes. If you are reading this, you do not have time for that. As Zora Neale Hurston says in our opening quote, if we don't all really understand what is being said, it's not useful to talk together. So, we begin this book with *clarify*. In this chapter, we attempt to sort out relevant terms, ideas, and initiatives so that we can get on to the business of *simplify* and *integrate*.

Clarify

You Might Hear . . . Differentiated Instruction. We Mean . . .

Differentiated instruction or the act of differentiating originally came from the ideas put forth by Carol Tomlinson (Tomlinson, 2017) as a framework for considering the individual needs of students when planning lessons. Meant originally for gifted and talented students, differentiated instruction directs teachers to consider student academic need and respond by varying the content, process, products, or learning environment during or after instruction (Tomlinson, 2017). According to the IRIS Center (2024), "Differentiated instruction is not a one-size-fits-all approach but instead should be shaped to meet the needs of students. This does not mean that teachers individually tailor instruction. Rather, they differentiate instruction for groups of students" (p. 2). Differentiated instruction includes ongoing assessment to better understand students' needs throughout instruction and flexible grouping of students depending on the areas of strength and need identified through assessment. In some cases, teachers discuss differentiated instruction based on learning styles (e.g., visual or auditory learner); however, there is little evidence of effectiveness of this type of differentiation. Evidence clearly exists for progress monitoring or ongoing assessment and flexible grouping though (e.g., Walker & Kearns, 2022). We discuss these in more depth in Chapter 4.

The term "differentiated" has also come to mean almost any change in instruction based on groups of students' needs. For example, in the vignette at the beginning of the chapter, Mr. Dixon and Ms. Welsch described allowing students to choose their final projects—a way to differentiate products by student strength. They used small groups and graphic organizers to differentiate the process—for all students in the classroom. So, they used ideas from differentiated instruction for the groups in the classroom, but those adjustments were not *individualized* specifically for Jada or other students with disabilities.

That is how differentiated instruction is different from SDI. Teachers differentiate instruction to meet the needs of groups of students in the classroom (e.g., active bilingual learners of English (ABLE); Przymus, Faggella-Luby, & Silva 2022) but not specifically to individualize instruction. We will use the word "differentiated" in this text to mean that instruction is different from typical class instruction or somehow changed to meet the needs of small groups of students either based on ongoing assessment or their previous performance. However, we want to be clear from the start that differentiated instruction is not the individualized instruction of SDI.

Reflection questions:

- How have you heard differentiated instruction used? How is it the same or different from what we have here?
- How is differentiation different from, but connected to, SDI?

You Might Hear . . . Universal Design for Learning (UDL). We Mean . . .

UDL is a "framework to guide the design of learning environments that are accessible, inclusive, equitable, and challenging for every learner. Ultimately, the goal of UDL is to support learner agency, the capacity to actively participate in making choices in service of learning goals" (CAST, 2024). There are three basic areas for consideration in UDL: (a) engagement, (b) representation, and (c) action and expression. Like differentiated instruction, UDL is built on consideration of the whole (whole class) by understanding the needs of the individuals (individual students) who make up that whole. Again, according to CAST (2024), "UDL aims to change the design of the environment rather than to situate the problem as a perceived deficit within the learner. When environments are intentionally designed to reduce barriers, every learner can engage in rigorous, meaningful learning."

For example, Ms. Welsch may understand that several of the students in her classroom access information better when it is presented in a visual manner (e.g., graphic organizers). She may also know that a handful of her students have difficulty with efficient processing of auditory material and therefore, uses guided notes. Ms. Welsch also knows that five of her students speak Spanish as their first language and therefore, uses both Spanish and English words to define critical vocabulary. These are not learning styles; they are learning strengths and needs. As you can see from these examples, there are many overlaps between the ideas of UDL and differentiated instruction, but they are both distinct from an *individualized* approach to instruction or SDI in that they are not usually specifically designed to meet the unique needs of a student with disabilities. They may offer opportunities to practice and reinforce knowledge and skills learned through SDI, but they do not meet the definition of the individualized instruction of SDI.

Reflection questions:

- How have you heard UDL used? Is it the same or different from what we have here?
- How is UDL different from, but connected to, SDI?

You Might Hear . . . Culturally Informed/Culturally Responsive/Culturally Sustaining Practices. We Mean . . .

Evolving from the ideas of Ladsen-Billings (1995), Gay (2010), and Paris (2012), culturally informed instruction (the term we will use in this book) builds on the idea that students are more engaged and learn better when their cultural identities are accepted, acknowledged, and incorporated into instruction (Kelly & Djonko-Moore, 2022). Teachers may use texts that include individuals from a variety of cultural backgrounds, involve community members in instruction, or make specific connections to students' lives. Teachers may differentiate their instruction to incorporate culturally responsive practices, based on the students or groups of students in their classroom. These changes may include specific means of accepting and acknowledging the culture of a student as part of the classroom in a variety of ways. Just like differentiated instruction and UDL, culturally informed instruction is not SDI or individualized instruction for a student with a disability to meet their unique needs. Culturally informed instruction could be incorporated into SDI by using relevant texts, materials, resources, and other means to accept and acknowledge the cultural background of the student with disabilities—such as teaching Jada reading comprehension strategies using texts with characters from the same background as Jada—but just incorporating these materials into instruction for the class or for a group of students in the classroom is not SDI (Faggella-Luby, Lindo, & Carlson, 2024).

Reflection questions:

- How have you heard culturally responsive practices used?
- Is it the same or different from what we have here?
- How is culturally responsive practice different from, but connected to, SDI?

You Might Hear . . . Access to Curriculum. We Mean . . .

The term "access" is often used in ways that do not reflect the original intent of IDEA or what is meant in SDI. In the phrase "access to the general curriculum," as in the definition of SDI in IDEA, the term means being able to *engage with* and *learn* the curriculum. In the phrase "access to nondisabled peers," the term means being able to *engage with* and *be a part* of activities with nondisabled peers. For example, for Jada to access the general curriculum standards in Ms. Welsch's fifth-grade classroom, she needs to learn specific reading comprehension strategies so that she can then identify critical characters, understand their character traits, follow the storyline, and identify major themes in *A Midsummer Night's Dream*. She also needs instruction, prompting, practice, and feedback on attention strategies so that she can focus enough to understand the events in the play. Without those strategies, and the instruction to use them effectively, Jada would be sitting in the classroom where the general curriculum was taught but she would not be *accessing* the curriculum. In other words, she would not be able to *engage with* and *learn* the general curriculum. As we use it in this book, "access" means engaging and learning, not just being present in a particular environment where the curriculum is taught and/or nondisabled peers receive instruction.

Reflection questions:

- How have you heard of access to the curriculum used?
- Is it the same or different from what we have here?
- How is "access to curriculum" different from, but connected to, SDI?

You Might Hear . . . Evidence-Based Practice or EBPs. We Mean . . .

According to Cook and Cook (2013), evidence-based practices or EBPs are "practices that are supported by multiple, high-quality studies that utilize research designs from which causality can be inferred and that demonstrate meaningful effects on student outcomes. EBPs are identified by applying specific criteria (for research design, quantity of research, quality of research, and effect size) to the empirical literature on a practice, a process often referred to as an "evidence-based review" (p. 73). EBPs are different from "best practices," "high leverage practices," and the like because they are proven effective through rigorous research studies. Many EBPs can be found on the What Works Clearinghouse website (https://ies.ed.gov/ncee/wwc/). These are interventions that have been proven to increase student outcomes based upon multiple, rigorous studies that involved many students, including students with disabilities. These EBPs provide more "bang for their buck" in that they have increased student outcomes over other practices and should be used whenever possible. Some examples of EBPs from intervention reports include the Good Behavior Game, Peer Assisted Learning Strategies, Self-Regulated Strategy Development (SRSD), and Functional assessment-based interventions (What Works Clearinghouse, 2024). There are currently sixty-three intervention reports that show varying levels of evidence of positive results for students with disabilities (What Works Clearinghouse, 2024). These are specific practices that can and should be included in the instruction of all students, particularly those students with disabilities. EBPs are instructional strategies that may be a part of SDI. For example, for a student with IEP goals related to writing, a teacher may use SRSD to teach specific writing skills. Or, for a student with behavior goals, a teacher may incorporate the Good Behavior Game into SDI. In other words, EBPs may be used to deliver SDI or to deliver general instruction. However, the EBP must be matched to the individual needs of the student with a disability for it to be SDI.

Reflection questions:

- How have you heard EBPs used?
- Is it the same or different from what we have here?
- How are EBPs different from, but connected to, SDI?

You Might Hear . . . High-Leverage Practices or HLPs. We Mean . . .

High-leverage practices or HLPs are defined as "those practices that are essential to effective teaching and fundamental to supporting student learning" (McLeskey et al., 2019, p. 2). The CEEDAR Center and Council for Exceptional Children have identified twenty-two HLPs that are critical teaching behaviors for collaboration, data-driven planning, instruction, and intensifying instruction (Aceves & Kennedy, 2024). They are very similar to the HLPs from the University of Michigan TeachingWorks group (https://www.teachingworks.org/high-leverage-practices/). These are the behaviors that all teachers should be able to use effectively, and they regularly include them in their instruction. Both sets of these HLPs are practices that increase the likelihood of positive student outcomes (Aceves & Kennedy, 2024). For example, HLPs include items such as use explicit instruction (HLP 16; TW HLP 2, 3, 18); collaborate with colleagues to increase student success (HLP 1; TW HLP 10); use multiple sources of information to develop a comprehensive understanding of a student's strengths and needs (HLP 4; TW HLP 12); and establish a consistent, organized, respectful learning environment (HLP 7; TW HLP 7, 8). Back to the vignette at the beginning of the chapter, Mr. Dixon and Ms. Welsch may have used some HLPs in their classroom instruction such as use flexible grouping (HLP 17; TW HLP 9), provide scaffolded supports (HLP 15; TW HLP 6), and systematically design instruction toward a specific goal (HLP 12; TW HLP 13). Just like the other terms we have covered, HLPs, in and of themselves, are not SDI because they may not have been selected and mapped to the individual needs of the student. However, they may (should) be used in the instructional delivery of SDI.

Reflection questions:

- How have you heard HLPs used?
- Is it the same or different from what we have here?
- How are HLPs different from, but connected to, SDI?

You Might Hear . . . Intensive Intervention or Intensify Instruction. We Mean . . .

Intensifying intervention or intensive intervention comes from literature on response to intervention, MTSS, and data-based individualization (Walker & Kearns, 2022). Briefly, intensifying intervention begins with setting student academic and/or behavioral goals with specific criteria for mastery. For example, a goal may be "By the end of the academic year, when given a grade level passage maze (close) activity, Jada will choose 8 of 9 correct responses on 4 of 5 trials." As part of an ongoing cycle of progress monitoring, Jada is assessed regularly to verify that the instruction she is receiving is increasing her accurate choices on the maze activity, indicating her reading comprehension is improving toward her IEP goal. If the ongoing assessment shows that she is not improving enough to meet this goal, then the related instruction needs to be *intensified*. That can mean a variety of things. It may mean that the dosage of instruction is changed—she receives more instruction directed at this area of need (e.g., 30 minutes per day instead of 15 minutes). It could mean the alignment of instruction is changed—during instruction, additional or different skills are taught (e.g., perhaps a focus on practicing sight words is added). It could mean that there is an increased use of explicit instruction principles during instruction (e.g., the teacher increased the number of opportunities for Jada to respond and the number of feedback statements delivered). Finally, it could mean that instruction in strategies of self-regulation or executive function is added to the instruction being delivered (Fuchs et al., 2017). In all cases, there is a change in instruction that is directly related to regular progress monitoring data that is collected by the teacher for the individual student. Intensive intervention or intensifying intervention may begin as part of tiered systems of support outside of special education (e.g., a student not responding to instruction in Tier 1 is provided additional, more intensive, instruction in Tier 2) where a student's performance is compared to group norms. But intensifying intervention is also a critical part of SDI when a student is not performing well enough to meet their annual IEP goals (Walker & Kearns, 2022). We will talk more about this in Chapter 6.

Reflection questions:
- How have you heard intensive intervention used?
- Is it the same or different from what we have here?
- How is intensive intervention different from, but connected to, SDI?

You Might Hear . . . Specially Designed Instruction or SDI. We Mean . . .

Specially designed instruction or SDI is the topic of this entire book so we will simply introduce the topic here. SDI is defined in the Individuals with Disabilities Education Act (IDEA, 2006) as

> adapting, as appropriate to the needs of the eligible child under this part, the content, methodology, or delivery of instruction—
>
> (i) To address the unique needs of the child that result from the child's disability; and
> (ii) To ensure access of the child to the general curriculum so that the child can meet the educational standards within the jurisdiction of the public agency that apply to all children (Section 300.39 (a)(3)).

The key words here are "adapting content, methodology, or delivery of *instruction*" and "*unique* needs of the child." Put together, these ideas mean that SDI is the instruction that a student with disabilities receives that is *different from* others in the classroom and will result in achieving IEP annual goals. It should be *individualized* (to meet that students' needs), *different* from the others in the classroom, and *relevant* to the general education curriculum. It can be delivered in any school setting—Tier 1, 2, or 3; general education classrooms or special education classrooms—but is distinguishable because it is individualized, different, and relevant. For example, in Jada's case, it might be individualized instruction in a reading comprehension strategy that is then practiced and generalized in her language arts class. SDI for Jada would not be the use of graphic organizers or guided notes—unless she received individualized instruction on how to create/use graphic organizers or guided notes that was different from the instruction given to her peers. Individualized, different, and relevant to unique needs: these are the critical features of SDI, and we will delve into them in more depth throughout the book.

Reflection question:

- How have you heard SDI used?
- Is it the same or different from what we have here?

So, we have clarified the differences between SDI and several terms or concepts that are used regularly in schools. It is critical to keep these differences in mind as you read through the text and learn more about what SDI is, what it looks like for students with disabilities, and how it fits into the system of schools.

Simplify

Though we could include many more terms related to SDI in this chapter, we will leave you with these for now as they are the most often used and confused with SDI. To review, we distinguished SDI from:

- differentiation,
- universal design for learning,
- culturally responsive practices,
- access to the curriculum,
- evidence-based practices, and
- intensive instruction.

Now, we need to *integrate* SDI into the school system.

Integrate

We write this book from the perspective of schools as complex educational systems that are organized in many, many ways. SDI is one component of that system, focused on meeting the needs of one, critical stakeholder in that system: a student with disabilities. However, providing SDI and meeting the needs of students with disabilities requires that virtually every other part of the system works together to make it happen. Special education, specifically SDI, is the federal mandate that students with disabilities receive instruction to help them succeed, just like every other student in our schools. For SDI to be successful, it must be integrated into all of the other instruction and experiences students with disabilities have with their K–12 peers. And that integration requires a system of personnel, resources, knowledge, and supports to make it happen. The image at the beginning of each chapter provides a visual representation of this integrated system and what aspect of the system is being addressed in that chapter.

Careful and intentional use of terms, particularly as they pertain to students with disabilities, is critical. Shared meanings and common understandings are important. Co-teachers, professional learning communities, individualized education program team members, and other school-based teams are made up of professionals from a variety of backgrounds and professional orientations. It is therefore critically important that we are clear in our communication. Figure 1.2 may help. As we think about SDI and meeting the unique needs of students with disabilities, we will describe instruction and instructional considerations for the entire class and for individual students, as well as how these integrate with—but do not substitute for—one another. SDI may include practices of culturally informed instruction just as whole group instruction may include differentiated instruction that allows for practice and reinforcement of what a student learns through SDI. But SDI and whole group instruction are not substitutes for one another. The critical features of SDI are that instruction is *individualized*, *different*, and *relevant* to the unique needs of students with disabilities.

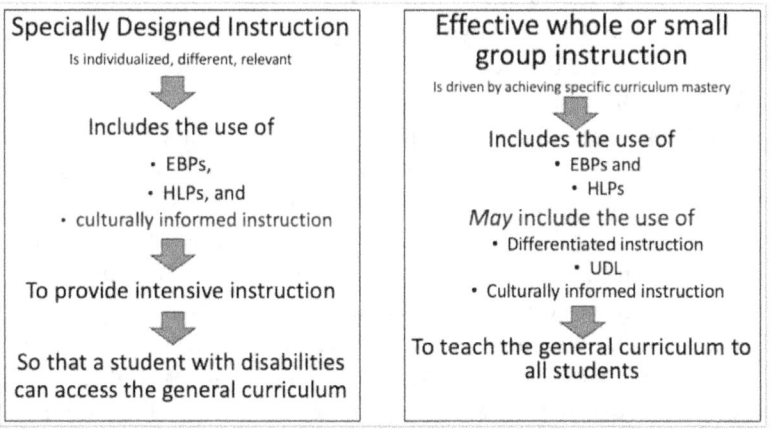

Figure 1.2 How SDI and whole group instruction are similar and different.

References

Aceves, T. C., & Kennedy, M. J. (Eds.). (2024, February). *High-leverage practices for students with disabilities* (2nd ed.). Council for Exceptional Children and CEEDAR Center.

CAST. (2024). *The goal of UDL: Learner agency.* https://udlguidelines.cast.org/more/udl-goal/

Cook, B. G., & Cook, S. C. (2013). Unraveling evidence-based practices in special education. *The Journal of Special Education, 47*(2), 71–82. https://doi.org/10.1177/0022466911420877

Faggella-Luby, M., Lindo, E., & Carlson, K. (2024). Decoding the disparities: Promising adolescent literacy intervention practices at the intersection of race & disability. *Literacy Today (July-Sept), 42*(1), 32–37.

Fuchs, L. S., Fuchs, D., & Malone, A. S. (2017). The taxonomy of intervention intensity. *TEACHING Exceptional Children, 50,* 35–43. https://doi.org/10.1177/0040059917703962

Gay, G. (2010). *Culturally responsive teaching: Theory, research, and practice* (2nd ed.). Teachers College Press.

Individuals with Disabilities Education Act (IDEA) Regulations. (2006). 34 CFR § 300 et seq.

IRIS Center. (2024). *Differentiated instruction: Maximizing the learning of all students.* https://iris.peabody.vanderbilt.edu/module/di/cresource/q1/p02/#content

Kelly, L. B., & Djonko-Moore, C. (2022). What does culturally informed literacy instruction look like?. *The Reading Teacher, 75*(5), 567–574.

Ladson-Billings, G. (1995). Toward a theory of culturally relevant pedagogy. *American Educational Research Journal, 32*(3), 465–491.

McLeskey, J., Billingsley, B., Brownell, M. T., Maheady, L., & Lewis, T. J. (2019). What are high-leverage practices for special education teachers and why are they important? *Remedial and Special Education, 40*(6), 331–337. https://doi-org.mutex.gmu.edu/10.1177/0741932518773477

National Center for Education Statistics. (2019). Characteristics of public school teachers. *U.S. Department of Education, Digest of Education Statistics.* https://nces.ed.gov/programs/coe/indicator/clr.

Paris, D. (2012). Culturally sustaining pedagogy: A needed change in stance, terminology, and practice. *Educational Researcher, 41*(3), 93–97.

Pressley, T., Marshall, D. T., & Moore, T. (2024). Understanding teacher burnout following COVID-19. *Teacher Development, 28*(4), 553–568. https://doi.org/10.1080/13664530.2024.2333982

Przymus, S., Faggella-Luby, M., & Silva, C. (2022). It's only a matter of meaning From English learners and emergent bilinguals to active bilingual learners/users of English (ABLE). *I-LanD Journal: Identity, Language, and Diversity, 4*(2), 30–50.

Quote from Zora Neal Hurston. https://empishthomas.com/2022/03/07/do-words-matter-heres-15-quotes-on-the-power-of-words/

Tomlinson, C. (2017). *How to differentiate instruction in an academically diverse classroom.* ASCD

U. S. Department of Education. (2024). *45th annual report to Congress on the implementation of the Individuals with Disabilities Education Act.* https://www.govinfo.gov/content/pkg/CMR-ED1-00187514/pdf/CMR-ED1-00187514.pdf

Walker, M. A., & Kearns, D. (2022). Provide intensive intervention using data-based individualization. In J. McCleskey, L. Maheady, B. Billingsley, M. T. Brownell, & T. J. Lewis (Eds.), *High leverage practices for inclusive classrooms* (2nd ed.; pp. 313–329). Routledge.

What Works Clearinghouse. (2024). https://ies.ed.gov/ncee/WWC/Search/Products?searchTerm=&&ProductType=2&&&&Populations=8&interventionId=&publicationDate=undefined).

2

Introduction to Specially Designed Instruction

Chapter Outline

Examples of SDI in Practice	19
The Legal Foundation of SDI	21
Legal and Ethical Considerations of SDI	22
The Individualized Education Program (IEP) and Components of SDI	25
SDI Must Address the Broad Spectrum of Needs of Students with Disabilities	27
What Roles do Teachers and Administrators Play in SDI?	30
Conclusion	32

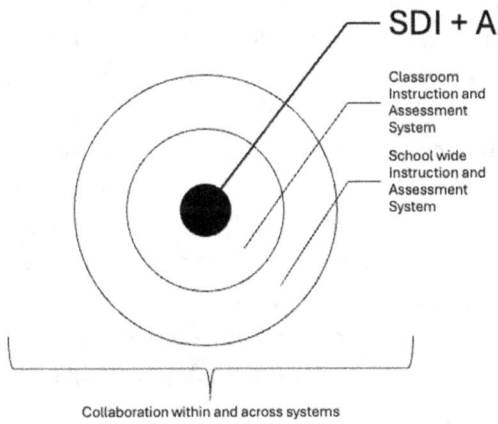

Figure 2.1 Specially Designed Instruction (SDI).

Chapter objectives:

- Situate SDI in the context of the Individuals with Disabilities Education Act (IDEA).
- Identify and describe significant court cases leading to our current understanding of SDI.
- Provide examples of SDI.

Pleased to meet you. Hope you guess my name. But what's puzzling you is the nature of my game.

—Mick Jagger

Reflection questions:

- What is specially designed instruction?
- How did our understanding of specially designed instruction evolve?
- How is specially designed instruction part of the individualized education program?

SDI is an essential component of special education as mandated by the IDEA,(2004). SDI ensures students with disabilities receive tailored educational experiences that meet their unique needs. According to 34 CFR 300.39 (b)(3), SDI involves adapting the content, methodology, or delivery of instruction to address the unique needs resulting from a disability and to ensure access to the general curriculum. These adaptations of content, methodology, and/or delivery of instruction help create an inclusive educational environment where all students, particularly students with disabilities, can succeed academically and personally (Individuals with Disabilities Education Act [IDEA] Regulations, 2006).

SDI is crucial for fostering an equitable education system with access for students with disabilities. It allows for individualized, different, and relevant teaching strategies and materials to ensure that these students can access and engage with the curriculum effectively. This individualization might include using assistive technologies, providing alternative formats for learning materials, adjusting curriculum, changing instructional groupings, and/or employing specialized instructional techniques (Bateman & Cline, 2016; Filderman & Toste, 2017). By addressing the individual learning needs of students with disabilities, SDI plays a pivotal role in promoting access to the general curriculum and ensuring all students receive a free and appropriate public education (FAPE).

Examples of SDI in Practice

What SDI looks like in schools is sometimes not clear, or, as Mick Jagger says above, can be "puzzling." To add to the confusion, whether a certain practice, strategy, grouping format, or accommodation is SDI varies across situations. For example, using explicit instruction may be SDI when a teacher uses it to teach a paraphrasing strategy to a student with a disability who has an individualized education program (IEP) that includes a goal related to reading comprehension. It is *not* SDI when explicit instruction is used by a teacher to teach an entire class how to solve a two-step math problem. What are some other examples of SDI?

- A student with a learning disability (LD) in reading may have difficulty making meaning from grade-level text. In this case, a teacher can provide individualized, different, and relevant instruction in a specific reading comprehension strategy that other students may not need to learn (e.g., self-questioning strategy). Alternatively, all students might learn a reading comprehension strategy, but the teacher provides additional, individualized instruction, practice with feedback, and cuing/self-monitoring for the specific student with LD.
- A student with dyslexia may have difficulty decoding and comprehending written text, which can impede their reading progress. To support this student, a teacher can implement individualized, specialized instructional techniques for this student, such as a multi-sensory approach to structured reading instruction. This method involves using visual, auditory, and kinesthetic-tactile strategies to enhance the student's reading skills

and is a vital part of Structured Literacy (Spear-Swerling, 2018). By using instructional techniques that include multiple learning pathways coupled with timely feedback, the teacher helps the student develop essential literacy skills for success in the general curriculum (Kearns, Lyon, & Kelley, 2022).

- A student with a speech and language impairment may struggle with verbal communication, making it difficult to participate in classroom discussions and activities. To address this, a teacher may help the student incorporate assistive technologies such as a speech-generating device or a tablet with communication apps into their classroom experience. These tools allow the student to express ideas and engage with peers and teachers effectively, thereby ensuring their participation in the general curriculum (Friend, 2022). While the availability of assistive technology (AT) can be thought of as an accommodation, the SDI occurs with instruction for the student on how and when to use the AT tools, as well as training for others in the school community (peers, teachers) on expectations around interacting with the student and AT to ensure participation and troubleshooting technology issues.
- A student with a visual impairment may find it challenging to access standard print materials. To accommodate this need, a teacher can provide learning materials in alternative formats, such as braille, large print, or audio recordings. Additionally, using screen reader software can help the student access digital content. These adaptations ensure the student can fully participate in reading assignments, research projects, and other academic activities (Harris, Schumaker, & Deshler, 2011). Providing adaptations is the first step, while providing explicit instruction and practice for how to engage with the learning access tools moves this from an accommodation to SDI.

Reflection questions:

- How do these examples compare to your thinking about SDI? What criteria make them SDI?
- What are some further questions you have about SDI in your school?

The Legal Foundation of SDI

The legal foundation for SDI is established in 34 CFR 300.39 (b)(3), which outlines the requirement for educational institutions to provide SDI to meet the unique needs of children with disabilities. This regulation is supported by significant court cases and rulings that have shaped the understanding and practice of SDI over time. These legal precedents underscore the broad scope of SDI and its critical role in ensuring that students with disabilities receive an appropriate and comprehensive education. The legal framework ensures that schools are accountable for providing the necessary individualized, different, and relevant instruction, support and adaptations to meet the diverse needs of their students (*Endrew F. v. Douglas County School District*, 2017; Hallahan et al., 2005).

For instance, the case of *County of San Diego v. California Special Educ. Hearing Office* (9th Cir. 1996) emphasized that the unique needs of students with disabilities encompasses more than just academic areas, to include social, health, emotional, physical, and vocational aspects. This case highlighted the importance of addressing a wide range of needs, all the student's needs, to provide a truly inclusive and effective education.

Another key case, *Timothy W. v. Rochester, N.H. Sch. Dist.* (1st Cir. 1989), highlighted that students with severe cognitive disabilities are entitled to SDI, even if their education focuses on daily living and self-care skills rather than traditional academic content. This ruling affirmed all students, regardless of the nature or severity of their disabilities, have the right to an education and the SDI that meets their unique needs.

Arlington Cent. Sch. Dist. v. Murphy (2006) further established the importance of providing SDI in accordance with the IDEA. The Supreme Court ruled the IDEA does not authorize parents to recover expert witness fees as part of the costs in litigation against school districts,[1] but the decision reaffirmed the necessity of SDI and the obligation of schools to provide it. This case reinforces the school's responsibility to ensure appropriate instruction and support for students with disabilities while also establishing that parents cannot be reimbursed for expert witness fees even if they win an IDEA due process case.

In *Endrew F. v. Douglas County School District* (2017), the Supreme Court clarified that schools must provide an education that is "reasonably calculated to enable a child to make appropriate progress in light of the child's circumstances," raising the standard from minimal progress to one that ensures meaningful educational benefits. This decision distinguished "de minimis" progress, which is merely trivial or barely more than nothing, from substantive progress, requiring that an IEP be ambitious and tailored to the child's unique needs. Meaningful educational benefits under *Endrew F.* necessitate SDI that enables measurable academic and functional growth, ensuring that students with disabilities receive opportunities to progress in line with their potential rather than settling for minimal advancement. This was significant because it moved the standard beyond de minimis (minimal) levels of progress set in *Board of Education v. Rowley* (1982) establishing emphasis on individualized and ambitious goals, progress aligned with potential, use of evidence-based instructional strategies, and the necessity of schools to show data as part of school accountability.

These legal precedents collectively affirm that SDI is essential for ensuring that students with disabilities receive a FAPE. They highlight the obligation of schools to adapt educational practices and provide SDI to meet the diverse and unique needs of each student, ensuring their right to an inclusive and equitable education (Yell, Bateman, & Shriner, 2022).

Legal and Ethical Considerations of SDI

"At No Cost" Requirement under IDEA

The IDEA mandates SDI must be provided at no cost to students and their families. This requirement ensures financial barriers do not impede access to appropriate education, making it a fundamental principle of IDEA. All services outlined in the IEP must be provided free of charge, including specialized instruction, related services, and necessary accommodations (Individuals with Disabilities Education Act [IDEA] Regulations, 2006). The "at no cost" requirement means all educational and related services specified in the IEP must be provided without charge to the parents or guardians of students with disabilities. This includes but is not limited to:

- Specialized instruction tailored to the student's unique needs (SDI).
- Related services such as speech therapy, occupational therapy, and physical therapy.
- Necessary accommodations like AT, extended time on tests, and modified assignments.

If a student's IEP includes weekly speech therapy sessions to address communication challenges, the school district must provide these sessions without charging the parents. This ensures the student receives the necessary support to succeed academically and socially (Friend, 2022).

While specialized services must be free, incidental fees that apply to all students may still be charged. These fees might include costs for field trips, extracurricular activities, or other non-instructional items. However, it is important that these fees do not become a barrier to participation for students with disabilities. For example, a school may charge a nominal fee for a class field trip that all students are expected to pay. However, the school cannot charge extra for any accommodations needed by a student with a disability to participate in the trip, such as providing a sign language interpreter or accessible transportation (Friend, 2022).

Ensuring SDI is provided at no cost is essential for promoting equity in education. Schools must ensure all students, regardless of their financial circumstances, have access to the support they need to succeed. This principle helps create an inclusive educational environment where all students can reach their full potential. For example, let's consider a student from a low-income family that requires an AT device to participate in classroom activities. The school must provide the device at no cost to the family, ensuring the student's financial situation does not hinder their educational progress (Friend, 2022).

Rights of Students and Parents

Ensuring transparency, collaboration, and compliance with legal requirements is essential in the special education process. Students and parents have specific rights under IDEA, including the right to participate in IEP meetings, access educational records, and receive prior written notice of changes to the IEP (Yell, Bateman, & Shriner, 2022). Parents and students have the right to actively participate in the development, review, and revision of the IEP. This collaborative process ensures the educational plan is tailored to the student's unique needs and reflects the input of all stakeholders. Parents and students have the right to access all educational records maintained by the school. This transparency allows them to stay informed about the student's progress and ensures that they can advocate effectively for necessary services and supports. For example, a parent can request copies of their child's progress reports, assessment results, and IEP documents. Reviewing these records helps parents understand their child's academic performance and the effectiveness of the services provided (Yell, Bateman, & Shriner, 2022). Schools must provide prior written notice to parents before making any changes to the student's identification, evaluation, or educational placement, or before initiating or refusing to initiate certain actions. This notice must include a description of the proposed action, an explanation of why the action is being proposed or refused, and a summary of the evidence and other factors considered.

Active participation and partnership between educators, students, and families are crucial for the successful implementation of SDI. Parents must be involved in all aspects of the IEP process, from initial evaluations to goal setting and progress monitoring. Their input and insights are valuable for creating effective and personalized educational plans. For example, a student with a disability is struggling with social interactions. During the IEP meeting, the parents suggest incorporating a social skills group into the student's plan based on their observations at home. The educators and specialists then discuss how to implement this recommendation, ensuring that the student's social and emotional needs are addressed (Friend, 2022). Educators must also ensure students understand their rights and are involved in decision-making processes to the extent appropriate. This promotes self-advocacy and self-determination, empowering students to take an active role in their education.

The Individualized Education Program (IEP) and Components of SDI

The IEP is the primary tool for implementing SDI. This is again why SDI is often so puzzling: there is usually no section in the IEP called SDI. So, if educators go looking for it, they are likely to be confused when it is impossible to locate. Instead, the IEP process involves developing an individualized plan outlining the specific educational goals, services, and accommodations for each student with a disability. This plan is created through a collaborative process involving educators, parents, specialists, and the student, when appropriate (Yell, 2019).

The IEP serves as a blueprint for delivering SDI, ensuring each student's unique needs are met. It outlines the present level of performance, goals, services, and supports that will be used to help the student achieve their educational goals. The collaborative nature of the IEP process ensures all stakeholders have a voice in developing and implementing the plan, promoting a shared commitment to the student's success (Friend, 2015). We will go into greater depth about the components of the IEP and their relation to SDI in Chapters 3 and 4.

Adapting Content, Methodology, and Delivery

One of the key components of SDI is adapting the content, methodology, and delivery of instruction to meet the unique needs of students with disabilities. This involves adjusting the curriculum, utilizing specialized teaching strategies, and employing alternative formats for instructional materials to ensure that all students can access and benefit from the education provided (Kavale & Forness, 1997). We provide an overview here and the rest of the book goes into depth about each of these key areas of SDI.

Adapting Content. Adapting content involves modifying the curriculum; teaching additional foundational skills; adding instruction in social skills, executive functioning, self-regulation, and the like to suit the learning needs of individual students. This can include simplifying language; breaking down tasks into smaller, more manageable steps; altering the content taught; and/or providing additional background information to enhance understanding. A teacher might teach a specific cognitive strategy to a student with an LD to help them understand complex concepts in science. Simplifying the language used in textbooks and providing concrete examples can make the material more accessible and engaging for the student also (Harris, Schumaker, & Deshler, 2008).

Adapting Methodology. Modifying methodology refers to the use of specialized teaching strategies that cater to the learning needs of students with disabilities. This might involve employing multi-sensory approaches, incorporating technology, or providing explicit instruction that other students are not receiving in specific skills (Scruggs, Mastropieri, & McDuffie, 2007). For a student with dyslexia, a teacher might use a multi-sensory approach for structured literacy instruction, which integrates visual, auditory, and kinesthetic-tactile elements to help the student develop phonemic awareness and decoding skills (Kearns, Lyon, & Kelley, 2022).

Adapting Delivery. Adjusting the delivery of instruction means altering how the content is presented to ensure it is accessible to specific students. This can involve offering one-on-one support, using small group instruction, in addition to providing accommodations such as extended time, alternative assessments, or the use of assistive technologies (Friend, 2015). A student with a hearing impairment might benefit from captioned videos and sign language interpreters during classroom instruction. The teacher could also provide written notes and use visual supports to ensure the student can follow along and participate fully in lessons (Meyer, Brandt, & Bluth, 1980). Or a student with an LD in math and attention deficit disorder may need explicit instruction in solving two-step word problems in a separate classroom.

By adapting content, methodology, and delivery, teachers can create an inclusive and supportive learning environment that addresses the unique needs of each student, ensuring they can succeed academically (Hall-Mills & Marante, 2022). Inclusion in the general education curriculum is a fundamental goal of SDI. As we mentioned in Chapter 1, ensuring access to the general curriculum means students with disabilities can engage meaningfully and learn the general curriculum while participating fully in the same educational experiences as their peers. This does not mean that they are just in the same classroom environment. Rather, it means that the SDI helps provide access to the same content and understanding as their peers. This requires thoughtful planning and the implementation of strategies to remove barriers to learning (Solis et al., 2012). Consequently, our focus for the rest of this book will be on identifying and delivering SDI within the context of classrooms and schools, as well as how to monitor student progress to make sure that the SDI being implemented is actually making a difference for the student with disabilities.

Reflection questions:

- What is the role of the IEP in determining SDI?
- What areas of need might SDI address? What examples of SDI in different areas of need can you think of?

SDI Must Address the Broad Spectrum of Needs of Students with Disabilities

Students with disabilities have a wide range of needs that must be addressed through SDI. These needs exist beyond specific disability labels (e.g., autism spectrum disorder, specific learning disability, intellectual disability), spanning various domains, including academic, social, emotional, health, physical, and vocational aspects. Recognizing and addressing these diverse needs is essential for providing an individualized, different, and relevant education (Brunsting, Sreckovic, & Lane, 2014; Meyer, Brandt, & Bluth, 1980).

Academic needs refer to the specific educational challenges that a student with a disability may face. These could include difficulties with reading, writing, mathematics, or other subjects. SDI aims to address these challenges through targeted interventions and instructional strategies that are tailored to the student's unique learning profile (Beck, McKeown, & Kucan, 2013). For example, a student with dyslexia may struggle with reading fluency and comprehension. To support this student, a teacher might implement an evidence-based reading program that incorporates a multi-sensory approach to teach phonemic awareness and decoding skills (adapting content and methodology). Additionally, providing audiobooks and text-to-speech software can help the student access grade-level content while building their reading skills (delivery).

Students with disabilities may also have social and emotional needs that require attention. These needs can include difficulties with social interactions, managing emotions, and building relationships. Addressing these needs is crucial for the student's overall well-being and success in school (Williams et al., 2009). For example, a student with autism might require individualized social skills training to navigate social interactions effectively. This training can include role-playing scenarios, social stories, and direct instruction on social cues and conversation skills (adapting content, methodology, and delivery). By providing this support, the student can develop the skills necessary to interact with peers and build meaningful relationships.

Health and physical needs encompass a range of conditions that can impact a student's ability to participate fully in school activities. These needs may include mobility impairments, chronic health conditions, or sensory impairments. SDI must address these needs through specific accommodations and modifications, *and the instruction on how to use those accommodations and modifications*, matched to address the unique needs of the learner to progress appropriately in the learning environment (Individuals with Disabilities Education Act [IDEA] Regulations, 2006). For example, a student with a physical disability might need adaptive physical education to participate fully in physical activities. This could involve modifying equipment, providing additional support during activities, or adapting the curriculum to focus on individual physical abilities. A student with a mobility impairment might participate in a wheelchair basketball program. This adapted activity allows the student to engage in physical exercise, develop teamwork skills, and enjoy the social aspects of sports. The program might include specially designed drills and modified game rules to accommodate the needs of all participants. Additionally, a student with an intellectual disability might have a peer buddy who assists them during PE classes. The peer buddy can help the student understand instructions, provide physical support during activities, and offer encouragement. Ensuring the student can engage in physical education promotes physical health and inclusion in all aspects of school life. Adapted PE programs focus on developing physical and motor fitness, fundamental motor skills, and skills in aquatics, dance, and individual and group games and sports. These programs are designed to meet the diverse needs of students with disabilities and ensure they have equal opportunities to participate in physical activities.

Vocational needs refer to the skills and experiences necessary for students with disabilities to prepare for post-school employment and independent living. SDI can include vocational training, career exploration, and work-based learning experiences (Vannest et al., 2011). For example, a high school student with a cognitive disability might participate in a vocational education program that includes on-campus jobs and internships at local businesses. This program can help the student develop job-specific skills, build a work history, and explore potential career paths. A student with a cognitive disability might learn to use a city bus to travel to a job site. The training could involve practicing how to read a bus schedule, identify the correct bus route, and safely board and exit the bus. Additionally, the student might learn how to handle unexpected situations, such as a missed bus or a route change (Yell, Bateman, & Shriner, 2022). A student with autism might receive instruction on pedestrian safety, including how to use crosswalks, understand traffic signals, and stay aware of their surroundings. Practicing these skills in real-life settings helps the student become more comfortable and confident when navigating the community independently (Yell, Bateman, & Shriner, 2022). A student with an LD might work in the school library, where they gain experience in cataloging books, assisting patrons, and managing library resources. This on-campus job helps the student develop organizational and customer service skills in a familiar setting (Yell, Bateman, & Shriner, 2022). Alternatively, a student with an intellectual disability might participate in a community-based vocational training program that includes a part-time job at a local grocery store. The student might receive support from a job coach, who helps them learn job tasks, interact with customers, and manage their work schedule. This paid employment experience helps the student develop important work skills and gain confidence in their ability to succeed in the workplace (Day, Nagro, & Mason-Williams, 2023). By providing these opportunities, the student is better prepared for life after graduation.

Reflection questions:

- In what other broad areas of need might students with disabilities need instruction or adaptation?
- Who are some of the partners with whom teachers might need to collaborate to provide SDI in these broad areas of need?

What Roles do Teachers and Administrators Play in SDI?

Teachers are at the heart of SDI's success. Their advocacy, ongoing professional development, and commitment to creating a supportive educational environment are vital. Educators must continually learn and adapt to meet their students' needs best, fostering an inclusive and equitable learning environment (Friend, 2015). Professional development is crucial for teachers to stay informed about the latest research and best practices in special education. This might involve attending workshops on new instructional strategies, collaborating with specialists, and participating in professional learning communities. For example, a teacher who attends a conference on meaningful inclusive education gains new insights into providing SDI and integrating technology into the classroom. By applying these strategies, the teacher can provide more effective support for students with disabilities (Friend, 2015).

Beyond professional development, teachers must also be strong advocates and collaborators. The role of the teacher extends beyond the classroom as they work to create a school culture that values and supports all learners. This involves organizing regular meetings with a student's support team, including the special education teacher, school counselor, and parents, to review progress and adjust instructional strategies as needed. Through such collaborative efforts, teachers ensure that students receive consistent and comprehensive support tailored to their unique needs (Friend, 2015).

School administrators play a pivotal role in the successful implementation of SDI. Their leadership and support are essential for creating an environment where SDI can be implemented effectively, and all students can succeed (Friend, 2022). Administrators must ensure that teachers and staff have the necessary resources and support to implement

SDI effectively. This includes providing access to professional development opportunities, ensuring adequate staffing, completing thoughtful scheduling, and securing funding for essential materials and technology. For example, an administrator might allocate funds to purchase AT devices for students with disabilities and provide training for teachers on effectively using these tools. This investment supports the successful integration of SDI into daily instruction, ensuring that all students can access the resources they need to succeed (Yell, Bateman, & Shriner, 2022).

Creating a culture of inclusion is another critical responsibility for administrators. They set the tone for the school environment by promoting policies and practices prioritizing equity and inclusion. This might involve implementing school-wide initiatives to celebrate diversity, such as hosting events that raise awareness about different disabilities and fostering activities that promote empathy and understanding among students and staff. By encouraging a positive and respectful school climate, administrators help create a supportive community where all students feel valued and included (Friend, 2015).

Ensuring compliance with legal requirements related to SDI and special education is also essential. Administrators must oversee the development and implementation of IEPs, monitor the provision of services, and address any issues or complaints promptly. For instance, an administrator might establish a system for regularly reviewing IEPs to ensure they are up-to-date and being implemented as intended. Additionally, providing training for staff on legal requirements and best practices helps ensure that the school meets its obligations and provides high-quality support for students with disabilities (Yell, Bateman, & Shriner, 2022).

Promoting collaboration and communication among all members of the school community is vital for effective SDI. Administrators must facilitate open lines of communication and encourage teamwork among teachers, specialists, parents, and students. Organizing monthly meetings for the special education team to discuss student progress, share strategies, and address challenges fosters a collaborative environment. By ensuring that all stakeholders work together, administrators help create a cohesive and supportive network dedicated to student success (Friend, 2022).

By recognizing the crucial roles that teachers and administrators play in implementing SDI, schools can ensure that all students receive the support they need to achieve their full potential. The combined efforts of dedicated educators and supportive leaders create an environment where students with disabilities can thrive academically, socially, and emotionally.

This collaborative and inclusive approach to education underscores the transformative power of SDI, highlighting its essential role in fostering equity and excellence in education for all students (Friend, 2015).

Conclusion

Effective SDI has the potential for a transformative impact on the academic and personal lives of students with disabilities and ensures compliance with IDEA regulations. By providing tailored instruction and support, SDI helps students overcome barriers to learning and achieve their full potential. Success stories and positive outcomes highlight the effectiveness of dedicated and individualized instruction (Friend, 2022). SDI enables students to make significant strides in their academic journey, often achieving milestones that might have seemed out of reach without such support. For instance, consider a student who received SDI for social skills training and successfully transitioned to a general curriculum classroom with his peers. This student was able to build meaningful relationships with peers, demonstrating how SDI fosters not only academic success but also crucial social development. Another example is a student who, with the help of SDI, overcame learning disabilities to achieve academic excellence and secure a college scholarship, illustrating how personalized support can unlock a student's potential and pave the way for future opportunities (Friend, 2022).

Reflecting on these success stories underscores the importance of SDI in promoting equity and meaningful inclusion in education. It shows how individualized, different, and relevant instruction can profoundly impact students' lives, enabling them to thrive both academically and personally. SDI not only helps students with disabilities succeed in school but also prepares them for a fulfilling life beyond the classroom, integrating them into society as confident and capable individuals (Yell, Bateman, & Shriner, 2022). As Mick Jagger once said, "It's all right letting yourself go, as long as you can get yourself back," and for many students with disabilities, SDI provides that essential structure—the puzzle piece that transforms what may at first seem confusing or overwhelming into a clear and purposeful path forward. As we close this chapter on the broad legal and ethical foundations of SDI, we look forward to Chapter 3's dive into how the IEP sets the stage for determining the SDI each student needs, ensuring they can navigate their education with direction, confidence, and success.

Note

1 Pub. L. No. 99-372, 100 Stat. 796 (1986) (codified at 20 U.S.C. § 1415(i)(3)(B)(i)(I) and authorizing the court "in its discretion" to "award reasonable attorney's fees . . . to a prevailing party who is the parent of a child with a disability").

References

Bateman, D. F., & Cline, J. L. (2016). *A teacher's guide to special education.* The Association for Supervision and Curriculum Development and the Council for Exceptional Children.

Beck, I. L., McKeown, M. G., & Kucan, L. (2013). *Bringing words to life: Robust vocabulary instruction.* Guilford Press.

Board of Education v. Rowley, 458 U.S. 176 (1982).

Brunsting, N. C., Sreckovic, M. A., & Lane, K. L. (2014). Special education teacher burnout: A synthesis of research from 1979 to 2013. *Education & Treatment of Children, 37*(4), 681–711.

Day, J., Nagro, S. A., & Mason-Williams, L. (2023). The nationwide trends and preparation requirements of alternative route programs in special education. *Teacher Education and Special Education, 47*(2), 93–109.

Endrew F. v. Douglas County School District, 137 S. Ct. 988 (2017).

Filderman, M. J., & Toste, J. R. (2017). Decisions, decisions: Using data to make instructional decisions for struggling readers. *Teaching Exceptional Children, 50*(3), 130–140. https://doi.org/10.1177/0040059917740701

Friend, M. (2015). Welcome to co-teaching 2.0. *Educational Leadership.* https://www.ascd.org/el/articles/welcome-to-co-teaching-2.0

Friend, M. (2022). *Interactions: Collaboration skills for school professionals* (9th ed.). Pearson.

Hall-Mills, S. S., & Marante, L. M. (2022). Explicit text structure instruction supports expository text comprehension for adolescents with learning disabilities: A systematic review. *Learning Disability Quarterly, 45*(1), 55–68. https://doi.org/10.1177/0731948720906490

Hallahan, D. P., Lloyd, J. W., Kauffman, J. M., Weiss, M. P., & Martinez, E. A. (2005). *Learning Disabilities: Foundations, Characteristics, and Effective Teaching* (3rd ed.). Pearson.

Harris, M. L., Schumaker, J. B., & Deshler, D. D. (2008). *The word mapping strategy.* Edge Enterprises.

Harris, M. L., Schumaker, J. B., & Deshler, D. D. (2011). The effects of strategic morphological analysis instruction on the vocabulary performance of secondary students with and without disabilities. *Learning Disability Quarterly, 34*(1), 17–33.

Individuals with Disabilities Education Act of 2004. (2004). 20 U.S.C. § 1400.

Individuals with Disabilities Education Act (IDEA) Regulations. (2006). 34 C.F.R. § 300 et seq.

Kavale, K. A., & Forness, S. R. (1997). Defining learning disabilities: Consonance and dissonance. In J. W. Lloyd, E. J. Kameenui, & D. Chard (Eds.), *Issues in educating students with disabilities* (pp. 3–26). Lawrence Erlbaum Associates.

Kearns, D., Lyon, C., & Kelley, S. (2022). Structured literacy interventions for reading long words. In L. Spear-Swerling (Ed.), *Structured literacy interventions: Teaching students with reading difficulties, Grades K-6* (pp. 43–64). The Guilford Press.

Meyer, B. J. F., Brandt, D. M., & Bluth, G. J. (1980). Use of top-level structure in text: Key for reading comprehension of ninth-grade students. *Reading Research Quarterly, 16*(1), 72–103. https://doi.org/10.2307/747349

Scruggs, T. E., Mastropieri, M. A., & McDuffie, K. A. (2007). Co-teaching in inclusive classrooms: A metasynthesis of qualitative research. *Exceptional Children, 73*, 392–416. https://doi.org/10.1177/001440290707300401

Solis, M., Vaughn, S., Swanson, E., & McCulley, L. (2012). Collaborative models of instruction: The empirical foundations of inclusion and co-teaching. *Psychology in the Schools, 49*, 498–510. https://doi.org/10.1002/pits.21606

Spear-Swerling, L. (2018). Structured Literacy and Typical Literacy Practices: Understanding Differences to Create Instructional Opportunities. *TEACHING Exceptional Children, 51*(3), 201-211. https://doi.org/10.1177/0040059917750160

Vannest, K. J., Hagan-Burke, S., Parker, R. I., & Soares, D. A. (2011). Special education teacher time use in four types of programs. *The Journal of Educational Research, 104*, 219–230. https://doi.org/10.1080/00220671003709898

Williams, J. P., Stafford, K. B., Lauer, K. D., Hall, K. M., & Pollini, S. (2009). Embedding reading comprehension training in content-area instruction. *Journal of Educational Psychology, 101*(1), 1–20. https://doi.org/10.1037/a0013152

Yell, M. L. (2019). *Legal issues in special education* (5th ed.). Pearson.

Yell, M. L., Bateman, D. F., & Shriner, J. (2022). *Developing educationally meaningful and legally sound IEPs*. Rowman & Littlefield Publishing Group.

3
Development of the IEP for Guiding Specially Designed Instruction

Chapter Outline

Overview of the Components of an IEP	37
Present Level of Academic Achievement and Functional Performance (PLAAFP)	37
Annual Goals with Progress Monitoring	40
Special Education and Related Services	42
Placement	44
The "Golden Thread" of the IEP	44
Extent of Non-Participation in General Education	45
Participation in Statewide Assessments	46
Accommodations and Modifications	46
Transition	47
Supplementary Aids and Services	48
Summary and Next Steps	49

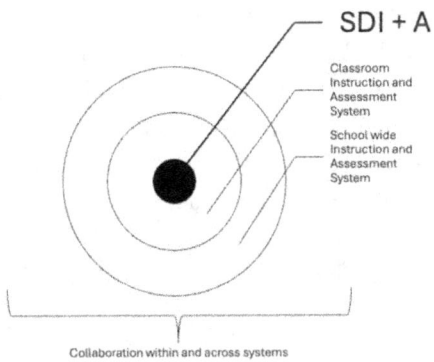

Figure 3.1 Specially Designed Instruction (SDI).

Chapter objectives:

- Provide an overview of the components of an individualized education program (IEP).
- Describe the SDI connections to the present level, goals, and services.
- Discuss internal consistency (the Golden Thread) of an IEP and its importance in determining SDI.

Planning is bringing the future into the present so that you can do something about it now.

—Alan Lakein

Reflection questions:

- What are the required components of an IEP?
- How is SDI connected to the present level, goals, and services listed in an IEP?
- What is the "Golden Thread" of an IEP and why is it important for determining SDI?

In Chapter 1, we met Mr. Dixon and Ms. Welsh as they were reflecting on their attempts to provide effective instruction for Jada, a fifth-grade student with a specific learning disability. While they clearly used evidence-based strategies in their instruction, such as small group instruction, graphic organizers, and student choice, we learned that these things alone may not be SDI.

In Chapter 2, we explored the definition of SDI as described in the Individuals with Disabilities Education Act (IDEA, 2004) and further refined through case law. A key concept to note is that SDI is *required* for every student with an IEP and that it must be individualized, different, and relevant for that student. That chapter highlighted multiple examples of SDI as implemented to address an individual student's educational needs. In this chapter, we highlight the direct connection between SDI and the student's IEP. Further, because SDI is not simply a single component of the written IEP, we will explore the components of the IEP and identify which ones help drive decisions about what SDI to offer for the student.

Overview of the Components of an IEP

Every student who qualifies for special education services through IDEA meets two criteria: (a) the student has a disability that impacts their ability to access the general education curriculum, and (b) the student requires special education services to address the impact (IDEA, 2004). Every student who receives special education services should have an educational program that the IEP team designs specifically to address that student's individualized needs. While every IEP contains content unique to that student, there are legally required components that must be included for all. These required components include information related to: (a) present level of academic achievement and functional performance (PLAAFP), (b) annual goals with progress monitoring, (c) special education and related services, (d) placement, (e) extent of non-participation in general education, (f) participation in statewide assessments, (g) accommodations and modifications, (h) transition, and (i) supplementary aids and services (IDEA, 2004). While each state has its own version of the IEP document, IDEA, the federal law that mandates a free and appropriate public education for students with disabilities, requires these nine components be included in each IEP. An astute reader will note that SDI is *not* one of these elements. Therefore, let's examine each of these components and how they relate to SDI.

Present Level of Academic Achievement and Functional Performance (PLAAFP)

The first thing most educators notice here is the long name and awkward acronym. Many states, authors, and teachers tend to abbreviate this to something more manageable such as PLAP, PLEP, or PLOP, but all are referring to the heart of the IEP: the statement of the student's present level of performance, the guide for the IEP team and reader to understand where the student currently functions. This is what helps the team make decisions for the rest of the program development so that they can identify what progress and goals to target for the IEP cycle.

It is important to note the present level statement includes both academic achievement and functional performance. As discussed in Chapter 2, academic achievement is what we traditionally think of when we think of school-related tasks: a student's performance in academic skills and areas, such as reading, writing, and mathematics. Functional performance is a broad term to encompass all the other knowledge and skills necessary to be successful in school and, arguably, in life after school. Functional skills include things like executive functioning, organizational skills, self-regulation, vocational, and daily life skills. Since IEPs are designed to address the needs of an individual student, the focus on academic and/or functional knowledge and skills will vary according to that specific student's needs. For example, a student who needs SDI in the academic skill of reading comprehension may receive direct instruction on a self-questioning strategy to support engagement with the text and reading for the purpose of finding evidence to support ideas. The same student may need SDI for a functional skill of organization, such as direct instruction on how to create and use a reference organizer for mnemonics and strategy steps to support independent skill practice across content areas (see *The Case of Jada* in Chapter 5 for more on this example). Addressing both is necessary to capture the full range of knowledge, skills, and behaviors a student exhibits currently to help drive the IEP team's discussion of what to target for the education program.

As we introduced in Chapter 2, the IEP must be "reasonably calculated to enable a child to make progress appropriate in light of the child's circumstances" (*Endrew F.*, 2017, p. 998). This substantive standard requires the IEP team to have a comprehensive picture of what the student currently can achieve, as well as what factors may be impacting the student's ability to access and engage in the general education curriculum and setting. The IEP team uses the PLAAFP to document student strengths and needs, concerns of the parent, future goals of the student, and what knowledge/skills/behaviors are needed to address the student's annual (and postsecondary) goals. To gain a full and clear picture of the unique strengths and needs of the student, the team uses the present level statement to document the student's interests both currently (e.g., loves dinosaurs, fascinated by planets and outer space, enjoys playing soccer, and recently started knitting) as well as longer term aspirations (e.g., archeologist, astronaut, or professional athlete). Awareness of these student interests can support discussions of short-term planning, such as connection to curricular standards or engagement in extracurricular activities, and long-term planning and goals related to skills needed for postsecondary transition. For example, a student who enjoys playing soccer may demonstrate more on-task engagement when reading and writing about soccer as opposed to swimming, so readings on soccer could be incorporated into lesson plan activities that require students to engage with or create a written passage. Similarly, a student with a career aspiration of becoming a professional athlete may want to try out for the school's soccer team or take an elective course on sports medicine when in high school. If the student struggles with knowing how and where to find information, the explicit instruction and practice activities could include learning about the requirements to join a school sports team or how to access/read the course catalog to identify what classes are offered. Knowing the student's postsecondary interests can support the team in identifying what knowledge and skills should be addressed within the IEP and transition goals.

Inclusion of parent input on the growth they are seeing as well as concerns they have regarding the student's academic and functional performance is not only legally required, but critical to the IEP team having a more complete picture of the student's needs. As mentioned before, the needs identified in the present level determine what should be targeted in the annual goals and connected services to be provided. It is important to note that each need documented in the present level statement should be addressed in the educational program, with the priority needs as the focus of the annual goals. Put simply, the present level drives the individualized goals, and the goals drive the individualized program. We get into more detail about the present level statements in Chapter 4, providing both examples and nonexamples to consider.

Reflection questions:

- How do the elements of the present level of academic and functional performance establish the baseline skills for students with disabilities?
- In what ways does the present level statement drive the development of the rest of the IEP?
- Why is it important to consider the student's postsecondary interests and parent input as part of the present level statement?
- Where does SDI "fit" in relation to the present level?

Annual Goals with Progress Monitoring

While the present level statement outlines the current academic and functional performance of the student, the annual goals set the target for where the student should be at the end of the IEP cycle. The goals are where the IEP team addresses the "reasonably calculated" plan regarding what progress is appropriate to expect within the timeline of the IEP. These goals should be "meaningful and measurable" annual goals written to address the individual child's needs and "the team's assessment of a student's potential for growth" (Goran et al., 2020, p. 335). IEP goals are not based on district curricula or external standards but on the student's individual needs (Hedin & DeSpain, 2018). That sentence may seem a bit confusing, so let's say it another way: the curriculum and standards don't drive the goals; the individual student's needs identified in the present level drive the goals. Goals should be geared toward the knowledge/skills the student needs to develop, which can support their access to the general curriculum standards but are not determined by the standards. Again, the general curriculum standards do not belong in an IEP. Rather, the goals should be targeted on the *skills* necessary to get the student to the general curriculum standard. This is the essence of a standards-based IEP: it does not include general curriculum standards as goals. It includes the *knowledge and skills* necessary to make those curriculum standards accessible for students with disabilities. See Table 3.1 for an example of standards and related IEP goals.

Once goals are written, they should be evaluated to ensure they are both *meaningful* to the individual student and *measurable*, with the necessary progress monitoring tools/methods identified. (More information on writing good annual goals can be found in Chapter 4.) After all, a goal isn't really a goal if it can't be measured, so it is imperative for the IEP team to determine both the goal and the tools/methods to measure progress toward that goal. Once the goals and progress monitoring tools have been determined, the IEP team determines what supports and services are required to address the goals. We dive into this more deeply in Chapter 4, too.

Reflection questions:

- How are the annual goals connected to SDI? What insights into the process did this section give you?
- Do the goals I write connect directly to the needs identified in the present level statement? Are they reflective of all my student's needs?

Development of the IEP 41

Table 3.1 Example Standards and Related IEP Goals

Example Curriculum Standard	Example Related Skills	Example IEP Goals
The student will solve multi-step linear equations in one variable algebraically, quadratic equations in one variable algebraically, and practical problems involving equations and systems of equations.	Knowledge and correct use of order of operations Accurate representation of an unknown value with a variable Knowledge and correct use of a constant with a variable Knowledge and fluent use of basic math facts (addition, subtraction, multiplication, division) How to represent practical problems algebraically	Given 10 problems that include addition, subtract, multiplication, division, and exponents, Antonio will solve 9 of 10 problems accurately on 3 attempts. Given 5 practical word problems that includes known and unknown values, Melissa will accurately represent 4 of 5 problems algebraically.
The student will orally identify and produce various phonemes (individual sounds) within words to develop phonemic awareness in support of decoding (reading) and encoding (spelling). Isolate sounds in four and five phoneme words. Demonstrate the ability to blend words with four and five phonemes, including words with consonant digraphs (e.g., th, sh, ch) and consonant blends (e.g., fr, st, bl). Demonstrate the ability to segment words with four and five phonemes, including words with consonant digraphs (e.g., th, sh, ch) and consonant blends (e.g., fr, st, bl).	Identify name and sound of individual letters. Isolate sounds in three phoneme words Blend words with fewer than 5 phonemes Identify sounds of consonant digraphs and consonant blends	When shown a letter, Monica will be able to accurately state the letter name and sound within 2 seconds with no prompt. When presented with a three-phoneme word, Jada will be able to isolate the three phonemes in 9 of 10 words.

Special Education and Related Services

The IDEA law requires each IEP to contain a statement of the services that will be provided to enable the student to advance toward attaining the annual goals, be involved in—and make progress in—the general education curriculum, and be educated with other children with and without disabilities (IDEA, 2006 §300.320(a)(4)). By "services," the law includes special education services, related services, supplementary aids and services, and supports for school personnel (Goran & Bateman, 2023). Special Education services are where we see the provision of SDI, and this is what makes special education "special"—it is the presentation of specially designed, targeted instruction for the specific student to meet their individualized needs as outlined in the present level and addressed in the goals. For example, as we learned about Jada in Chapter 1, she receives special education services to teach her specific reading comprehension strategies that allow her to identify critical characters, understand their traits, follow a storyline, and identify major themes in the assigned text (in this case *A Midsummer Night's Dream*). Chapter 4 provides more in-depth examples of special education services and Chapter 5 includes how Jada's required services are delivered within the context of a classroom.

Related services are additional services (beyond special education services) that are required for an individual child to receive a FAPE as described in IDEA (2004; Goran & Bateman, 2023). The federal regulations (34 CFR §300.34) provide the following definition:

> Related services means transportation and such developmental, corrective, and other supportive services as are required to assist a child with a disability to benefit from special education, and includes speech-language pathology and audiology services, interpreting services, psychological services, physical and occupational therapy, recreation, including therapeutic recreation, early identification and assessment of disabilities in children, counseling services, including rehabilitation counseling, orientation and mobility services, and medical services for diagnostic or evaluation purposes. Related services also include school health services and school nurse services, social work services in schools, and parent counseling and training.

You'll notice the definition indicates related services are "required" and are intended to "assist" a child in benefiting from special education. The definition also goes on to provide examples of various related services, such as speech-language pathology and audiology services, physical and occupational therapy, and school health services, which often are familiar to educators and parents. It is important to note there are other services listed that may be less familiar, such as interpreting services, orientation and mobility services, and parent counseling and training, and all these related services are provided by professionals with training in that field. A final important point here is that the list in the federal regulations is not exhaustive; the specific related services identified for an individual child should be based on the needs and abilities of that specific child (Goran & Bateman, 2023).

Supplementary aids and services and supports for school personnel are covered in a later section in this chapter. That's because they are listed under services AND as their own stand-alone required component of the IEP. This should alert the reader to their importance in the decision-making process the IEP team engages in to identify what supports and services are required for that individual child to access both special education services and have access to a free appropriate public education.

More in-depth coverage of these service-related terms is beyond the scope of this book, but we encourage you to use this introduction as a starting point, and explore the great resources that exist, such as books (Goran & Bateman, 2023) and learning modules (The IRIS Center, 2011).

Reflection questions:

- How are the special education and related services connected to SDI?
- Do the services I list for my students connect directly to the needs identified in the present level statement and the annual goals? Are they reflective of all my student's needs?
- What are distinguishing differences between special education services, related services, and supplementary aids and services? What are recommended resources to learn more about each of these?

Placement

Along with determining the types and extent of services required to provide the SDI needed for the student, the IEP team must consider where the services take place. Some required services may occur in locations other than the general education setting, such as a special education setting or even an alternative setting. The IDEA law includes the determination of placement to address a key principle: least restrictive environment (LRE). This principle states that the student with an IEP should be educated with general education peers to the "maximum extent possible" while meeting their individualized educational needs (IDEA, 2004). The concept of LRE is not the same thing as full inclusion, rather, it ensures the student receives the appropriate services without being unduly segregated from peers (Markelz & Bateman, 2021; Yell, Bateman, & Shriner, 2021). In fact, LRE makes it possible to provide a continuum of student placements, ensuring that inclusion is meaningful when appropriate, and instruction is always beneficial as defined by the *Endrew* standard. (See Chapter 5 for discussion of where the various services are provided for Jada, Nolan, and Derrick.)

The "Golden Thread" of the IEP

For our current purposes, it is important to remember that the present level drives the goals, the goals drive the services, and the services drive the placement. There should be a clear connection across these components of the IEP. This has been referred to as "internal consistency" or the "golden thread" of the IEP (Yell, Bateman, & Shriner, 2021). This "golden thread" pulls all the way through the IEP, but the anchor point goes through the present level, annual goals, services, and placement. One should be able to read the present level statement, find goals related to the areas of need (goals that are meaningful and measurable), see services that will provide the appropriate time and personnel for instruction to reach those goals, and understand the placement for the services. Services might appear as 3 hours of individualized instruction from a reading specialist or 30 minutes per day of specialized instruction from a special education teacher. And placement may be in a general education classroom, a resource or self-contained room, a co-taught

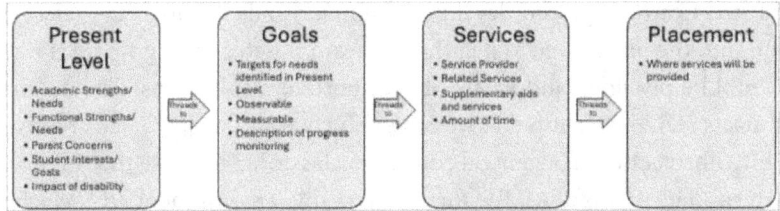

Figure 3.2 Internal consistency ("Golden Thread") of the IEP.

classroom, or any other place on the continuum of services. The specifics about the instruction (e.g., what intervention, what instructional method), in other words the SDI, are not necessarily written into the IEP, but are determined from the information provided. This is why it is critical there be consistency from present level needs to annual goals to services to placement. Figure 3.2 offers a visual representation of this needed internal consistency in the IEP.

Extent of Non-Participation in General Education

Along with the consideration of placement, the IEP must include a statement describing the extent to which the student is educated outside of the general education setting. Again, as the IEP team considers LRE for the student (see the Placement section), the legal responsibility is to make it clear how much of the school day/week is spent in specialized settings versus the general education setting, with the goal of the student being educated with typically developing peers to "the maximum extent possible" while providing an appropriate education. The idea of including students with disabilities into the general education curriculum and setting can be seen throughout the IDEA law and is a key part of that legislation since children with disabilities previously had been excluded from public school opportunities (Markelz & Bateman, 2021). This extent of participation is typically represented by a percentage, such as "more than 80% of the time in the general education setting," and is calculated from the total number of minutes in the school day or week.

Let's connect this back to the "golden thread" of the IEP and to SDI. As we've discussed, the IEP should have an internal consistency that can be tracked from the present level to the annual goals, through the services, and into the placement. When the IEP team is determining what services should be provided and where, it is important also to consider how that impacts SDI. For example, as we explore further in Chapter 5, Jada receives ELRA instruction in a general education classroom because the IEP team determined this is the LRE for her. For this environment to meet her academic and instructional needs, Jada also receives explicit instruction in cognitive learning strategies (this is her SDI for reading comprehension) to support, practice, and offer feedback on her ability to use these strategies while reading grade-level text as part of the general education classroom instruction.

Reflection questions:

- How does the "golden thread" of the IEP influence team discussions and decisions about appropriate placement and extent of time in the general education setting?
- How might SDI be impacted for a student receiving the majority of their content instruction in a general education classroom?

Participation in Statewide Assessments

In the same way the IEP team must consider—and document—time spent outside of the general education setting, the team must also consider participation in assessments. Statewide assessments are part of the educational program for all students, so the IEP team must identify which assessments the student will take, along with what accommodations and/or modifications are required for the student to participate in the assessments in a fair manner. Many school districts include both state- and district-wide assessments in this section of the IEP document.

Accommodations and Modifications

As stated in the previous section, the IEP team identifies and documents the accommodations and/or modifications a student with a disability needs for the state- and district-wide assessments. Accommodations and modifications also must be considered for participation in the general education setting. As a review, accommodations are things such as a calculator, read aloud, small testing setting, that level the playing field for the student by allowing the student to access the general education curriculum by bypassing the impact of their disability without changing the essential task. For example, if a student with a learning disability that affects their reading fluency is asked to identify themes in a novel, using a text reader bypasses the reading fluency issue and allows the student to accomplish the learning task of identifying themes. There is no change in the essential task of identifying themes.

Modifications, on the other hand, alter (or "modify") the task/expectation for the student. Using the example above, if the essential task was pronouncing words in connected text, having a text reader read the passage would fundamentally change the task—it would read, not the student. If students were assigned a five-paragraph essay that is graded for syntax, capitalization, and organization, but a student with a writing disability was assigned a shorter essay to be graded only on organization, that would be a modification of the task. Please note this example isn't simply shortening the task; it is also reducing the number of expectations from three criteria to one (i.e., organization). Modifications may support the student in both academic and functional activities. It is important to remind ourselves there is no exhaustive list of available accommodations or modifications; these are determined by the IEP team for the individual child based on the needs identified in the present level statement. (Refer back to Chapter 1 for a reminder of how accommodations and modifications are not SDI.) The accommodations and/or modifications needed by a student contribute to the "golden thread" mentioned above. The IEP document is designed to be a cohesive representation of the student's needs and the goals, services, accommodations, modifications, and supports required to allow that student to access the general education curriculum and setting.

Transition

IDEA (2004) requires the IEP team to address transition planning, supports, and services for students with disabilities. This is an essential part of the IEP development and includes the concepts of preparing students with disabilities for postsecondary life and success. Transition planning must be included in the IEP by age sixteen according to IDEA, and is required earlier in some states (e.g., Texas, Florida, Illinois, Pennsylvania). It is important to know what the requirements are for your state. Additionally, while transition is legally required to be addressed by a certain age, it can be addressed earlier in the process as determined by the IEP team, especially for skill development that may take longer than the two to three years of high school in a typical graduation plan. Often, this discussion is documented in the present level statements. For example, the student mentioned earlier who is interested in a career as an archeologist, astronaut, or professional athlete may consider courses focused on geology, astronomy, or sports medicine as electives in either middle or high school. Additionally, along with the information provided in the Present Levels section above, the IEP team may explore options for courses or job shadowing experiences available through the local career-technical center, as well as services targeting the identified IEP goal areas connected to postsecondary employment (e.g., organizational skills, financial literacy, self-regulation). Collectively, each of these goals is likely to require SDI as students with disabilities seldom develop these skills on their own and without explicit instruction, assessment, and feedback.

Supplementary Aids and Services

The term "supplementary aids and services" appears in IDEA within the section stipulating statements that must be included (§300.320(a)(4)). The terms are defined as follows:

> ***Supplementary aids and services*** mean aids, services, and other supports that are provided in regular education classes, other education-related settings, and in extracurricular and nonacademic settings, to enable children with disabilities to be educated with nondisabled children to the maximum extent appropriate. (§300.42)

There are several important components to this definition. First, it includes "aids, services, and other supports," which encompass SDI, accommodations, modifications, and adaptations required to enable the student with the IEP to be educated with nondisabled peers "to the maximum extent appropriate" (Yell, Bateman, & Shriner, 2021). As part of the services component of the IEP, these supports are part of the "golden thread" of consistency that determines what SDI is needed for that individual student.

Next, these supports are provided in "regular education" classes and settings, including extracurricular and nonacademic settings. These could include the supports necessary for a student with an IEP to participate in extracurricular activities such as school sports teams, or engage in nonacademic settings, such as field trips or clubs. As the team develops the IEP, these settings and opportunities for engagement "beyond the classroom" should be considered.

Finally, supplemental aids and services can include both direct services for the student as well as support and/or training for the staff who work with the student (Center for Parent Information and Resources, 2024). As is true with accommodations and modifications, there is no exhaustive list of supplemental aids and services to be provided for a student with an IEP; these supports are to be determined based on the individualized needs of the student.

Reflection questions:

- When thinking about the components of the IEP, how can the IEP team ensure a "golden thread" of consistency across all components? How does SDI contribute to the "golden thread" of the IEP?
- In your experience, where do IEP teams focus the most energy in an IEP? PLAAFP? Goals? Services? Placement? Transition? How might the team focus its discussions to ensure a "golden thread" throughout the IEP that incorporates clear information on the SDI needed for the student?

Summary and Next Steps

In this chapter, we reviewed the required components of an IEP and provided an overview of the importance of each to the overall document. We highlighted the direct connection necessary across the present level statements, goals, services, and placement to establish the internal consistency or "golden thread" of the IEP and provided Figure 3.2 as a visual reminder of these important connections. This connection allows us to identify how the IEP team uses the components of the IEP to drive decisions about what SDI to offer for the student. As we discuss throughout this chapter, the specific SDI needed for the individual student is impacted by the student's needs and goals, as well as the environment in which services are provided. To connect back to Alan Lakein's quote at the beginning of this chapter, the IEP is the plan to address the student's future and do something about it now. The SDI for the student is the "something" provided. We dive further into SDI in the classroom in Chapter 5, after outlining the steps necessary to develop a general statement of SDI for a student with a disability in Chapter 4. We've developed a two-step test for determining SDI and share that, along with examples and reflection questions to help you connect this to your work with students.

References

Center for Parent Information and Resources (2024). *Supplementary Aids and Services (Component of the IEP)*. Retrieved February 12, 2025, from https://www.parentcenterhub.org/iep-supplementary/

Endrew F. v. Douglas County School District, 580 U. S. 386 (2017), 798 F.3d 1329 (10th Cir. 2015), 137 S. Ct. 988 (2017), 290 F. Supp. 3d 1175 (D. Colo. 2018).

Goran, L., & Bateman, D. F. (2023). *Related services in special education: Working together as a team*. Rowman & Littlefield.

Goran, L., Harkins Monaco, E. A., Yell, M. L., Shriner, J., & Bateman, D. (2020). Pursuing academic and functional advancement: Goals, services, and measuring progress. *TEACHING Exceptional Children*, 52(5), 333–343. https://doi.org/10.1177/0040059920919924

Hedin, L., & DeSpain, S. (2018). SMART or not? Writing specific, measurable IEP goals. *TEACHING Exceptional Children*, 51(2), 100–110. https://doi.org/10.1177/0040059918802587

Individuals with Disabilities Education Act (IDEA) of 2004 (2004). 20 USC § 1400 et seq.

Individuals with Disabilities Education Act (IDEA) Regulations (2006). 34 CFR § 300 et seq.

Markelz, A. M., & Bateman, D. F. (2021). *The essentials of special education law*. Rowman & Littlefield.

The IRIS Center. (2011). *Related services: Common supports for students with disabilities*. Retrieved from https://iris.peabody.vanderbilt.edu/module/rs/

Yell, M. L., Bateman, D. F., & Shriner, J. G. (2021). *Developing educationally meaningful and legally sound IEPs*. Rowman & Littlefield.

4
Steps for Determining Specially Designed Instruction

Chapter Outline

Getting from IEP to SDI	53
Quality PLAAFP Statements to Answer, "How Is the Student Performing Now?"	55
Annual Goals as "How Do We Want the Student to Perform at the End of the IEP?"	59
PLAAFP + Annual Goal to Guide SDI	63
Specially Designed Instruction	64
Summary and Next Steps	67

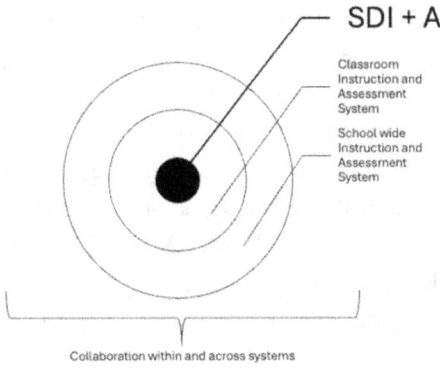

Figure 4.1 Specially Designed Instruction (SDI).

Chapter objectives:

- Identify the information necessary to determine the SDI for a student with a disability.
- Describe where to find this information.
- Give examples and nonexamples of SDI statements that identify instructional need, specific instructional content, methodology, and/or delivery of instruction necessary for appropriate student growth.
- Guide the reader through a strategy to determine SDI for a student with disabilities.

Have a bias toward action—let's see something happen now. You can break that big plan into small steps and take the first step right away.
—Indira Gandhi

Reflection questions:

- What do I need to know to begin to develop an SDI plan for my students?
- What should I be looking for when examining the PLAAFP statement? Am I writing complete PLAAFP statements?
- What should I be looking for when examining annual goals? Am I writing complete and useful annual goals?

As you read in Chapters 2 and 3, a student with a disability has an individualized education program (IEP), crafted by their IEP team. This IEP includes information related to: (a) present level of academic achievement and functional performance (PLAAFP), (b) annual goals with progress monitoring, (c) special education and related services, (d) placement, (e) extent of non-participation in general education, (f) participation in statewide assessments, (g) accommodations and modifications, (h) transition, and (i) supplementary aids and services (IDEA, 2004). As we stated in Chapter 3, what you might notice is that SDI is not included in this list. The SDI that occurs to advance a student toward their annual goals is not specifically written in the IEP. However, special educators, along with other members of the IEP team, use many components of the IEP to identify exactly what the SDI needs to be for each student. As detailed in Chapters 1, 2, and 3, SDI is the instruction necessary to (a) address the unique needs of the child that result from the child's disability AND (b) ensure access of the child to the general curriculum (IDEA, 2006). This includes adapting, as appropriate to the needs of the eligible child . . . the content, methodology, and/or delivery of instruction (IDEA, 2006). If SDI is not in the IEP, how do we identify it? Translate it into practice?

Getting from IEP to SDI

As most teachers have heard in their IEP training over the years, specific instructional methods or programs should not be included in an IEP. For example, an IEP should not indicate that a student will receive instruction using the Wilson Reading System (https://www.wilsonlanguage.com/programs/wilson-reading-system) or Red Light Purple Light! (https://ies.ed.gov/ncee/wwc/EvidenceSnapshot/725). An IEP is a binding document that should include the goals for student performance but not the specific instructional means to get there because, should progress monitoring indicate that the student is not making progress with that specific instructional method or program, then the method or program would need to be changed and the IEP would need to be amended for each instructional change made. This is not an efficient or effective way to operate.

But how then does one determine the SDI for each student with a disability if it is not written in the IEP? As Indira Ghandi says in the introductory quote, this is where we break things into small steps and start acting on them. In order to determine the SDI for each student with a disability, educators must determine the unique needs and present level of performance of the student (identified in the PLAAFP), identify the annual goals the student must meet, and describe the instruction necessary to get the student from their current performance to their annual goal. Determining the instruction necessary for a student with disabilities to achieve their annual goals lives in the "black box" or "toolkit" of special educator expertise. It is what fills the space between the present level statement and the annual goals. Take a look at Figure 4.2 for what we call the two-step test for SDI.

In the figure, one starts with the question, how is the student performing *now*? By examining the PLAAFP statement (see Chapter 3 for more), one can answer the following questions:

1. What are the strengths of the student?
2. What are the areas of weakness/need for the specific student?
3. What are the current skill levels for the student in these areas, and how do those compare to peers/general curriculum?

Then one moves to the question, how do we want the student to perform at the *end* of the IEP? By examining the annual goals, one can answer the following questions:

1. What are the goals and how will they be measured?
2. How are they related to the student's PLAAFP?

Then one asks:

1. What instruction is necessary to get from the PLAAFP to the annual goal (adaptations to the general curriculum content, delivery, methodology)?

The instruction necessary for SDI, the adaptations of content, delivery, and methodology, may span service delivery models, classrooms, and

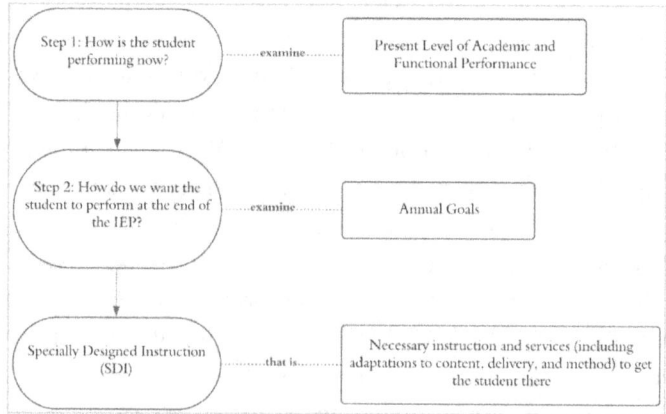

Figure 4.2 The two-step test for determining SDI.

teachers. It will include individualized instruction but will also include cuing, prompting, and reinforcing those new skills in new settings. The collaboration required across professionals to make this happen is why we think about SDI as a part of a system in this book. So, the process of examining where a student is, where we want them to be, and determining how to get them there is a continuous process that occurs across settings. We will talk about that more as we continue.

The process of determining SDI is predicated on the fact that both the PLAAFP and the annual goals are well written and include the information necessary to understand what the needs of the student are. If they are not, it will be very difficult to make decisions about SDI. We provide some examples and nonexamples below to further describe the two-step process for identifying SDI.

Reflection question:

- What is the two-step test for determining SDI and how can I use that in my practice?

Quality PLAAFP Statements to Answer, "How Is the Student Performing Now?"

Well-written and useful PLAAFP statements include specific data to guide decision-making (Goran et al., 2020; Harmon et al., 2020). Vague terms such as "struggles with" without specific data to define the term are useless in determining SDI. Let's look at some examples and nonexamples of PLAAFP statements.

Nonexample

Monica is performing below grade level in language arts and mathematics. Monica exhibits deficits in oral expression, and she often has a difficult time following oral and written directions to complete the given tasks. Monica requires a lot of repetition for her to master content and information. She can recall previously learned information and concepts inconsistently. It is noted in the Psychological report that one of Monica's weaknesses is her associative memory, and it impacts her learning. She has a difficult time retrieving words, facts, and details. Overall, Monica's performance is inconsistent in all academic subjects, and it affects her ability to access the general education curriculum. Currently, she is diagnosed with ADHD and taking medication for her ADHD.

In this nonexample, there are several areas in which Monica clearly has a need for instruction, including, for example, oral expression, following directions, and recalling previously learned information. However, there are many questions about Monica that are unanswered with this statement. Here are a few examples:

1. What deficits in oral expression does she exhibit? Under what conditions? In all classes? With all tasks?
2. Does she have trouble following one-step, two-step, or other oral and written directions? Under what conditions? With all tasks?
3. What does it mean to "require a lot of repetition" to master content? In what ways does repetition help her learn? Does she need feedback with that repetition? Are there other ways that she learns more consistently? Is this need for repetition different from her peers?
4. How does ADHD impact any areas of performance for Monica?

Before we can identify what instruction Monica needs, we need specifics about these areas of need. This means data-based information about performance, under what conditions, and with what impact.

Let's look at an example areas of need in a PLAAFP statement for Ernesto. This statement includes specific, data-based descriptions of his performance and relates that performance to his peers.

Example

Reading Fluency: Ernesto has an outside diagnosis of dyslexia. Reading fluency is an area of significant deficit as he struggles with it across content areas. The expected DRA level entering 3rd grade is 28. Ernesto began 3rd grade with a DRA 16. His Fall 2023 FastBridge Fluency screening was 35 Correct Words Per Minute (CWPM). His FastBridge progress monitoring showed growth, increasing to 56 CWPM in the Winter, and 75 CWPM in the Spring. Expected fluency at the end of 3rd grade is 130 CWPM.

Encoding: As evidenced in work samples, Ernesto is inconsistent in applying spelling rules that have been previously taught, particularly with medial sounds. He is able to recognize the rules when words are presented, but when asked to apply the rules independently in writing (e.g., in a spelling test or in a writing assignment), he often misapplies rules. For example on a recent spelling test, he spelled tray "tra," stairs "staers," chair "caer," and steal "stell."

Behavioral: Teachers report that Ernesto is impulsive across all classes and most frequently during small group or whole group discussion. During instruction in all classes, he does not raise his hand consistently and frequently provides a response before the teacher has called on him for the answer. Teacher data samples over three quarters show he gains attention appropriately during teacher-led instruction 49 percent of the time (1st quarter), 42 percent of the time (2nd quarter), and 56 percent of the time (3rd quarter).

In this example, one can see terms such as "struggles with" or "significant deficit" but these terms are followed by data that provides a clear indication of the student's current level of performance. In essence, each term is operationalized by specific data to remove ambiguity for anyone working with the IEP. In the first section related to reading fluency, the writer also included information about average performance in the grade level to help all parties understand the data in relation to peers. From this PLAAFP statement, it is clear that Ernesto shows unique needs in the areas of reading fluency, spelling rules (particularly those related to vowel sounds), and effectively gaining teacher attention. These needs differ from other students in his class.

Clearly identifying the relevant data in a student's PLAAFP statement is critical to determining the SDI for that student. In order to better understand this information, it is sometimes helpful to *clarify* and *simplify* the relevant data into a table or spreadsheet similar to the consolidated data sheet in Table 4.1.

Reflection questions:

- What makes a quality PLAAFP statement? What should I be including in the PLAAFP statements I write?
- What should I avoid writing?

Table 4.1 Consolidated Data Sheet (Example with Ernesto)

Student Name	Area of Strength	Area of Need	Data to Indicate Current Performance in This Area	Under What Conditions?	Performance in Relation to Typical Peers?	Annual Goal
Ernesto	Math calculation	Reading fluency	Fall 2023 FastBridge Fluency screening was 35 (CWPM). 56 CWPM in the Winter, and 75 CWPM in the Spring.	FastBridge Fluency	Expected fluency at the end of 3rd grade is 130 CWPM.	Given a grade-level narrative text, Ernesto will read 130 CWPM on 4 out of 5 trials.

Annual Goals as "How Do We Want the Student to Perform at the End of the IEP?"

Once there is a data-based starting point or baseline for the student, it is time to then look at the target or annual goal. (We use annual goals here knowing that many IEPs include short-term objectives that may also be used as targets. However, though we recommend them as best practice, short-term objectives are not required in all IEPs, so we wanted to include text that was relevant to all.) A well-written IEP annual goal sets a *measurable, observable, achievable, and relevant* target for students to reach by the end of the IEP year. This goal ensures that students with disabilities are making meaningful progress in their areas of need so that they can access the general curriculum as much as possible (*Endrew F.*, 2017). Again, the quality of these goals will determine how well a special educator can determine the SDI that is appropriate for the student.

To be a complete goal, the statement must include a *task* (what the student will do— not what the teacher will do), a *condition* (under what conditions the student will perform the task), and *criterion* (how accurately or appropriately the student will perform the task in order for it to be determined that the student has mastered it). These components go by many different names and acronyms (e.g., ABCs or ABCD-T); however, what the student will do under what conditions to what criterion are the critical components of every annual goal (Goran et al., 2020; Hedin & DeSpain, 2018). Many school districts/divisions have standard types of phrases (e.g., "use a % accuracy and a number of trials") or formats (e.g., "always start with a condition-given XXX") so it is important to understand those requirements but to also make those requirements and the resulting criterion (or criteria), meaningful. For example, it is hard to determine if someone raises their hand with 90 percent accuracy on 4 of 5 trials. What does "accuracy" mean here? The student raised their hand above their head? They put their hand in the air and did not speak or wave it around? They raised their hand before the teacher finished asking a question? After the teacher answered a question? Instead, in many cases, the goal is for the student to gain teacher attention appropriately. So, the goal might be, "During teacher directed instruction in science, Mary will gain teacher attention appropriately in 8 of 9 attempts." In this case, the conditions are specific (teacher-directed instruction in science); the task is clear (gain teacher attention—so this might be raising a hand and waiting to be recognized, signaling to a co-teacher who is not delivering instruction, or any other option that the teacher accepts or is teaching the student to use); the criterion is also clear (on 8 of 9 attempts—so when the student attempts to get the teacher's attention, did the student do it appropriately?). In another example, it is also difficult to determine what someone means when they say, "the student will solve a multi-step word problem with 90% accuracy." Does that mean it is *almost* correct? Does that mean they skipped one step? They calculated incorrectly? How can a math problem be 90 percent accurate? What the writer really means is that the student will solve 9 of 10 of those problems accurately and they should just say that in the goal. Let's look at some nonexample goals (taken from real IEPs) that would make it difficult to determine the required SDI.

Nonexamples

1. *Given a text, Ernesto will read 130 words per minute with 90 percent accuracy on 4 out of 5 trials.*

   Task: student will read (clear)

   Condition: given a text (here we don't know what type of text, what level of text—basically we need to know more about what the condition/text would be in order to think about how to develop instruction)

   Criterion: 130 words per minute with 90 percent accuracy on 4 of 5 trials (usually, the number of words read per minute means the total number of words read minus the errors. Therefore, we might want to specify 130 words read correctly per minute. It is not clear what 90 percent accuracy means in this scenario, but we want to make sure that the student can do this task multiple times and not just get lucky and do it once!)

2. *Kevin will improve attention during teacher-directed lessons 80 percent of time.*

   Task: improve attention (Can Kevin constantly be improving attention? What does "improve attention" look like?)

Condition: teacher-directed lesson (Is this in every class? It would be very difficult to collect accurate data across all of Kevin's classes to know whether he is achieving his goal. However, if it is a specific area of need, it would be beneficial to focus on particular parts of lessons to observe and collect data.)

Criterion: 80 percent of time. (80 percent of what time? Is he only supposed to be improving attention 80 percent of time? All day? All classes? How does one quantify and observe this?)

3. *Given support, Mary will set up and solve equations with 85 percent accuracy on 4 out of 5 trials.*

    Task: set up and solve equations (Do we want to separate these—it's actually two tasks and she might accomplish one and not the other? Are there particular types of equations that are critical for Mary to know and understand? This would come directly from data in the PLAAFP.)

    Condition: given support (It's not clear what this means. What is support? What does support look like? If it varies, it will be hard to assess whether Mary is meeting her goal through her own efforts.)

    Criterion: with 85 percent accuracy on 4 out of 5 trials (What does 85 percent accuracy mean? Does it really mean that Mary can accurately set up and solve 3 of 5 given equations on 4 out of 5 trials? Or does it mean that the set up and solving is 85 percent correct?)

4. *Given direct instruction and strategies in identification of prefixes, suffixes, and root words, Amber will increase her ability to read and understand using grade-level vocabulary with 100 percent or higher on all assignments.*

    Task: increase her ability to read and understand using grade-level vocabulary (It is not clear at all what this task is! Is she increasing her reading and understanding ability on grade-level vocabulary? Can she constantly be increasing her reading and understanding? How do we know if she's increasing?)

    Condition: given direct instruction and strategies in identification of prefixes, suffixes, and root words; using grade-level vocabulary (Instruction is not meant to be a part of the condition of an IEP goal. The understanding is that the student will receive instruction—specially designed instruction—to meet all of the annual goals written into their IEP. Therefore, putting the instruction in the goal is not an appropriate condition. Rather, here, the condition is meant to be the condition under which the student will perform the task.)

Criterion: 100 percent or higher on all assignments (This one always makes us chuckle! There really isn't supposed to be a "higher" than 100 percent. And, quite frankly, we are still wondering 100 percent of what? And this 100 percent applies to all assignments—meaning all classes, all work. This is impossible to measure!)

Examples

1. *Given a grade-level narrative text, Ernesto will read 130 correct words per minute on 4 out of 5 trials.*

   Task: student will read;
   Condition: given a grade-level narrative text;
   Criteria: 130 word read correctly per minute on 4 out of 5 trials.

2. *By the end of the school year, Kevin's on-task behavior will increase from 37 percent to 85 percent of teacher-directed instruction time in language arts.*

   Task: on-task behavior will increase;
   Condition: by the end of the school year, teacher-directed instruction time in language arts;
   Criteria: from 37 percent to 85 percent.

3. *Given a graphic organizer to cue her solution strategy, Mary will accurately set up and solve 9 of 10 three-step equations on 4 of 5 trials.*

   Task: set up and solve three-step equations;
   Condition: given a graphic organizer to cue her solution strategy;
   Criteria: accurately set up and solve, 9 of 10 equations, 4 of 5 trials.

4. *Given a list of ten grade-level vocabulary terms in any content area, Amber will accurately spell and define the terms.*

   Task: spell and define;
   Condition: given a list of ten grade-level vocabulary terms in any content area;

Criteria: accurately (meaning all ten terms).

In these examples, the task, conditions, and criterion are clear, observable, and measurable. Each can provide a guide to what the SDI might be.

Reflection questions:

- Why is it important to have a clear, observable, and measurable task, condition, and criterion in annual goals?
- How could a consolidated data sheet help support my thinking about and planning for SDI?

PLAAFP + Annual Goal to Guide SDI

Now, let's put everything together using information from Ernesto in Table 4.1. According to the reading fluency component of the PLAAFP statement:

> *His Fall 2023 FastBridge Fluency screening was 35 Correct Words Per Minute (CWPM). His FastBridge progress monitoring showed growth, increasing to 56 CWPM in the Winter, and 75 CWPM in the Spring. Expected fluency at the end of 3rd grade is 130 CWPM.*

His IEP team has identified an annual goal of

> *Given a grade level narrative text, Ernesto will read 130 correct words per minute on 4 out of 5 trials.*

There are many reasons that the IEP team may have identified this annual goal for Ernesto. As he finishes 3rd grade and enters into 4th, he is reading at approximately 75 CWPM. By the end of 4th grade, his peers are probably reading at about 152 CWPM. Getting Ernesto to 130 CWPM will not get him to the average rate of his peers, but it will almost double his current rate and reduce the discrepancy between him and his peers significantly.

Knowing that the special educator has to start with Ernesto at 75 CWPM and move him to 130 CWPM means a rapid rate of improvement, above that of his peers. Through the third grade here, his rate of improvement was high, moving from 35 CWPM to 75 CWPM. The instruction he was receiving made an impact! So continuing it or intensifying it for fourth grade might be his SDI.

Specially Designed Instruction

By SDI, we mean the broad idea of the instruction and services necessary. Day-to-day planning for SDI and its implementation will be the topic of Chapter 5. SDI is the adaptation of delivery, methodology, and content to address the unique needs of a student with disabilities and provide access to the general curriculum (IDEA, 2004). So, it is critical to think about all three of these areas when determining how best to provide instruction for a student with disabilities. Figure 4.3 provides a graphic with just a few examples of evidence-based practices and strategies to consider when thinking about SDI particularly for our example students.

Ernesto

In considering Ernesto's PLAAFP and annual goals, it is clear that he will need SDI related to reading. In the *services* area of the IEP, the team might identify that Ernesto would receive "specialized reading instruction" for 30 minutes a day. But the *SDI* that Ernesto needs would clearly need to include adaptations to delivery, content, and methodology to the general curriculum instruction in reading. Specifically, Ernesto would probably benefit from small group or individualized instruction that would include content that

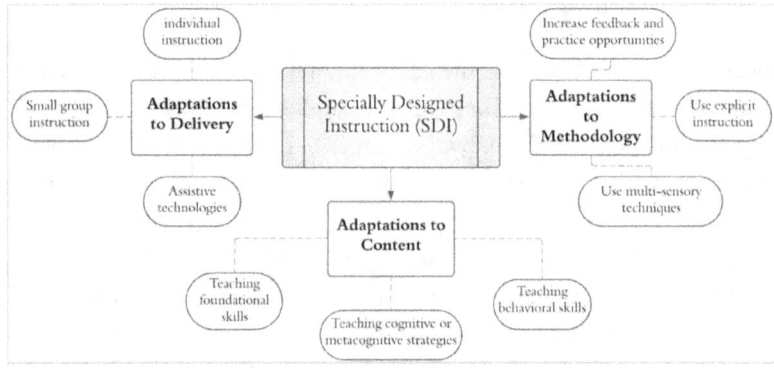

Figure 4.3 Three areas and examples of SDI.

is focused on phonics and decoding skills, along with fluency practice, that is different from his peers. So, his SDI would be specialized reading instruction that includes small group, multi-sensory instruction with a focus on phonics, decoding, and additional reading skills. In addition, it would probably also include the accommodation of using text-to-speech software when reading content for meaning and increased practice opportunities with prompting and feedback related to his improving decoding skills when in the general curriculum. We will talk a bit more about what that looks like day to day in Chapter 5. Let's take a look at another example.

Jack

Step 1: Data-based PLAAFP statement. Jack's scores on the KTEA-2 math composites are within the average range (SS: 97) for same-age students. However, his math calculation standard score is 115 and his applied problems standard score is 70. His math teacher states that he has strong rote math calculations and will often participate in class discussions. His teacher also states that Jack consistently solves single and multi-step math equations when given in a list format; he can use a calculator for various calculations with decimals and fractions; and he is able to substitute values for variables to solve math problems. Jack's teacher notes that analytical processes prove more difficult for him, as he will often shut down and not attempt problems when confused or frustrated. Jack is inconsistent on math tests and quizzes. He has earned the following test scores: 65 (unit test on determining sums and differences of polynomial expressions); 98 (quiz on evaluating algebraic expressions); 52 (unit test on determining products of polynomial expressions). His classwork grades are also inconsistent, and some samples show evidence of not following directions. Jack cannot follow multi-step tasks and recall information at the same level as his peers, as indicated by below-average scores on the Differential Abilities Scale-2.

Step 2: Observable, measurable, relevant annual goal. Given a set of ten multi-step word problems, Jack will accurately translate them to algebraic expressions and correctly solve all ten problems on three out of four opportunities.

SDI. Jack shows an area of weakness in math; specifically, his teachers indicate he can usually accurately calculate items, including multi-step equations. However, it seems it is difficult for him to actually apply that knowledge and determine what algorithm to use in a given applied situation. We do not have specific grade-level standards here but a special educator determining the SDI for Jack probably would have that information. For now, it would be appropriate to concentrate instruction on reading, interpreting, and applying a strategy to solving word problems that he may encounter at his grade level. In order to do this, Jack's SDI would require an adaptation to delivery, either small group or individually delivered instruction given the content of it. He would also require an adaptation of content to teach Jack to use specific problem-solving strategy routines that include graphic organizers or a cuing system (e.g., schema-based instruction) that would be taught using explicit instruction with multiple practice and feedback opportunities. Finally, he would need explicit instruction and prompting in how to generalize these strategies to the general curriculum.

Not all students will need adaptations in all three areas of content, delivery, and methodology. However, many will need combinations that make them worthwhile. For example, a general educator may be teaching a cognitive strategy to an entire class but the student with a disability might need more explicit instruction and an increased number of practice opportunities (adapting methodology) using simplified text (adapting content) in a small group setting (adapting delivery). In most cases, it is difficult to imagine that a student with a disability who is eligible for special education services would only need an adaptation to methodology or to delivery but that *might* be the case. For example, a student with ADHD may be able to progress in the general curriculum without significant changes to content and methodology if instruction is delivered in a way that removes distractions (e.g., small group, small room, online, or other). As these examples have indicated, SDI complements instruction in the general curriculum. They work synergistically to build on one another—SDI is meant to make the general curriculum more accessible by the development of knowledge and skills in areas that are not fully developed for students with disabilities. Because SDI and instruction in the general curriculum are complementary, there is a requirement for collaboration across professionals who are delivering this instruction. While it is incumbent upon the special educator and related service providers to identify the SDI, it is also incumbent upon the general educator to help generalize, cue, and practice these knowledge and skills essentials, along with ensuring that accommodations are implemented. As we have said over and over, SDI may be focused on academics, behavior, life skills, executive function skills, and other areas for students with disabilities but all of those areas are critical for success in the general curriculum. Therefore, educators must *integrate* their areas of expertise to improve outcomes for students with disabilities.

Note: We recognize that some students with disabilities will access an adapted curriculum as part of their IEP and SDI. Because IDEA uses the general curriculum as a target, we also use that throughout the book. However, because SDI is based upon a student's IEP goals and the goals are based on the present level of performance, the SDI is targeted on achieving these goals.

Reflection question:

- How is this process the same or different from what you already do?

Summary and Next Steps

This chapter outlined and provided examples of the steps necessary to develop a general statement of SDI for a student with a disability. The first step is to identify the starting point or a student's present level of performance, given multiple sources of data. From there, the teacher examines the corresponding annual goal to identify the target. Then, the special education teacher identifies the instruction necessary to get the student from the present level to the goal. The IEP may indicate services such as "specialized reading instruction" or "cognitive strategy instruction" but the delivered SDI would include specific adaptations to content, methodology, and/or delivery. Once it is clear what is necessary for SDI, the special education teacher can move to developing plans for day-to-day SDI implementation which is our topic in Chapter 5.

In the next chapter, you will engage in identifying SDI for three students with disabilities; allow us to introduce them briefly here.

Jada is a 12-year-old student with a specific LD related to reading comprehension, specifically her ability to read long sentences with multisyllabic words that results in habits of skimming and missing big ideas. Jada also has a comorbid diagnosis of ADHD that often results in incomplete assignments, frequently talking out of turn and disrupting small group work. Her SDI includes an adaptation of content in teaching her a self-questioning strategy, adaptation in delivery of small group instruction, and adaptation of methodology by providing instruction using the Strategic Instruction Model with graphic organizers and mnemonic cues.

Nolan is a 13-year-old student with Down syndrome whose understanding of letter-sound correspondence has improved dramatically over the last few years but is still below grade level. Specifically, he is below grade level in blending sounds that results in lower reading fluency. Moreover, challenges with speech make expressive reading difficult and cause embarrassment that results in a reluctance to participate orally in class during group discussions. The SDI for Nolan is an adaptation in content by using below grade-level reading passages, generated by a software program that also produces comprehension questions. There is also an adaptation in delivery by using small groups and in methodology by teaching cognitive strategies with a significant number of repetitions, practice opportunities, and by chunking the strategy into smaller parts.

Derrick is an 11-year-old student with ASD who has excellent verbal skills and language comprehension. He is a strong reader and is usually assigned to one of the highest ability reading groups during small group instruction. However, Derrick struggles to read social cues, frequently talking over his classmates, interrupting them, or ignoring their conversation to read ahead. His SDI includes adaptations in content by instruction in behavior strategies for turn taking and maintaining personal space, adaptations in methodology by using explicit instruction, and adaptations in delivery by providing that instruction individually and cuing it during small group instruction.

It is evident to us, and we hope to all readers, that determining SDI may begin with the IEP team and assigned special educator but the implementation of SDI requires a systems approach across educators, school personnel, and placement options.

References

Endrew F. v. Douglas County School District, 137 S. Ct. 988 (2017).

Goran, L., Monaco, E. A. H., Yell, M. L., Shriner, J., & Bateman, D. (2020). Pursuing academic and functional advancement: Goals, services, and measuring progress. *TEACHING Exceptional Children*, *52*(5), 333–343.

Harmon, S., Street, M., Bateman, D., & Yell, M. L. (2020). Developing present levels of academic achievement and functional performance statements for IEPs. *TEACHING Exceptional Children*, *52*(5), 320–332.

Hedin, L., & DeSpain, S. (2018). SMART or not? Writing specific, measurable IEP goals. *TEACHING Exceptional Children*, *51*(2), 100–110.

Individuals with Disabilities Education Improvement Act of 2004. (2004). 20 U.S.C. § 1400 et seq.

Individuals with Disabilities Education Act (IDEA) Regulations. (2006). 34 C.F.R. § 300 et seq

5

Specially Designed Instruction in the Classroom

Evidence-Based Instructional Strategies and Interventions

Chapter Outline

Connecting the Dots	72
Effective Instructional Design	79
Applying the Framework to Create SDI	81
Conclusion	95

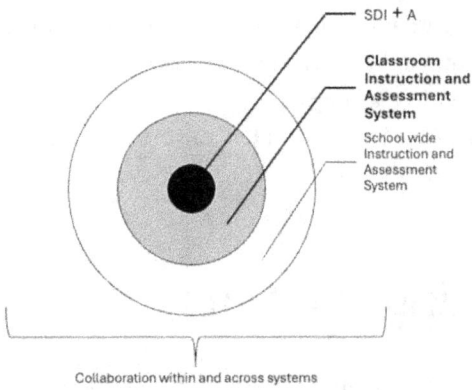

Figure 5.1 Specially Designed Instruction (SDI) + Classroom Instruction and Assessment System.

Chapter objectives:

- Illustrate a classroom case with three students with disabilities to demonstrate how SDI might look in an inclusive general education classroom.
- Describe how elements of the IEP from the previous chapter are operationalized into short-term objectives and then lesson plans to meet group and individual needs.
- Introduce the concept of evidence-based practices (EBPs) aligned with specific student skill development.
- Provide information about where to begin searching for EBPs for specific skills.
- Operationalize the Two-Step Test of SDI within the context of lesson planning.
- Warn against common pitfalls of planning for SDI.

Our goals can only be reached through a vehicle of a plan, in which we must fervently believe, and upon which we must vigorously act. There is no other route to success.

—Pablo Picasso

Reflection questions:

- When planning lessons for a whole class, how do you ensure alignment with individual student's IEP goals and objectives?
- What resources are currently available to you for incorporating EBPs into your teaching?
- In what areas of SDI do you feel the most confident? Where do you feel you need more guidance or resources?

Connecting the Dots

When it comes to planning classroom instruction, educators have a variety of resources that provide guidance on what to teach. For example, state standards, purchased curriculum, pacing guides, and guidelines from professional organizations (e.g., NCTM, NCTE) all provide suggestions for crafting instructional delivery. However, equally important to designing general education instruction is the composition of the classroom—who are the students? While all classrooms are filled with wide ranges in learner variability (i.e., strong readers and struggling readers, students with persistent levels of attention and those with attention issues, etc.), in a case where the classroom includes students with disabilities, it is essential that educators draw upon the IEP for guidance to ensure that each student's SDI is appropriately created. If the standards and curriculum provide the initial *what* of instruction, SDI from the IEP will now incorporate emphasis on *how* the individual with a disability will receive access to the general education curriculum by matching the unique needs and goals of the student with instruction and instructional delivery that meets those needs and goals (see Two-Step Test, Chapter 4). SDI specifically addresses the skills that may be necessary for students with disabilities to learn to acquire, store, and express their learning (IDEA, 2004). In the previous chapter, we described how special educators use a three-phase process for using the PLAAFP to identify learning barriers, choose practices to address these barriers, and then implement to assess efficacy. In this chapter, we will describe the dual process educators, both special and general education, take in the words of Picasso to create the vehicle of a plan to guide their vigorous action on behalf of students with disabilities.

Let's start with the big-picture reality of the general education classroom. Consider the example below as Ms. Welsch's fifth-grade ELAR class uses the district-mandated amplify curriculum to deliver an introductory lesson on Shakespeare's *Midsummer Night's Dream*. Her classroom has twenty-eight students, including three students with disabilities whose SDIs have been crafted as outlined in Chapter 4 to ensure that while moving through the assigned curriculum, the students not only have access to the general education curriculum, but are working toward their annual goals within the whole-group lesson and beyond. Ms. Welsch has consulted with Mr. Dixon, the school's special education teacher, on the specific SDI for each student with a disability, but only Mr. Jordan, a paraprofessional, is available for classroom support during this period of ELAR instruction.

The Classroom Case

Lesson Overview. Ms. Welsch has learned from previous years of instruction that while many of her students have heard of Shakespeare, very few have sufficient background knowledge in the world of the Elizabethan Theater or the Greek myths informing *Midsummer Night's Dream* to easily make meaning from the school-provided texts. Therefore, to begin the unit, she has chosen to start with a lesson using a set of readings on the life of William Shakespeare and the Elizabethan theater of his time. In addition to addressing student background knowledge, Ms. Welsch has also decided to use this unit to reinforce self-questioning as a reading strategy to keep her students engaged with the text, and small group cooperative learning routines that ensure everyone participates appropriately during seat work. The self-questioning strategy was introduced during the last unit, but many students have not developed automaticity (i.e., they cannot yet use the strategy without significant effort or attention) when using the strategy causing too much short-term memory use and sacrificing reading comprehension (e.g., Faggella-Luby, Schumaker, & Deshler, 2007; Sweller, 1988). Finally, small group routines were taught earlier in the year but, based on the project presentations from the last unit, roles and procedures need to be re-prompted and practiced (e.g., Slavin, 2012).

Lesson Components. In brief, the lesson includes the following components: Ms. Welsch gathers the students as a whole group for a brief lecture on the theater in Shakespeare's day, some common Elizabethan words, and an overview of the Greek society portrayed in *Midsummer*. Using the Smartboard in her classroom, the 12-minute presentation draws on textual descriptions, short video and audio clips, and even sharing two Elizabethan period costumes with the students to touch and feel as modalities for learning. She concludes the guided discussion by introducing a short reading in the textbook to be used in small groups as their next activity. She also briefly introduces the self-questioning strategy and demonstrates for the class how they might ask themselves questions while reading the passage in groups. Ms. Welsch used a modified verbal think-aloud related to the title and the first paragraph of the reading, generating two factual questions, and one higher order question.

Next, the students slide into cooperative learning small groups. Mrs. Welsch uses a verbal prompt and a visual cue toward the poster in the classroom to remind each group of the guidelines for small group work including special emphasis on assigning roles and turn taking. Groups are homogeneous, organized for this lesson based on overall reading comprehension ability. Each group of students gets three items: (a) a reading on Shakespeare and the Elizabethan Theater written at their ability level, (b) a worksheet to record self-questions, and (c) one laminated card per group with the reminder of small group routine procedures. At the conclusion of cooperative learning, it is expected that each student will have a set of questions, predictions, and answers related to big ideas in the reading. Ms. Welsch then conducts a class-wide debrief, asking for example questions and answers from each group. It is expected that the reporter from each group will share out, with Ms. Welsch recording and providing feedback with strong group questions written on the whiteboard. She concludes the class with a review of the relevant big ideas that students were to draw from the reading for their notes, and a statement about the utility of self-questioning in their future reading.

Embedding SDI. Ms. Welsch's lesson design was also mindful of the long-term outcomes for three students with disabilities in her class: Jada, Nolan, and Derrick. During the beginning of the school year, she met with Mr. Dixon, and they outlined a model of service delivery between the general education classroom and the 1:1 and small group resource room instruction that each student received as outlined in their IEP. Below, we provide insight into how each student was meaningfully included in the classroom, engaging with relevant content, and progressing toward both lesson and IEP goals.

The Case of Jada

Jada is a 12-year-old student with a specific LD related to reading comprehension that causes her frustration when reading long sentences with multisyllabic words and results in habits of skimming and missing big ideas. Jada also has a comorbid diagnosis of ADHD that impacts her learning by allowing small distractions to take her away from her assignments, frequently talking out of turn and disrupting small group work. As a result, Jada frequently concludes assignments without connecting ideas or finding evidence to support claims. To address this need, Ms. Welsch and Mr. Dixon have decided to teach her the Self-Questioning Strategy from the *Strategic Instruction Model*™ (SIM) because it directly addresses Jada's reading comprehension needs by providing a problem-solving approach that engages Jada with the text while surfacing evidence to support claims. This is Jada's SDI for reading comprehension. Mr. Dixon provides explicit instruction in the strategy, using the SIM steps and materials during Jada's resource room individualized instruction time. As Jada is learning and practicing in the resource room, Mr. Dixon works with Ms. Welsch to prompt its use in the ELAR classroom.

To help cue the use of the SQ Strategy during Ms. Welsch's class, Mr. Dixon has helped Jada to create a page in her notebook for easy reference that includes the mnemonics and strategy steps. Ms. Welsch helps remind Jada when to use the strategy and corresponding notebook page during different reading activities. In this way, the targeted strategy instruction as part of her SDI can be practiced with leveled texts during pullout time with Mr. Dixon, as well as applied with grade-level readings during her ELAR class with Ms. Welsch. Ongoing progress-monitoring data is showing that Jada has mastery of the strategy steps and can use them with novel texts of increasing complexity. Moreover, in-class formative assessments are showing that Jada is more engaged with the text because the problem-solving process helps her focus, resulting in increased self-monitoring, increased persistence in reading tasks, more questions asked per reading assignment, and improved evidence to support claims. Finally, these skills, along with the class-wide emphasis on small group routines have decreased the number of interruptions Jada causes during cooperative learning time because she is learning she can wait her turn to share and still contribute meaningfully.

The Case of Nolan

Nolan is a 13-year-old student with Down syndrome who attends Ms. Welsch's ELAR class daily with his paraprofessional, Mr. Jordan. As outlined in his PLAAFP, Nolan's understanding of letter-sound correspondence has improved dramatically over the last few years, though at times he struggled with blending sounds which can impact his fluency. Moreover, challenges with speech make expressive reading difficult and cause embarrassment that results in a reluctance to participate orally in class during group discussions. To meaningfully include Nolan in Ms. Welsch's small group reading lesson on Shakespeare, Mr. Dixon, Mr. Jordan, and Ms. Welsch have agreed to address two of his critical reading needs. They will use *Diffit*™ (http://beta.diffit.me/#topic), an AI-enhanced tool for teachers that allows Ms. Welsch to upload the 5th grade reading passage the rest of the class will be using so that Diffit will provide both a 3rd grade version of the passage and suggest comprehension questions related to the passage content that will be similar to those generated by other students using the SQ Strategy.

As SDI, and in preparation for Ms. Welsch's lesson, Mr. Dixon and Mr. Jordan have agreed to use Nolan's IEP mandated additional small group literacy time in a self-contained learning environment with them to use pre-teaching of vocabulary and key phrases and echo reading during their three 20-minute sessions with him during the week prior. Specifically, Mr. Jordan will help Nolan work on his fluency, prosody, and confidence. Mr. Dixon has secured from Ms. Welsch the appropriate version of the text and, using *Diffit*™, differentiated the reading to a third-grade level that is appropriate for Nolan. He also has identified key vocabulary and phrases, providing visual supports to reinforce meaning and noting syllabication for polysyllabic words. Mr. Jordan can then begin instruction with a brief overview and explicit practice with the key vocabulary and phrases. Nolan is given multiple opportunities to respond with practice in isolation before they collectively turn their attention to the pre-selected connected text. Mr. Jordan will then read the passage to Nolan, modeling articulation, expression, and proper intonation. Nolan will repeat each sentence or passage (depending on length) and receive immediate feedback from Mr. Jordan. This process will be repeated with gradually increasing passage lengths based on Nolan's accuracy and confidence over several days. At the conclusion of the passage, Nolan will follow the same echo reading steps with the *Diffit*™ generated questions.

On the day of the whole-group lesson, Nolan will still benefit from some additional supports in the general education environment. Fortunately, Mr. Jordan has agreed to run a small, homogeneous reading group because Ms. Welsch has several students reading below grade level and she wants to have these small number of students practice the SQ Strategy with an ability-level text to reduce cognitive load from the reading task in a way that will shift their thinking toward asking questions. This will allow Mr. Jordan to work with Nolan and three other students. Together, the group will read the short passage with Mr. Jordan prompting the steps of the SQ Strategy at predetermined stopping points throughout the passage. After the group has finished generating questions, Nolan will be encouraged to review his list of *Diffit*™ generated and practiced questions and share aloud with the group any additional questions that might be related to the content at each stopping point. Once the questions are recorded and predictions made, the group works together to continue reading and searching for answers to the questions in the text. Because Nolan is using the *Diffit*™ generated questions, it is guaranteed that the group will find an answer to at least his questions thus adding to his connection to the group. Mr. Jordan is pleased that the design of this instructional opportunity not only allows Nolan to read a passage on a similar topic to his neurotypical peers in the rest of the class, but also to practice his speech by contributing during small group conversations using the suggested questions.

The Case of Derrick

Derrick is an 11-year-old student with autism spectrum disorder (ASD) who has excellent verbal skills and language comprehension. He is a strong reader and is usually assigned to one of the highest ability reading groups during small group instruction. However, Derrick struggles to read social cues, frequently talking over his classmates, interrupting them, or ignoring their conversation to read ahead. Ms. Welsch and Mr. Dixon have agreed, based on Derrick's IEP and behavioral intervention plan (BIP), that he needs explicit instruction and practice in turn taking, a skill that is valuable throughout his day, but particularly during small group reading time. Like Jada, for Derrick's SDI, Mr. Dixon has taken advantage of his pullout time with Derrick to teach him a strategy for turn taking. Using social narratives (NPDC, 2015) to explain other people's perspectives and the social ramifications of his actions, Derrick and Mr. Dixon have co-created a visual support (https://afirm.fpg.unc.edu/visual-supports) that mirrors the steps on the laminated card used by Ms. Welsch with the reminder of small group routine procedures. Mr. Dixon and Derrick have practiced using the visual support during his pullout class time, and he is now ready to try generalization practice in Ms. Welsch's classroom during the reading activity.

When the students transition into small groups, Ms. Welsch would remind all students about the procedures for using the laminated card, suggesting that each member of the group is assigned a role. She can then circulate around the room allowing her to cue Derrick individually before the small group activity begins so he knows the expectations to use his own visual support. During the lesson, Ms. Welsch will take behavioral data on whether Derrick is allowing each member of his group to participate, taking turns, and saving what he wants to share until it is his turn. She is hoping that two immediate results of this experience are that (1) the other students in the group will turn to look at Derrick when he is speaking, rather than ignoring him because he has interrupted them, and (2) because Derrick has had an opportunity to share, she believes he will refrain from reading ahead, instead listening to the contributions of others. Perhaps when the small group time is up and their group has completed the activity, Ms. Welsch will overhear one of Derrick's group members complement one of his suggested questions!

Reflection question:

- How has Ms. Welsch designed the lesson above to address the specific IEP goals of Jada, Nolan, and Derrick while also ensuring their SDI connected to the class learning objective for the day?

Effective Instructional Design

The cases of Jada, Nolan, and Derrick—and for that matter Ms. Welsch, Mr. Dixon, and Mr. Jordan—is the story of specially designed instruction. Effective instructional design for whole groups that also includes the appropriate service delivery tailored to the unique needs of students with disabilities requires collaboration with a systemic mindset, the knowledge and skill to put research into practice, and careful planning to avoid common pitfalls. SDI is part of the guarantee of special education services to enable a student with a disability to make appropriate progress, and while initially may require more coordination and planning for educators, can also positively transform the least restrictive environment, especially when it includes typical achieving peers in an inclusive classroom. We believe that translating student PLAAFP into annual goals and providing SDI to reach those goals is one of the most rewarding and meaningful efforts an educator can have in their career. Below we detail just how you can move from planning to action with coordinated plans for each student.

The Systemic Mindset

Planning for SDI with one student can be challenging. Planning for an inclusive class with multiple students with disabilities may feel overwhelming to some. However, because SDI is not only the right thing to do, but also is required for compliance with the law, it is worth our efforts. Therefore, we have found that it is most efficient when educators adopt a systemic mindset when approaching classroom implementation of SDI. As we detailed in Chapter 4, at its most basic level, the Two-Step Test can be operationalized into three stages in the classroom. In that example, we looked specifically at the role of the special education teacher, their review of the PLAAFP for barriers, identification of practices to address the barriers, and then implementation with feedback by a host of educators. As an expansion of that model, let's review a collaborative version of that model when the general educator is involved and considering meaningful inclusion in the general education classroom (see Figure 5.2).

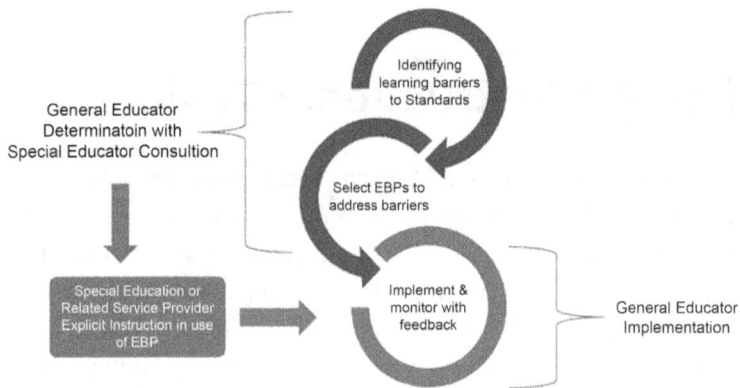

Figure 5.2 SDI problem-solving mindset.

First, the general educator identifies the barrier to standards-aligned learning for an individual student. This barrier is most commonly observable in the gap between the lesson objective and the appropriate learning assessment (more on this in Chapter 6). Barriers might include challenges with reading multisyllabic words (as with dyslexia or ID), the ability to brainstorm writing ideas (as in communication disorders, dysgraphia, or ASD), or completing multi-step math equations (as in dyscalculia or ADHD). Next, the general educator, in consultation with the special educator, determines an EBP that is aligned to address the specific barrier to the objective. SDI may require additional time to teach the student the components of the EBP and, therefore, it is essential that coordination between special education and general education occur on a regular basis around short and long-term objectives. Finally, the general educator implements the EBP with the student as part of whole group or small group instruction and monitors progress to provide feedback and ensure that the practice is implemented with fidelity, mastered by the student, and sufficiently addressing the lesson objective.

One important caveat to the model described above is the need for the special educator or a related service provider to use explicit instruction when teaching the student with an EBP. In some cases, as in Nolan's echo reading example, the use of an explicit framework when offering modeling, practice, and feedback is sufficient. However, in cases like Jada and Derrick, it is necessary for the explicit instruction to target mediation for the learner as mastery is transferred from the educator to the student, developing self-regulated use. Without this parallel process, the general education teacher is likely to be unsuccessful in cuing the student to use the strategy as the student does not have sufficient mastery to use it on their own.

Applying the Framework to Create SDI

Let's reconsider our example cases involving Jada, Nolan, and Derrick. For Jada, her inattention and struggle to connect ideas or find evidence to support claims were the most important barriers to accessing the general education curriculum. Ms. Welsh and Mr. Dixon had lots of choices for interventions but decided that the metacognitive components embedded in the steps of the Self-Questioning Strategy were an important step in addressing the executive functioning challenges Jada was facing while reading. Specifically, the Self-Questioning Strategy would support her reading with a mnemonic for remembering the seven types of questions to ask, as well as a formula for (a) asking questions, (b) making related predictions, and (c) continuing to read and record the actual answers to the questions based on textual evidence.

Moreover, because the strategy helps build engagement with the text through the question-prediction-search-for-answers formula, Jada was likely to see improvements in overall comprehension. Mr. Dixon knew that Jada would not likely master the strategy if she was just told the steps and given opportunities to practice. Therefore, her teachers decided to provide Self-Questioning Strategy instruction during her pullout reading time (30 minutes, two times per week) using an explicit eight-stage model of instruction (see Table 5.1 for differences in sample dialogue). This would allow her to build automaticity with the strategy, allowing Ms. Welsch to cue its use during regular class time. To complete the three-stage problem-solving process, Mr. Dixon conducted regular progress monitoring to measure Jada's knowledge of the strategy steps and her ability to use the strategy with novel passages. This provided him with data to guide specific corrective feedback that accelerated her ability to master the strategy so that he knew she would be ready to try the strategy on her own during a lesson with Ms. Welsch.

When it comes to applying this problem-solving framework to ensure SDI, the case is similar for Nolan. Specifically, for Nolan, his struggles with fluency and speech were identified as barriers to accessing the general education curriculum. As detailed above, this led to teacher-directed differentiation by creating passages with AI at his reading level to reduce the fluency challenge. In doing so, this freed critical cognitive capacity for making meaning regarding the content in which the rest of the class was engaging. Nolan can then practice his speech in the small group run by Mr. Jordan, scaffolded by sharing predetermined questions.

What we do not see in Ms. Welsch's class that is critical to SDI is that, prior to this lesson, during pullout instruction with Mr. Jordan and Mr. Dixon, Nolan practiced blending activities using words from the AI Diffit-created passages related to Shakespeare's Theater. After isolated practice, Mr. Jordan then used a repeated reading strategy with Nolan to

Table 5.1 Differences in Sample Dialogue between Tiers during Instruction of the Self-Questioning Strategy

Whole Group (Tier 1)

Mrs. Welsch: Today, we're going to practice a strategy that can help us better understand Shakespeare's *A Midsummer Night's Dream*. This strategy involves asking ourselves questions while we read. This technique can keep us engaged and help us make sense of the text. A self-question is simply a question you ask yourself about what you're reading. It can be about the characters, the plot, or even the language Shakespeare uses. For example, let's look at Act 2, Scene 1. One question you might ask yourself could be, "Why is Oberon so upset with Titania?" This question helps you focus on the motivations of the characters and the conflict between them. Now, who can give me another example of a question we might ask ourselves while reading this scene?

Jamie: Um, maybe, "What does Puck's mistake mean for the other characters?"

Mrs. Welsch: Excellent! That's a great question to think about while reading. Now, I want each of you to practice this strategy as you read Act 2 on your own. Remember to pause occasionally and ask yourself questions about what's happening. This will help you stay engaged and understand the play better. Alright, start reading, and keep those questions in mind!

Small Group (Tier 3)

Mr. Dixon: Hi, Jada. Today, we're going to work on a strategy that can help you better understand *A Midsummer Night's Dream* by Shakespeare. This strategy involves asking ourselves questions while we read. Remember last week we talked about character motivations and plot development? Well, this is a continuation of that. We're going to use a specific method to generate questions and make predictions. This technique can be really helpful for you, especially when you come across challenging texts in the future.

Jada: Okay, sounds good.

Mr. Dixon: Great. So, let's define what we're doing today. I'm going to model how to generate questions using different question words. I'll also show you how to make a prediction based on each question and then read on to find the answer. This strategy can help you understand the text more deeply and keep you engaged. You can use this in any subject, not just English.

Jada: Got it.

Mr. Dixon: Let's start with Act 2, Scene 1 of *A Midsummer Night's Dream*. I'll think aloud so you can see how I apply the strategy. Ready?

Jada: Ready.

Mr. Dixon: (Thinking aloud) Okay, let's start with "who." Who is in this scene? I see that Oberon and Titania are the main characters here. So, my question is, "Who are Oberon and Titania, and what is their relationship?" I predict that they are important characters with a complicated relationship because they are arguing. I am going to record my question and prediction on my Self-questioning Note sheet.

Jada: Okay.

Mr. Dixon: (Writing) "Who are Oberon and Titania, and what is their relationship?" Prediction: They are the king and queen of the fairies with a complicated relationship. "What are Oberon and Titania arguing about?" Prediction: A specific disagreement related to their roles. And so on for the rest of the questions. Now, let's read on to find the answers. (Reading) Ah, here it is. Oberon is upset with Titania because of the changeling boy. That confirms our prediction for the "what" question.

Jada: I see. So you predict first and then check if you're right by reading further.

Mr. Dixon: Exactly. Now it's your turn. Let's think about another part of Act 2. Can you come up with a "who" question and predict the answer? **Jada:** Sure. Who is Puck, and what is his role? I predict Puck is a mischievous fairy who works for Oberon.

Mr. Dixon: Great job, Jada. Let's write that down and read to see if your prediction is correct. (Reading) Yes, Puck is indeed a mischievous fairy who serves Oberon. Well done! Let's read the next section together. I will stop you periodically and ask you to make a new self-question and prediction. Let's try to ask a variety of questions from the seven types we learned including who, what, when, where, which, why, and how.

practice his fluency until his rate of reading the passage was sufficient to make meaning. To assess Nolan's progress, it was determined he was ready to move on when his rate of accuracy was above 90 percent and his words correct per minute averaged between 90 and 100 meeting fall benchmark scores.

Similarly, the list of self-questions generated became part of Nolan's practice with his speech-language pathologist (SLP), Ms. Madden, during one of their bi-weekly sessions. In this case, related services would target both speech and language skills that are involved in successful participation in oral reading activities as part of Nolan's SDI. Specifically, to help improve Nolan's articulation, pacing, and functional communication, Ms. Madden first evaluated Nolan's current skill level when initially reading the questions out loud. Together, they set a goal of working on his articulation first, helping her to identify a series of visual and tactile cues with multi-sensory feedback to guide Nolan's progress. Together, they used drill practice with word lists and sentences containing target words by practicing sounds in isolation, then in whole words, phrases and short sentences. When Nolan's speech was measured to be 90 percent intelligible (the percentage of words or phrases understood by the SLP) and he made fewer than two articulation errors in a three-sentence reading, Ms. Madden knew he was ready for Ms. Welsch's lesson.

Finally, in the case of Derrick the desire to address his barrier with reading social cues led to the identification of social narratives as a potential intervention to provide clear, structured, and personalized explanations of Derrick's expected small group behavior. Together during pullout instruction, Mr. Dixon and Derrick used the structure of the social narratives to clarify social expectations and group norms, demonstrate through the narratives how he might reduce his own anxiety about the unpredictable nature of small group conversations, and provide cues as to what he should do to respond appropriately. Practice sessions included promoting perspective-taking and appropriate behavior was positively reinforced in preparation for Ms. Welsh's lesson. When Mr. Dixon and Mr. Jordan provided a role-playing small group scenario using one of Derrick's favorite puzzles, they were able to assess that he could independently apply the strategy from the social narrative when using the laminated card with eight out of ten positive interactions.

Data-Based Individualization

Our three-step systemic mindset can be used as a holistic way to view SDI in the classroom. A more in-depth version of this process has been described in the research literature as data-based individualization (DBI) and may provide additional insight into the mechanics of planning for SDI. To summarize, DBI contextualizes different kinds of assessment data to inform intervention selection and adaptation (e.g., NCII, 2013). The DBI process begins with a validated intervention program for selected students found to not respond to the research-based core curriculum. Implemented when students have not responded to typical classroom instruction (likely as a standard treatment protocol) given previous patterns of student struggle, students are progress monitored to see how they respond to the intervention program. If students are responsive, the intervention is continued until the student makes sufficient progress to warrant discontinuation (see Chapter 6 for more on this process). While an important part of DBI, this may not yet be SDI as standard treatment protocols are *standard* and not individualized yet to student need. Therefore, if a student is nonresponsive to the intervention program, additional diagnostic data is collected, and SDI really begins.

Specifically, imagine the case of a second-grade student struggling with early reading. Diagnostic data on fluency of letter naming, letter sound, reading nonsense words, and oral reading might be collected and analyzed to determine what additional intervention adaptations are necessary. Frequent adaptations might include explicit instruction in foundational skills, more practice with corrective feedback, or structured literacy interventions. Progress monitoring is then continued to measure student response or nonresponse. In the case of nonresponse, the diagnostic data is reexamined (or when necessary, collected in new areas) to further individualize instruction and improve the likelihood of response to the intervention. In these latter examples, we see the exact process of SDI in the DBI framework as PLAAFP (i.e., diagnostic data) leads directly to the selection or adaptation of the appropriate validated intervention with progress monitoring to guide implementation.

Reflection question:
- How do you currently identify EBPs or instructional strategies to address specific barriers to learning for students with disabilities?

The Role of Research in Practice

For the team of Mr. Dixon, Mr. Jordan, and Ms. Welsch, it was essential not to just select interventions or strategies that they felt might work well for their students or that they were used to doing. In each case, their conversations focused on the needs or barriers the students were having when trying to achieve a particular learning objective. The selected EBPs were then directly aligned to address the barrier. Further, in all three cases, the students were receiving explicit instruction in the EBP during time with either Mr. Dixon or Mr. Jordan to build their skills prior to cuing in the general education classroom with Ms. Welsch.

SDI requires a match between the specific needs of Jada, Nolan, and Derrick with practices supported by research to show that they can address exactly these types of barriers. While it may be popular for educators to groan when they hear terms like *evidence based, research based, high leverage, validated, or scientifically research-based* to describe curricula, interventions, and practices, the role of research to inform practice is a critical step forward in our field and much more than a punchline. One need only reflect on the differences in medicine from 1825, 1925, and 2025 to see why it is critical for a field to use research to inform its practice. Sadly, it is likely that if we placed a teacher from 1825 or 1925 in a modern classroom, they would likely feel quite comfortable with the practices they observed and be ready to jump in to help. Yet there are significant attempts being made in education to change this trend. To move the field of education forward, the No Child Left Behind Act (2001) referenced the use of "scientifically research based" over 110 times to connect practices to particular standards. Specifically, scientifically based research should include the items in Table 5.2.

Fortunately, scholars in the field of special education are ever mindful of the need to align research to clear standards outlining high-quality research. This is because before educators working with students on IEPs like Jada, Nolan, and Derrick can implement effective strategies to meet their annual goals, the research community must determine which practices, instruction, and interventions are reliably the most effective. Following the lead of medicine, scholars seeking to reform practice and identify a broad continuum of EBPs with established standards related to the quantity, quality, research design, and amount of impact necessary in studies to warrant this nomenclature. Example quality indicators of special

Table 5.2 Characteristics of Scientifically Based Research

When evaluating research, it's important to recognize the key features of scientifically based studies:
- They follow a structured, evidence-driven approach.
- Data is analyzed thoroughly to ensure findings are valid and conclusions are well-supported.
- Results must be consistent and reliable, even when different researchers, measurements, or studies are involved.
- Studies use experimental or quasi-experimental methods, meaning participants, programs, or activities are placed in different groups—ideally through random assignment—to assess their impact under controlled conditions.
- The research is described in enough detail that other researchers can replicate the study.
- Findings undergo independent peer review to ensure they meet high scientific standards.

education research from Bryan Cook and colleagues (2009) include studies with specific research designs (e.g., experimental groups, single-case, and correlational), clear participant descriptions, measuring treatment integrity (fidelity), controlling for internal and external validity, and clear data analysis procedures. A practice becomes an EBP when there are a sufficient number of high-quality studies showing beneficial effects for targeted students. The actual number of studies varies based on research designs, number of participants, and effect size among other factors.

Yet every day, there are students in schools who cannot sit by and wait for ongoing research to accumulate sufficient evidence to call everything an "EBP." Recognizing this reality, Travers and colleagues (2016) have described a model of selecting EBPs based on a continuum of evidence (see Figure 5.3). Educators can use this model by initially looking for effective EBPs with several high-quality studies demonstrating the practices' effectiveness with their population. If that is not available, educators might then move toward "research-based practices" that have a few well-designed studies or a "promising practice" in which experts provide theoretical foundations for why this practice might benefit students like those in their classroom. At the extreme end of SDI practice selection might be "best practices," those with unknown effects but that have been tried and have some social validity. The model also includes

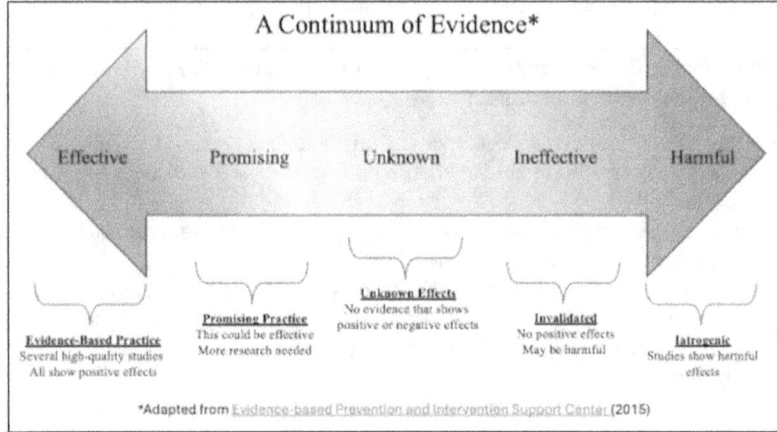

Figure 5.3 Continuum of evidence.

clear avoidance of ineffective or harmful (Iatrogenic) practices that research has demonstrated have no positive effects or even negative/harmful effects. Maintaining these standards of intervention and practice selection help meet immediate student needs during design of SDI but also allow for the evolving field of special education research to continue to inform ongoing classroom practice.

If, like us, you had been in education during the late twentieth century, you would recall it was popular to reflect that educational paradigms and practices seemed to swing like a pendulum, with one method, resource, or perspective dominating for a period of time, before that method was found wanting and another would take its place. As cycles of change swung from whole language to phonics instruction or constructivism to direct instruction, educators frequently found themselves periodically in and out of step with the recommended practice *de jure*, without ever changing what they were doing! In many ways, the real goal of NCLB was to use scientifically research-based practices to change the swinging pendulum into a grandfather clock, using research to mark progress during each pendulum swing to truly identify: what interventions, for what kids, and under what conditions. Though remaining a multivariable problem (studying human beings, especially children, can be quite challenging), the last quarter century has been marked by a growing continuum of research-based practices in education to meet the needs of each learner.

Using this mindset, Mr. Dixon was able to find several resources that indicated the benefits of self-questioning for Jada. Materials were available both online at TeachingLD.org and in several textbooks he had acquired during his graduate program. Knowing less about speech, Mr. Dixon consulted with a speech-language pathologist to learn about research-based practices in her field that would help with articulation issues. Finally, drawing from freely available IRIS Modules and the National Professional Development Center on Autism (https://autismpdc.fpg.unc.edu/) Mr. Dixon and Mr. Jordan were able to review the research on social narratives and see that it was well aligned with Derrick's needs.

Organizing Practices by Skill, Not Disability

It may seem intuitive to organize EBPs by disability diagnosis, as one might assume that the characteristics of individual disabilities are unique and drive intervention and instruction selection. However, as Barbara Bateman and others have noted, a disability diagnosis in K–12 schools provides a mechanism for passing through the gateway of special education to access services based on individual needs, not categorical labels. Specifically, once criteria for one of the thirteen categories of disabilities covered under IDEA are sufficiently reached, the student receives an IEP and accompanying access to whatever services they require. Put simply, the eligibility category provides access to services, but the specific services are determined by the student's individualized needs. In fact, as we have described (see more in Chapter 2), the IEP is designed by constructing a plan (or program) of SDI based on student strengths and needs in the PLAAFP, and a set of agreed-upon annual goals. The collaboration between Mr. Dixon, Mr. Jordan, and Ms. Welsch cataloged throughout this chapter embodied these principles. They have selected interventions and practices to directly address the skill areas identified in the PLAAFP for each student.

Consequently, it is more functional to organize EBPs based on the specific skill areas the student will need to address to make educational or functional progress. We find the work of Harmon and colleagues (2020) a helpful framework for organizing student-specific factors for consideration when designing instruction. While not exhaustive, this list of skills related to learning and human development includes the following categories: (a) cognitive, (b) executive functioning, (c) communication, (d) behavior, (e) social skills, (f) emotional, (g) motor skills, (h) adaptive skills, and (i) transition (see Harmon et al., 2020 for more). Even this sample list of skills is significant enough in number to impede the practicality of making a list of EBPs in each skill area.

Moreover, as pointed out by Ed Kame'enui, former Founding Commissioner of the National Center for Special Education Research (NCSER) in the Institute for Education Sciences (IES), to truly list EBPs would require completing a three-dimensional matrix in each skill area by grade level, disability diagnosis, and appropriate content area. Regrettably, our current research base and pages within this book are not sufficient to take up that examination here. Therefore, rather than attempting a quixotic and comprehensive list, we have attempted to collect a set of digital resources from government agencies, grant-funded projects, professional organizations, and significant groups within the field of special education as a starting place for readers interested in learning more about EBPs. Interestingly, and in support of our thesis here to focus on skills, readers exploring these links will likely find common interventions and instructional recommendations across categorical disability organization websites and resources.

Finally, when thinking about the selection of EBPs, we think it is helpful to remind all educators that there is frequently little necessity to reinvent the wheel when it comes to intervention and instruction. We have great empathy for educators attempting SDI, knowing that while there may not be an exhaustive list of practices available, there are frequently many solid places to begin your research. It is highly unlikely that an overworked educator will invent the most appropriate intervention out of thin air. It is unfair and unrealistic to expect today's educators to bear this additional burden. Instead, we hope that the list of resources will provide teachers with a starting place for selecting, adapting, and measuring student progress as part of SDI in the classroom.

Reflection question:

- How does the IEP team at your school match learner needs and annual goals to specific accommodations, modifications, or interventions?

Table 5.3 Sample Resources for Finding Evidence-Based Practices

---

Government or Grant Funded Resources
What Works Clearinghouse: https://ies.ed.gov/ncee/wwc/
National Center on Intensive Intervention: https://intensiveintervention.org/
IRIS Center: https://iris.peabody.vanderbilt.edu/resources/iris-resource-locator/
STEM: https://www.centeroninstruction.org/topic.cfm?s=1&k=ST&c=2
UFLI: https://ufli.education.ufl.edu/foundations/toolbox/
FCRR: https://fcrr.org/
NTACT: https://transitionta.org/
NCELA: https://ncela.ed.gov/
CTD: https://www.air.org/project/center-technology-and-disability
ECTA Center: https://ectacenter.org/
OCALI: https://www.ocali.org/
OSEP: https://osepideasthatwork.org/federal-resources-stakeholders/tool-kits/tool-kit-teaching-and-assessing-students-disabilities#content
IES Practice Guides: https://ies.ed.gov/ncee/wwc/practiceguides

Professional Organizations
CEC Subdivisions: https://exceptionalchildren.org/engage/special-interest-divisions
NDSC: https://www.ndsccenter.org/
Center on PBIS: https://www.pbis.org/
ASHA: https://www.asha.org/
NPDC: https://autismpdc.fpg.unc.edu/
NCLD: https://www.ncld.org/

Other Organizations
PBIS World: https://www.pbisworld.com/
Best Evidence Encyclopedia: https://bestevidence.org/
Intervention Central: https://www.interventioncentral.org/
Swift Education Center: https://swiftschools.org/
National Library of Virtual Manipulatives: http://nlvm.usu.edu/en/nav/vlibrary.html
The Meadows Center: https://meadowscenter.org/
Reading Rockets: https://www.readingrockets.org/
Understood: https://www.understood.org/en
CEEDAR Center: https://ceedar.education.ufl.edu/
AIM: https://autisminternetmodules.org/
CASEL: https://casel.org/#content
Doing What Works: https://dwwlibrary.wested.org/
OAR: https://researchautism.org/
IDA: https://dyslexiaida.org/

EBP as a Verb

While each of the resources above can serve educators interested in learning more about specific practices, interventions, or tools supported by research as part of their commitment to SDI, the term EBP can also be understood as a verb, not just a noun. We believe this subtle but important difference in thinking about EBP is critical given that research has not exhausted all of the potential areas for intervention, nor isolated each population that might benefit from research-based practices (see Faggella-Luby, Lindo, & Carlson, 2024).

The conceptualization of EBP as a verb involves three corresponding elements. First, as indicated in detail above, is the need for sufficient research evidence to support a practice as not only avoiding harm, but in fact is at least *promising* or hopefully *effective* as defined by Travers and colleagues (see Figure 5.3 for the continuum of evidence and Table 5.3 for a review of resources; Travers et al., 2016). Additionally, EBP as a verb includes value for the clinical (or pragmatic) expertise of the educator. SDI is to be thoughtfully designed based on the training, local norms, and experience of teachers, paraprofessionals, and related service providers working with the student. This unique perspective will ensure SDI is designed with the specific student in mind rather than retrofitted or standardized. Finally, EBP as a verb is student-centered (and a critical part of person-centered planning) by aligning to student and family values, expectations, and goals. Educators embracing all three of these elements are more likely to design instruction that is powerful, likely to be implemented, and aligned to the student's self-determination.

Common Pitfalls

Clearly providing appropriate, specialized instruction designed to meet Jada, Nolan, and Derrick's needs can happen in a variety of ways—yet may not match the process you observe in your school. This can be unsettling, when your reality may reflect a lack of compliance at best and be harmful to students at worst. Our hope is that by providing clarity about how to translate the PLAAFP and annual goals of the IEP (outlined in Chapter 3), you can now see that translating SDI into your classroom requires knowledge of student barriers to learning as well as skill at identifying related EBPs to enable students to make appropriate progress. Unfortunately, in our experiences of schools across the country, SDI is frequently confused as either an element of the IEP or a general framework intended to meet the needs of all learners (rather than specially designed for individual students). To help you put SDI into practice in your own school and classroom, we conclude this chapter by identifying a few common pitfalls that can occur in the SDI process.

First, some educators may believe that the IEP contains specific recommendations for SDI, and it does—but only as breadcrumbs for your planning. Specifically, the PLAAFP outlines the student's current strengths and challenges relevant to the learning environment. This gives a baseline for where the student is and establishes what barriers might exist to the learning for that year. Additionally, the annual goals provide a target for where the student will need to be by the end of the year, with short-term objectives to provide benchmarks along the way. Frequently, well-written IEPs also include a section on accommodations or instructional practices that might help the teacher address student barriers while working toward annual goals (see Chapter 3 for more on this). However, at the classroom level, educators work on lesson objectives, not annual goals or even short-term objectives. Educators must then focus attention on planning lessons that accomplish short-term objectives on the way to realizing annual goals. In this way, lesson objectives are how classroom planning and instruction helps meet IEP goals for each student.

Second, we must not confuse EBPs for SDI. While we have spent a great deal of time explaining the importance of research in education, we must consider this as only a piece of EBP. Just as a wrench may be a tool but is not the appropriate match when trying to install a screw, SDI is only accomplished when the EBP matches the specific skill barrier for the student, and in a specific learning context. SDI does not come from using specific interventions unless those interventions are matched to specific student need. Later we will explain how using interventions with an entire class is also *not* SDI unless it also fits the needs of a particular child.

Third, SDI does not occur, even in the conditions described above, without also measuring whether it is working for the student. Progress monitoring data used to inform intervention adaptation and implementation is essential during SDI. Without regular assessment, the student may not make appropriate gains at the rate and level outlined in the IEP goals (e.g., Hendricks & Fuchs, 2020). In the words of Yogi Berra, without measurement, we risk being lost, "but making good time!"

Fourth, another common pitfall is to confuse teaching behaviors with SDI. Teaching behaviors (or strategies) are instructional routines or pedagogical practices like advance organizers, corrective feedback, ability-level practice, grade-level practice, teaching for generalization or other components of explicit instruction. Neither are broad frameworks like Universal Design for Learning, Multi-tiered Systems of Support, Content Enhancement Routines, or even Structured Literacy as part of the Science of Teaching Reading alone examples of SDI. This is because teaching behaviors, like EBPs, must be matched to the unique needs of the child. While it may be a good idea to use the UDL framework for planning in your inclusive classroom, it is not designed to meet the individual barriers or needs for the student with a disability (e.g., Meyer, Rose, & Gordon, 2014). Please don't throw the baby out with the bathwater here—UDL, MTSS, and other listed components of explicit instruction are well placed on the continuum of evidence, but what makes something SDI is the individualized match to student need (see Chapter 6 for much more on this topic of what is and what is not SDI among popular school and class-wide practices). Consequently, there is great importance for classroom routines that increase the skills of all students, and they are particularly inclusive (and become SDI!) when they reinforce the specific learning outcomes for students with disabilities (as in the case of small group behavioral routines to reinforce appropriate behavior for all students, but students like Derrick in particular).

Fifth, and very much connected to the above, is the desire to make available to students different cognitive learning strategies or instructional interventions (e.g., providing graphic organizers, suggesting students ask themselves questions while they read, speech-to-text, etc.). Such practices become pitfalls when there is no plan to explicitly teach students *how* to use these practices independently and with self-regulation. Just as in the examples of our students above, time must be made for instruction and practice in skills for mastery to become possible and only when aligned to individual student goals. This also likely requires coordination between general education, special education, and/or related service providers to ensure students learn how, when, and why to use the tool during related learning to address a specific skill barrier.

Finally, a common pitfall for teachers is when they operate as the executive functioning for their students. A signal this may be happening to you, is if you feel like you spend most of your day answering questions like, "Where is my notebook?" or "What page are we on?" "Can I go to my locker to get it?" or "What is the password again?" This kind of feedback tells us that SDI is not being met for students and that they likely need additional instruction or practice in using a particular organizational, listening, or recall strategy. The nature of mediated instruction is that initially teachers will always have to initiate and provide this information, but to achieve the IEP outcomes in the long run, students must be able to do them independently—otherwise the students have not truly developed the self-regulation expected in the goal. When independent self-regulation is mastered, it is a win for the students and a win for the educator because it frees up more of their capacity to tackle other barriers to learning for the student and other classroom challenges for the teacher!

Reflection question:

- Aligning instruction to address student barriers and needs is essential for helping students progress toward their IEP goals. What specific pitfalls or challenges have you observed in your school that may be preventing the implementation of high-quality SDI? What evidence or data supports your observations? Who among your colleagues or school staff could collaborate with you to address these challenges effectively?

Conclusion

To wrap up, specially designed instruction (SDI) is essential to ensuring students with disabilities can make appropriate progress in an inclusive classroom. The stories of Jada, Nolan, Derrick, and their teachers highlight how effective instructional design requires a systemic mindset, the ability to translate research into practice, and careful planning to avoid common pitfalls. Implementing SDI starts with adopting a systemic mindset, recognizing the barriers to learning for each student, selecting appropriate evidence-based practices (EBPs), and ensuring regular coordination between special and general education.

Research plays a crucial role in informing practice, guiding educators to use scientifically validated methods to address specific skill areas rather than relying on disability diagnoses alone. By organizing practices by skill, educators can better address the diverse needs of students, using resources from reputable agencies and organizations as starting points for selecting EBPs. However, common pitfalls include misunderstanding the role of IEPs in providing specific recommendations for SDI, confusing EBPs with SDI without proper alignment to student needs and failing to progress monitor effectively. Additionally, strategies like UDL and MTSS, while beneficial, do not substitute for individualized SDI unless tailored to the student's specific barriers. In summary, successfully implementing SDI in the classroom involves recognizing and addressing individual barriers, using EBPs effectively, and continuously monitoring progress.

References

Cook, B. G., Tankersley, M., & Landrum, T. J. (2009). Determining evidence-based practices in special education. *Exceptional Children, 75*(3), 365–383. https://doi.org/10.1177/001440290907500306

Evidence-based Prevention and Intervention Support. (2015). *What does it mean when we say a program is "evidence-based"?* Penn State College of Health and Human Development. https://epis.psu.edu/sites/default/files/2024-08/What%20does%20it%20mean%20when%20we%20say%20a%20program%20is%20evidence%20based%20-%20rev%2005-07-2024_0.pdf

Faggella-Luby, M., Lindo, E., Carlson, K. (2024). Decoding the disparities: Promising adolescent literacy intervention practices at the intersection of race & disability. *Literacy Today, (July-Sept),* 32–37.

Faggella-Luby, M., Schumaker, J. S., & Deshler, D. D. (2007). Embedded learning strategy instruction: Story-structure pedagogy in heterogeneous secondary literature classes. *Learning Disability Quarterly, 30*(2), 131–147.

Harmon, S., Street, M., Bateman, D., & Yell, M. L. (2020). Developing present levels of academic achievement and functional performance statements for IEPs. *TEACHING Exceptional Children, 52*(5), 320–332. https://doi.org/10.1177/0040059920914260 (Original work published 2020).

Hendricks, E. L., & Fuchs, D. (2020). Are individual differences in Response to Intervention influenced by the methods and measures used to define response? Implications for identifying children with learning disabilities. *Journal of Learning Disabilities, 53*(6), 428–443. https://doi.org/10.1177/0022219420920379

Individuals with Disabilities Education Act (IDEA), 20 U.S.C. § 1401 (2004).

Meyer, A., Rose, D. H., & Gordon, D. (2014). *Universal design for learning: Theory and practice.* CAST Professional Publishing.

National Center on Intensive Intervention (NCII). (2013). *Data-based individualization: A framework for intensive intervention.* U.S. Department of Education. Retrieved from https://intensiveintervention.org/

National Professional Development Center (NPDC) on Autism Spectrum Disorder. (2015). *Evidence-based practices for children, youth, and young adults with autism spectrum disorder.* Retrieved from https://autismpdc.fpg.unc.edu/

Slavin, R. E. (2012). Classroom applications of cooperative learning. In K. R. Harris, S. Graham, T. Urdan, A. G. Bus, S. Major, & H. L. Swanson (Eds.), *APA educational psychology handbook, Vol. 3. Application to learning and teaching* (pp. 359–378). American Psychological Association. https://doi.org/10.1037/13275-014

Sweller, J. (1988). Cognitive load during problem solving: Effects on learning. *Cognitive Science, 12*(2), 257–285. https://doi.org/10.1016/0364-0213(88)90023-7

Travers, J. C., Cook, B. G., Therrien, W. J., & Coyne, M. D. (2016). Replication research and special education. *Remedial and Special Education, 37*(4), 195–204. https://doi.org/10.1177/0741932516648462

6

Classroom and Individual Assessment to Inform Specially Designed Instruction

Chapter Outline

SDI or SDI&A?	101
The Role of Diagnostic and Individualized Assessment in SDI	104
Linking Assessments to PLAAFP	107
Creating Measurable and Observable Learning Objectives for SDI	108
Leveraging the Value of Summative Assessment for SDI	110
The Critical Role of Formative Assessment Types in SDI	112
Formative Assessments in Classroom Instruction	113
Introduction to Progress Monitoring	115
Curriculum-Based Measures (CBMs) as Progress Monitoring	117
Benefits of CBMs to SDI	119
Practical Guidelines for Aligning Effective Classroom Assessments to SDI for SWD	120
Conclusion	129

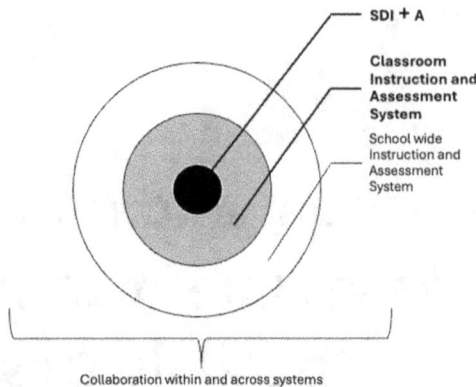

Figure 6.1 Specially Designed Instruction (SDI) + Classroom Instruction and Assessment System.

Chapter objectives:

- Explain how diagnostic, formative, and summative assessments contribute to designing and delivering SDI aligned with IEP goals.
- Demonstrate how strategies can be used to develop measurable and observable learning objectives that align with IEP goals and to select appropriate assessments to monitor progress toward SDI.
- Explore that assessments differ in their purposes and applications within the SDI framework to support individualized student learning.
- Introduce how assessment data can be analyzed and applied to guide instructional decisions, evaluate intervention efficacy, and make adjustments to SDI strategies.
- Confirm that laws like IDEA and ethical guidelines influence the administration and use of assessments to inform SDI for students with disabilities.

We are lost, but we are making good time.

—Yogi Berra

Reflection questions:

- What types of assessments do you use most often? How do you select the right type of classroom assessment to measure the effectiveness of SDI over time?
- How do you regularly measure student progress toward annual goals and short-term objectives as part of lesson planning?
- How do you currently collect, analyze, and use data from classroom assessments to monitor student progress and make instructional decisions regarding SDI?

SDI or SDI&A?

SDI in the classroom is just as much about assessment as it is about instruction (Salvia, et al., 2016; Yell et al., 2012). Fundamentally, when assessment is blended successfully within SDI, its utility guides student learning, informs instruction, and provides immediate feedback to both the teacher and the student about the student's progress toward individualized learning goals. Measures appropriate for use within an SDI framework can include formal and informal assessments of every kind if they align appropriately to the individualized learning objectives for an annual goal, given lesson, or course of study. In this chapter, we provide a comprehensive analysis of how classroom and individual assessments inform each step of the SDI process, taking care to note how unique types of assessments provide differing perspectives on student learning trajectories. We highlight two aspects of assessment: assessment of progress toward IEP goals and assessment of learning within individual lessons.

Assessment is a bit of a lightning rod topic, isn't it? If your experience was like that of most students, even as an educator, you likely have considerable thoughts and feelings about measuring student performance. For some, and with apologies to the classic Motown song "War" (1969), testing might be described by many educators with the phrase, "Testing, huh, yeah; What is it good for? Absolutely nothing (say it again!)." We think it is possible to take a different perspective even when acknowledging that tests are not always used for their intended purpose. Test usefulness must be tied to competency in choosing a measure and administering, scoring, and interpreting the related data. Therefore, we need to always think critically about why and how we assess student performance, answering questions like:

- Does the measure align with its intended purpose? Are we choosing more than one?
- Are the measures administered and scored with fidelity?
- Are the results being interpreted reliably and appropriately?
- In what ways are the outcomes of the assessment being applied to inform instruction?
- What legal considerations govern the implementation and use of this type of assessment?

When the answers to the questions above are appropriate and aligned to the needs of students, classroom assessment becomes a necessary and vital component of the education of each child. It provides evidence that learning has occurred, can motivate students and teachers to maintain their persistence, and, most importantly, will guide educators in providing students with feedback about their learning.

Right from the start, let us contextualize the relationship between the IEP goals and SDI level learning objectives. First, the IEP takes a macro perspective. Though it may include short-term objectives (not always required), even these are usually spaced quarterly. For educators, it is critical to have this long-term target to chart student learning, but it is hardly practical in the day-to-day world of delivering instruction to students. Instead, the level of focus for teachers is either the unit, or, more practically, a set of connected daily lesson plans. Consequently, it is essential to SDI that the micro focus on lesson plans does not create a situation where, in the words of Yogi Berra, "We are lost, but making good time." This kind of thinking risks daily accomplishments and considerable teacher (and student) work in the service of tasks and activities not aligned to the agreed-upon (and legally required) direction established during the IEP meeting. Rather, SDI aligns the annual goals with the individualized student learning objectives present in the daily lessons. Assessment then becomes an essential piece for measuring student progress toward learning targets at both the macro and micro levels (Fuchs & Fuchs, 2006). Moreover, this view makes clear the necessity to ensure assessment is compliant with IDEA requirements.

Reflection question:

- What is the relationship between learning objectives and classroom assessments when you are lesson planning? How is assessing learning for students with disabilities included in the lesson part of the process?

Let us consider Figure 6.2, illustrating the relationship of selected types of measures within the SDI process and relating them to learning objectives. First, as we have described previously in this book (see Chapters 3 and 4), individualized student learning objectives aligned to SDI are selected for a particular lesson. These may match larger classroom goals for all students or be a result of individualized instruction to access the general education curriculum. Regardless, the SDI learning objectives are aligned to the annual goals for the individual student and operationalized within the context of current instruction. Second, educators identify barriers to accomplishing the learning objective. This might include limited attention, inability to fluently read polysyllabic words, or fine-motor challenges that prevent suitable note-taking. As mentioned in Chapter 2, it is the needs of the students rather than the specific disability that are critical at this point in the process. Labels get students access to services, but their unique needs are what drive SDI.

Consequently, the third step in the process is to select evidence-based practices (see Chapter 5 for a discussion and definition of EBPs) aligned to address identified barriers. EBPs may come in the form of

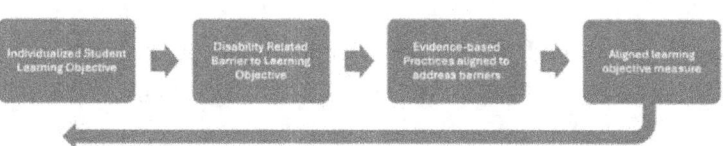

Figure 6.2 The alignment of learning objectives and assessments to guide classroom and individual assessment.

accommodations, modifications, or interventions, but they must be selected with the explicit purpose of accomplishing the individualized student SDI learning objective. Finally, and the focus of this chapter, specific measures aligned to the SDI learning objective are chosen to evaluate student progress and outcomes. Together, these four elements ensure that, within and across lessons, the student is guaranteed SDI because of clear alignment between objectives, instructional planning, and measures of progress. In fact, as we see from the figure, there is additional utility in the model because the data gleaned from the aligned learning objective measure is used to inform instructional decisions, including adjusting teaching strategies or revising individual student learning objectives for the next lesson!

The rest of this chapter will explore how different types of classroom and individual measures provide data within the SDI process. We will touch on the use of diagnostic assessments to provide a window into specifically what the barriers to learning might be for an individual student. We will then consider the role of summative assessment, the time-honored (and perhaps abused) measure of student outcomes. Formative assessments are then offered as an irreplaceable and core feature of SDI for classroom and individualized assessment. Specific attention is paid to a type of formative assessment called progress monitoring, with curriculum-based measures (CBM) serving as a reliable and valid means of measuring student rate and level of progress toward learning objectives and annual goals. Finally, we illustrate practical ways of collecting, analyzing, and sharing classroom and individual assessment data across multiple stakeholder groups.

The Role of Diagnostic and Individualized Assessment in SDI

The catalyst behind SDI is clearly understanding the characteristics of the individual student. What are the student's strengths and areas of need in all areas impacting their education? If needs are creating barriers to student success, how can interventions help address these needs? Diagnostic assessment is a lens for magnifying student abilities and skill gaps in specific areas in relation to their typically achieving peers (Hosp, Hosp, & Howell, 2016). For example, Jada is struggling in reading comprehension—but what does that mean? Diagnostic assessment for Jada would be an in-depth examination of the specific knowledge and skills in reading comprehension and Jada's performance in those areas, leading to the identification of a need for a self-questioning strategy. On the other hand, diagnostic data for Nolan and Derrick might provide critical information about underlying skills like speech, fluency, or appropriate social interactions in small groups. We most frequently think of diagnostic assessment as occurring following screening measures that have identified students at-risk for failure or informing decisions related to eligibility for special education services or present level of performance statements. However, it is equally true that teacher use of pre-assessment data to determine student prior knowledge and/or skill level with new content before starting a new unit of study is a type of diagnostic assessment! The diagnostic lens identifies specific skill areas of strength and need and informs the selection of targeted interventions to allow students to accomplish learning goals or access the general education curriculum.

Perhaps the most well-known diagnostic measures are those used by educators, diagnosticians, and school psychologists to understand students' cognitive, academic, behavioral, and language strengths and challenges. Listed in Textbox 6.1, these measures represent elements of common batteries, or collections of tests, intended to more deeply probe student present levels of performance using a multidimensional approach. Each is administered in a standardized way, with sufficient data to provide age- or grade-level norms. Typically, these measures are given as one-time, deep explorations of the learner rather than as periodic or formative assessments. Sufficient research has been conducted on these measures to ensure reliability and validity in assessing student needs.

> **Textbox 6.1.** *Common Standardized and Norm-Referenced Diagnostic Measures*
>
> - BASC-3 (Behavior Assessment System for Children, Third Edition): This tool assesses a wide range of behaviors and emotions in children and adolescents to identify both strengths and areas needing behavioral or emotional support.
> - CELF-5 (Clinical Evaluation of Language Fundamentals, Fifth Edition): This diagnostic tool assesses a child's language and communication skills, identifying areas that may need intervention.
> - KTEA-3 (Kaufman Test of Educational Achievement, Third Edition): This assessment measures academic skills in areas like reading, math, written language, and oral language to support the diagnosis of learning disabilities.
> - PPVT-5 (Peabody Picture Vocabulary Test, Fifth Edition): A test that measures receptive vocabulary and is often used to estimate verbal ability and language development.
> - WISC-V (Wechsler Intelligence Scale for Children, Fifth Edition): This intelligence test evaluates cognitive ability in children, measuring various intellectual skills across multiple domains.
> - WJ-IV (Woodcock-Johnson IV Tests of Achievement): This measure assesses academic strengths and weaknesses across reading, math, and writing skills, commonly used for identifying specific learning disabilities.

Yet, not all "well-known" measures should serve as diagnostic assessments, even if they are norm-referenced. For example, the Measures of Academic Progress (MAP) testing and iStation are common *nonexamples* of diagnostic assessments. While both are designed as general assessments for academic progress, neither is intended to provide in-depth diagnostic information. While they measure overall performance, and if given as periodic benchmark assessments three times per year can show growth, these two assessments do not provide the specificity beyond academic skills necessary to identify underlying cognitive, language, or behavioral issues impacting learning. As we noted above, it is essential that in any discussion of assessment, selection of the measure matches the intended, and researched, purpose behind the measure.

Reflection question:

- How does student diagnostic data from the PLAAFP help guide your classroom instruction? How is the PLAAFP connected to lesson-related assessments?

Linking Assessments to PLAAFP

The process for aligning learning objectives and measures to guide assessment begins with an accurate picture of the learner. Diagnostic assessments provide information about a student's specific strengths and weaknesses in multiple domains. They can also identify underlying factors contributing to a student's academic or behavioral challenges. As norm-referenced measures, diagnostic measures provide comparison between the student's performance and that of their peers which can be helpful when determining some disabilities or judging selection of appropriate interventions. Taken as a snapshot, each battery of assessments provides what the IEP identifies as PLAAFP.

The PLAAFP is critical for two specific reasons related to this chapter. First, it helps indicate the needs to be addressed by SDI. Areas of challenge or struggle that interfere with the student's ability to accomplish learning objectives or access the general education curriculum require SDI as discussed in depth in Chapter 4. Additionally, and of great importance in this chapter, is the PLAAFP guides the development of annual goals which include individualized measures for use to monitor student progress once SDI has been implemented. For example, if you have a student who is struggling with reading slowly and making frequent mistakes, SDI might focus on a reading fluency intervention so a measure of oral reading fluency would be appropriate. If students are struggling to recall information from reading at the sentence level, SDI might focus on a reading comprehension intervention so a Maze passage would be an appropriate measure to see how students are deriving meaning from text.

If a student has limited oral language skills and expressive language, SDI might target modeling or expansion techniques so an expressive vocabulary or oral language CBM would be appropriate (lots more on these specific measures below!).

Creating Measurable and Observable Learning Objectives for SDI

The next step in the SDI process is to use the PLAAFP data and annual goals to create measurable and observable learning objectives for each SDI lesson. Using annual goals and short-term objectives to design unit and lesson plan construction is the most efficient way to ensure individualized instruction because it keeps the specific needs or barriers to learning for the individual student in mind.

While there are many schools of thought regarding the characteristics of well-written learning objectives, we are partial to ensuring each objective includes the audience, behavior, conditions, degree of student success, and timeline (Goran, et al., 2020;Mager, 1997; see Chapter 4 for more on determining SDI) or, said another way, the task, condition, and criterion. The ABCD+Ts of objective writing always begin with the specific student in mind. Thus, the annual goals and short-term objectives are for an individual student (audience) as the target. The to-be-learned content (i.e., curriculum and standards) is then operationalized specifically with that student in mind. Next, the behavior or task is identified (e.g., reading, writing, synthesizing, and identifying) as it relates to the cognitive, language, or behavioral skill in question. Third, the conditions (e.g., interventions, accommodations, modifications) or other supports necessary to address the student's individual needs to accomplish the learning target in question are listed. Next, the degree or criteria of success is outlined relevant to measuring student learning of the specific behavior or skill. Finally, the timeframe for mastery is determined.

The step related to student degree of success is exactly where classroom and individualized assessments fit into teacher lesson planning. As illustrated in Figure 6.3, a well-designed lesson will include a clear

Classroom and Individual Assessment   109

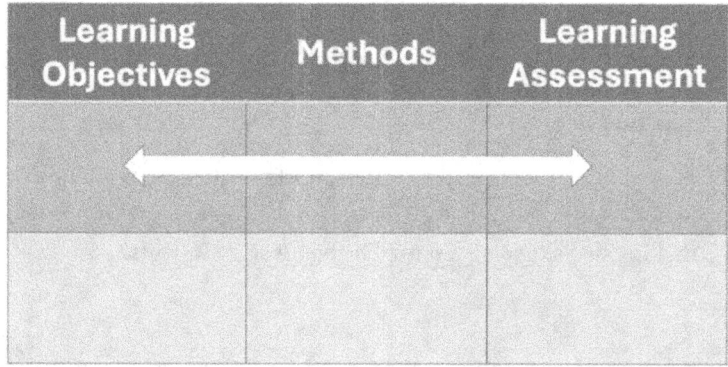

Figure 6.3 Methods of instruction as pedagogical bridge between learning objectives and aligned learning assessments.

throughline between (a) the learning objectives (what is to be accomplished), (b) the methods of instruction (the how or conditions of instruction targeted to address specific student needs or barriers to learning), and (c) the learning assessment. Like the discussion above about linking the PLAAFP to goals, selection of measures must meaningfully evaluate the specific behavior or skill included in the learning objective. To reiterate the above—if the target skill is slow reading, the assessment would measure oral reading fluency, if the target skill were sentence level comprehension, the assessment would measure words restored correctly in a Maze passage, and so on. Revisiting our cases, Nolan would require both a speech related goal, aligned intervention, and appropriately sensitive measure of growth to measure response to the work with a speech-language pathologist. Jada and Derrick, on the other hand, would need appropriately aligned measures of their specific strategies (self-questioning and social narratives) that included both their knowledge of the components and their ability to use the strategy as they progress toward independent mastery. These latter measures would initially be administered by Mr. Jordan or Mr. Dixon but would also have utility for Ms. Welsch to assess generalization of the skills to the general education environment.

What is essential is that the chosen measure reliably aligns to the behavior or skill. It is preferred that the measure be as low inference as possible, meaning the skill required is matched in the assessment results (e.g., words read correctly, words restored correctly). When inference is low, teacher use of data for instructional decision-making has a better chance of seeing an immediate impact when putting interventions, accommodations, or modifications in place.

Reflection question:

- How do you balance summative and formative assessment in your lesson planning? What evidence or data is helpful from each for making decisions related to SDI for specific students?

Leveraging the Value of Summative Assessment for SDI

General Summative Assessments

For educators, likely the most thought-of assessment to measure student learning objectives is summative assessment. In general, summative assessments are a type of evaluation that helps gauge how well students have met standards and learning objectives over a period of instructional time once instruction has concluded. Typically, the instructional time is a unit, semester, or school year. Summative assessments are concerned with learning outcomes, rather than the process, as the instruction has concluded, and the teacher is measuring the sum of knowledge and skills acquired. Borrowing a metaphor from our friends in the restaurant industry, summative assessment is when the guests taste the food at the table, judging the final product. Summative data can be used to make decisions about overall student progress, curriculum or intervention effectiveness, and areas for instructional improvement. Finally, summative assessment data provides essential information when communicating with parents and other educators about student outcomes.

There are many specific examples of summative assessments commonly found in K–12 classrooms, including end of unit (or chapter, or story) tests and quizzes with response types ranging from true/false and multiple-choice to short answer and extended essay response. However, additional examples less frequently encountered may include projects, portfolios, or reports exploring essential questions from a unit of study. Occasionally teachers will use oral presentations (sometimes in combination with the additional examples above) or multimedia products for student demonstration of learning outcomes. More formal testing might include curriculum-based reading assessments, district benchmark assessments, or state-mandated assessments. These assessments provide a bottom-line evaluation of student learning over a defined time.

SDI and Summative Assessment

While typically viewed for the benefit of measuring achievement, summative assessments also have an important role to play in SDI. As we have detailed, in SDI, educators tailor instruction to meet the unique needs or barriers to learning for individual students based on their IEP goals and objectives. Summative assessment can be used to determine if the individualized goals have been accomplished over a set period, indicating areas of progress or need for further intervention (e.g., Black & Wiliam, 1998). For Jada, summative assessments might be used to show if the reading strategies she is learning to master are having an overall impact on her unit test or midterm/final grades. This is particularly relevant during IEP annual reviews while reflecting on intervention, accommodation, or modification efficacy as goals and interventions for the new year are reviewed and selected.

Moreover, summative data helps to identify gaps in learning (skills or knowledge), especially related to grade-level expectations and student progress within the general education curriculum. Such data can even help the team reveal trends in student performance across subject areas, shedding light on the need for additional or alternative instructional strategies or supports. Standardized assessments, and assessments across the school or district, may also help compare the performance of students with disabilities to their peers, exposing systemic barriers to instruction and local norms (more on this in Chapter 7 about school-wide assessment). Finally, summative assessments can help the IEP team to determine student readiness for transitions between grade levels, and schools (e.g., elementary school to middle school), or into postsecondary education. In the case of Derrick, a measure of his social skills in small groups will be vital to his transition to high school where he wants to study science at a

STEM school but will have to work collaboratively in the lab. Consequently, it is critical within the SDI framework that summative data be collected with immediate analysis to inform the IEP team and families about student outcomes and progress.

The Critical Role of Formative Assessment Types in SDI

Formative assessment involves collecting data during the process of instruction to inform student feedback and instructional decision-making relative to whether (or not!) students are making adequate progress. Moreover, when highly correlated with desired student outcomes (even those measured by summative assessments discussed above), formative assessments are the most effective and efficient way to ensure daily student progress, make instructional changes, reteach in real time, and guide the design of future instruction. These characteristics make formative assessments particularly powerful for assessing and helping to revise individual student SDI.

Whereas summative assessments tell us at the end of instruction whether students have mastered specific knowledge or skills, formative assessments can tell us while we are teaching whether or not the students are learning the critical content under study or benefiting from the selected SDI to support learning. Who among us has not gotten to the end of a unit, only to learn when examining summative test scores that many of our students were not with us (remember Mr. Dixon and Mrs. Welsch in chapter 1)? More colloquially, summative assessments are like closing the barn door after the horse is running down the hill! This is a frustration of inefficiency for teachers at best, and critically lost opportunities for individualized learning that risks continued student failure, frustration, and loss of faith in their efforts as a learner. On the other hand, formative assessment provides teachers with ways to monitor student progress based on SDI and make in-the-moment teaching (or reteaching!) decisions to ensure higher rates of student learning and SDI effectiveness for the individual learner.

Hosp and colleagues (2016) capture the value of formative assessment used generally when they note, "Every minute spent on assessing takes time away from teaching. Therefore, assessments should be efficient and

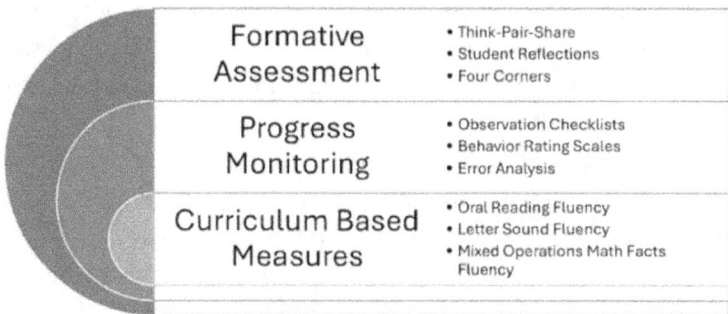

Figure 6.4 The hierarchical relationship of different types of formative assessment with examples.

provide information that will guide instruction and improve student outcomes." For our purposes, there are three hierarchical types of formative assessment (see Figure 6.4) that are fundamental to SDI. First is the broader category of formative assessment providing information during regular instructional intervals about both teacher effectiveness and student learning. Next, progress monitoring provides formative assessment data both in the moment and over time, measuring student change in terms of knowledge or skill development which is critical for determining SDI efficacy. Finally, CBMs are a particular type of research-based, reliable and valid progress monitoring assessments providing rate and level of student growth for many SDI learning objectives. We explore each of these types of measures below.

Formative Assessments in Classroom Instruction

Formative assessments are a type of intentional activity, tool, or process used by teachers during instruction to gauge how well students are progressing toward learning objectives with the explicit purpose of guiding student feedback and instructional decision-making. Typically, formative assessments are ongoing and embedded within the regular instructional intervals. It is common for some formative assessments to be employed multiple times during a single lesson to measure student response to instruction (e.g., thumbs-up-thumbs down, think-pair-share, lecture pauses). Each of these purposes is well aligned to measuring the impact of instruction for individual students, avoiding wasting student and teacher time with what is not working while staying closely aligned to the to-be-learned content.

Formative assessments are concerned with the learning process over learning outcomes as SDI implementation is ongoing, giving the teacher an opportunity to shape how student knowledge and skills are acquired. Borrowing again from our friends in the restaurant industry, formative assessment occurs in the kitchen by the cooks, before the guests taste the food at the table, providing an opportunity to add ingredients before the final product is served. Formative data can be used to make decisions about where students are excelling or struggling, what they have learned, and how much more they must learn. Educators working with Jada, Nolan, and Derrick interested in knowing if they are progressing in learning toward their goals require formative assessment data that provide an ongoing picture of their learning. This data then guides student feedback and what SDI-related changes to amounts of practice, model problem use, formation of student groups, or other types of pedagogical enhancements might be employed. Some formative assessments can be helpful in providing information over time to parents and other educators about student growth trends relative to their annual goals and short-term objectives, but the primary user of formative assessment is the educator in the classroom.

Specific examples of formative assessments include traditional quizzes whether they are handwritten or digital (e.g., Peardeck or NearPod) that include true/false, multiple-choice, or long or short answer formats. Other examples include cooperative learning structures like Think-Pair-Share, or one of our favorites, Write-Pair-Share, that provides a product for later teacher review to document student progress toward SDI learning goals. Formative assessment can also have students move around the classroom as in the Four Corners activity, with students moving across the room to represent their responses to questions or statements by the teacher. Some teachers also use a mix of self-reflections and peer reviews throughout a unit of study to help develop self-efficacy and assess progress over time in a non-evaluative way. Many teachers use pre-prepared questions during guided practice with students to keep track of rates of student response and levels of accuracy across the group during new topics or when reviewing at the end of a lesson as formative data.

In many cases, formative assessment is a common standard of practice in general education classes used to track whole group progress. Popham's work on adjustment triggers is a good example. Using this model, teachers track two critical elements: (a) required level of individual student performance, and (b) required level of total-group performance. While these methods in combination with predetermined adjustment triggers help guide group instruction, clearly the utility of formative assessments is that they also provide information about SDI. Teachers may find that by blending these formative assessments into the general education class, with alignment to measuring SDI for students with disabilities meaningfully included in the class, they are improving outcomes for all students. Such a pedagogical decision not only ensures the rights of students with disabilities, but the utility of formative measures can also be seen as part of best practice rather than as something "more" they need to do for individual students. One particularly powerful example of formative assessment is called progress monitoring. Progress monitoring provides additional critical information to guide SDI while continuing to be of great utility to the educator on all fronts.

Reflection question:

- Are the formative measures you are using reliable and valid? Do they provide evidence of student rate and level of growth in specific areas? What additional information do you want classroom assessments to provide when making instructional decisions?

Introduction to Progress Monitoring

Progress monitoring is a systematic type of formative assessment that involves routine, ongoing tracking of academic and behavioral growth over time (e.g., Stecker et al., 2005). As a type of formative assessment, it occurs during instruction, guides responsive teaching, and provides data for feedback to students. However, what distinguishes progress monitoring and makes it a critical component of SDI is the combination of ongoing assessment aligned with individualized student goals. Unlike general formative assessments that primarily focus on measuring content knowledge, progress monitoring occurs at routine intervals (e.g., weekly, bi-weekly), is aligned to specific goals or behaviors from the IEP and can be used to make data-based decisions about intervention efficacy. These measures answer questions like, how is the student progressing toward specific annual goals? How effective are the selected teaching strategies or student interventions? And what changes, if any, might be needed to support continued or accelerated student progress?

Specific examples of progress monitoring related to SDI might include classroom observation checklists used to record the presence or absence of specific behaviors, skills, or steps. A teacher might use the checklist during a classroom discussion to ensure that an individual student raises their hand to contribute to class discussions 4 out of 5 times per day. Similarly, a behavior rating scale could be used by a teacher (or students themselves) to capture the frequency, intensity, or quality of a behavior (e.g., staying in seat, keeping hands to self, staying calm during corrective feedback) over a specific time as seen in the case of Derrick. Another common measure is error analysis which involves examining the types and patterns of errors a student makes on tasks (e.g., missed steps, miscalculations, decoding unfamiliar words). In the latter case, error analysis might be appropriate for a student with a decoding IEP goal (e.g., student will correctly decode 90 percent of unfamiliar grade-level words) by allowing the teacher to analyze decoding errors as related to vowel patterns, blends, sight words, or a combination of skills. Other types of progress monitoring include collecting student work samples of a particular skill (e.g., writing) over time, using time sampling to observe and record specific behaviors at regular intervals, and so many more. We hope you realize these are exactly the types of measures that would help assure Jada, Nolan, and Derrick are progressing toward their annual goals and short-term objectives mentioned above!

An additional characteristic of progress monitoring related to SDI is the value of sharing or displaying trends in learning visually. By using repeated direct measures of a particular skill, this apples-to-apples dataset provides opportunity for comparison over time when determining if instructional adaptations are necessary. In fact, the research on progress monitoring has found that there are two critical elements in the process. First is data use. This may sound simple, but in reality, teachers have so much going on that data is frequently collected but goes unanalyzed in service of putting out the next (frequent) fire. However, analysis of data at regular intervals is critical to SDI because it ensures that students are on track to accomplish the short-term objectives and therefore the annual goals spelled out in the IEP. Only regular review of data allows teachers to make course corrections in terms of teaching strategies or intervention selection. Additionally, the second critical element is graphing (or visualization) of student data. While we believe this process should be done with, and, preferably, by the students working with a teacher, visual representation of data is essential to the process. Graphing facilitates accuracy of data review, brings transparency to the shared effort to accomplish IEP goals, builds student self-efficacy, and guides feedback to students (e.g., Fuchs et al., 1991). In fact, there is a type of progress monitoring called CBM that so reliably predicts student performance that it can function like a crystal ball, signaling an early warning to teachers, students, and families about when a change is necessary.

Curriculum-Based Measures (CBMs) as Progress Monitoring

Perhaps the most reliable and valid progress monitoring system for assessing individual (and group) student performance is CBMs(e.g., Deno, 1985; Fuchs, 2017). CBMs use repeated, equivalent measures aligned to alterable areas of student growth and specific curricular domains (e.g., word-level reading, passage-level reading, math calculations). Benefits of CBM include that they mimic tasks usually performed in class (e.g., identifying letter sounds, reading aloud, computing equations), and include both data analysis guidance and data for graphing. Moreover, CBM data is low inference, requiring no conversion of results. Data is reported as fifty-two words read correctly per minute, or eighteen letters correct per minute—clearly communicating the level of performance. The research literature on CBMs is robust, with sufficient technical adequacy and positive effects on student achievement to warrant reliable use as part of the SDI process.

There are three types of CBM measures, general outcome measures, skill-based measures, and mastery measures. Each shares a set of common elements consistent with CBM including standard directions, the need for a timing device, a set of ability or grade-level materials, specific scoring rules, standards for judging performance, and forms or charts to report results. Unlike portfolio or performance assessments, these types of CBM provide data utilization rules and allow for graphing aligned to subskills or on equivalent forms representing general outcome measures (Espin, Shin, & Busch, 2000). Moreover, CBM norms allow for national comparison to typical achieving peers rather than local norming or skill inflation.

In a book about SDI, it is particularly inadvisable to provide grade-level estimates for specific CBMs as individual students developing academic and behavioral skills do not always have IEP goals aligning to grade-level expectations. That said, for illustrative purposes we provide example CBMs for reading and their common grade-level for use (see Table 6.1). Example areas for CBM in math include Math Computation Fluency (MCF),

Table 6.1. Example Curriculum-Based Measures (CBMs) for Reading and Common Grade Levels

CBM Reading Measure	Grade Levels	Description
Oral Reading Fluency (ORF)	1–8	Measures the number of words read correctly per minute from a grade-level passage. Often used to monitor reading accuracy, fluency, and prosody.
Letter Naming Fluency (LNF)	K–1	Assesses the ability to quickly and accurately name random letters of the alphabet, a foundational early reading skill.
Phoneme Segmentation Fluency (PSF)	K–1	Measures the ability to segment spoken words into individual phonemes, critical for developing phonemic awareness.
Nonsense Word Fluency (NWF)	K–2	Evaluates a student's ability to decode consonant-vowel-consonant (CVC) nonsense words to assess phonics skills.
Word Identification Fluency (WIF)	K–2	Measures the ability to quickly and accurately identify sight words or high-frequency words from a word list.
Maze Fluency (Reading Comprehension)	2–8	Assesses reading comprehension by requiring students to select appropriate words to fill in blanks within a passage.
Vocabulary Matching or Cloze Tests	3–8	Measures understanding of word meanings and the ability to apply vocabulary knowledge in context.

Number Identification Fluency (NIF), and Quantity Discrimination. Writing CBM is also common with measures of Correct Word Sequences (CWS), writing fluency and spelling. Behavior and social-emotional skills also follow the CBM format with examples such as the Behavior Observation of Students in Schools (BOSS), Social Skills Improvement System (SSIS) Rating Scales, or Direct Behavior Rating (DBR).

Going back to our students, given her reading comprehension goals, the teacher working with Jada may collect the number of correct choices in a thirty item, five-minute maze probe. The teacher working with Nolan might collect words-read correctly in one minute in a grade-level text. For Derrick, the emphasis would be on collecting ongoing data related to his interactions and interruptions in the classroom perhaps through the Direct Behavior Rating scale.

Benefits of CBMs to SDI

CBMs provide substantial benefits over regular formative assessments. First, CBMs provide consistency. Using standardized administration procedures, equivalent protocols, and comparable time periods, CBMs bring reliability to data comparisons over time. Further, their design ensures dependable measurement for all students. Second, CBMs provide a reliable and valid measure of student learning, offering a low-inference picture of student achievement in relation to the expected curriculum. This data is most robust and related to SDI when it is aligned to IEP goals and reporting of progress. Third, CBM measures are specifically designed to target alterable and small-scale changes in student performance. This specificity helps track the effectiveness of instructional strategies and interventions without having to wait extended periods of time. Fourth (and related to the above), CBMs support the practice of data-based decision-making which is critical to SDI. Educators can analyze data to make informed decisions about the need for individual student adjustments. Such data is also consistent with larger models of delivering multi-tiered systems of support particularly synonymous with the identification of specific learning disabilities. Fifth, CBM data is clear (low-inference) and objective regarding individual learner impact. Such data is particularly valuable for reporting IEP progress and program accountability, ensuring compliance with IDEA requirements. Finally, while SDI is concerned with individual student performance and growth, CBM data also allow for comparison of individual student progress to normative data, supporting goal setting.

Practical Guidelines for Aligning Effective Classroom Assessments to SDI for SWD

While some of the above may be a review for you, the purpose of this book is to align commonly occurring school elements, like our focus on classroom assessment in this chapter, specifically to SDI. It can be helpful to connect summative and formative assessments, especially those that are used for progress monitoring and CBMs, to a set of guidelines for ensuring SDI is in place for students with disabilities. Guidelines can be used as a procedural checklist (see Textbox 6.2) during educator reflection or collaborative team meetings (see Chapter 8 on collaboration) on a regular basis. Below we detail a series of guideline elements for consideration.

> **Textbox 6.2.** *Procedural Checklist for Ensuring SDI Alignment with Classroom Assessments*
>
> 1. Align IEP Goals with Classroom Assessments
>   - ☐ Review IEP goals and short-term objectives for each student.
>   - ☐ Use backward planning to align lesson objectives with IEP goals.
>   - ☐ Ensure lesson objectives are clear, measurable, and written in ABCD+T format (Audience, Behavior, Condition, Degree, Time).
>   - ☐ Match assessments (formative and summative) to the individualized lesson objectives.
>   - ☐ Develop rubrics or scoring guides for subjective measures aligned with desired skills.

2. Implement Curriculum-Based Measurements (CBMs)

    ☐ Determine if learning objectives align with areas measurable by CBMs (e.g., fluency, writing, math).
    ☐ Select reliable and valid CBMs appropriate for the objectives.
    ☐ Schedule CBM implementation on a regular basis (e.g., weekly or bi-weekly).
    ☐ Administer CBMs with fidelity to ensure consistent data collection.
    ☐ Review CBM data to assess progress toward short-term objectives and annual goals.
    ☐ Adjust SDI frequency, intensity, or methods based on CBM results.

3. Collect and Use Data Meaningfully

    ☐ Commit to daily or weekly assessments aligned with student objectives.
    ☐ Use tools (e.g., spreadsheets, LMS) to log and organize data for easy access.
    ☐ Ensure the accuracy and reliability of assessment data (e.g., timing, administration fidelity).
    ☐ Regularly analyze data to inform instructional decisions.
    ☐ Involve students in tracking and graphing their progress, consider adding goal-setting activities.

4. Review Data Routinely

    ☐ Schedule regular intervals for reviewing data (e.g., weekly, quarterly).
    ☐ Analyze formative data to make timely instructional adjustments (e.g., regroup students, modify interventions).
    ☐ Use summative data to determine mastery and identify areas requiring reteaching or review.

5. Analyze Data Collaboratively

    ☐ Schedule bi-monthly or monthly team meetings to review assessment data.
    ☐ Include grade-level teams, IEP teams, and administrators in data discussions.

- [ ] Share data and progress with families during conferences or quarterly updates.
- [ ] Foster a community mindset, encouraging shared problem-solving and support.

6. Use Multiple Data Analysis Techniques

- [ ] Examine growth trends from CBM and progress monitoring data.
- [ ] Combine formal and informal assessment data for a comprehensive view.
- [ ] Identify the relationship between informal assessments (e.g., homework) and summative outcomes.
- [ ] Use analysis to forecast future outcomes and adjust interventions as needed.

7. Focus on Patterns and Trends

- [ ] Track student progress over time to identify recurring challenges or growth areas.
- [ ] Compare individual data to class-wide trends for local norming.
- [ ] Use longitudinal data to refine interventions and instructional strategies.
- [ ] Review data for systemic trends that may require curricular adjustments.

8. Translate Data into Action

- [ ] Use data to adjust SDI elements (e.g., strategies, materials, environment).
- [ ] Plan reteaching or additional practice based on identified student needs.
- [ ] Document changes in interventions and outcomes for future reference.
- [ ] Reflect on instructional practices and SDI effectiveness regularly.

Aligning IEP Goals with Classroom Measures

Effective lesson planning for SDI begins by aligning the learning objectives (or annual goals) with instruction and identifying the appropriate measure for student outcomes. This ensures that whether teachers are interested in process (formative assessment) or product (summative assessment), the measure of instructional effectiveness is unique to the needs of the students. This of course also requires clear and measurable lesson objectives (we like the ABCD+Ts listed above) so that SDI conditions for supporting student learning are unmistakably identified. Further, the appropriate measures will help indicate if students have reached the desired degree or criteria of success. In the case of more subjective measurement, assessment may require developing rubrics or scoring guides specifically targeting the desired knowledge and skills in the individualized learning objectives.

Consider Implementing CBMs When Aligned to Objectives

Second, when learning goals are related to areas measured by CBMs (i.e., early literacy skills, fluency, passage comprehension, spelling, writing, calculations, etc.), they are most effectively leveraged when implemented on a regular basis. Educators attempting to embed CBMs in their classrooms will find countless (and many free; e.g. easyCBM, Intervention Central, https://www.interventioncentral.org/curriculum-based-measurement-reading-math-assesment-tests) resources to guide step-by-step implementation for administration, scoring, and interpretation of results. Individual educators or teams of educators can then reflect on data to ensure SDI is resulting in appropriate rate and level of response to accomplish short-term objectives and ultimately annual goals for each student. Further, the team can determine frequency of assessment and intervention based on the reliable and valid data, collecting and recording data to make recommendations when SDI requires revision or alternative dosage.

Collect and Use Data Meaningfully

Third, assessment related to SDI requires certain best practices to ensure that data is used meaningfully, rather than as "just another thing" teachers must do. This begins with a commitment to ongoing, daily and weekly measurement directly aligned to student learning objectives. Educators may find specific tools and strategies to help facilitate data collection and analysis. For example, a learning management system (LMS) may allow each educator to log student scores on a regular basis, ensuring easy access to both individual and group data for easy analysis. Nothing is more of an impediment to data analysis (beyond not collecting it at all!) than not having the data organized and easy to access. Other tools can include spreadsheet programs with built in graphing features that are easily learned using YouTube videos—don't be intimidated! We have also found that committing with a partner to administer and log student data on a regular (weekly) basis helps to "routinize" the process so that it becomes a regular part of classroom activity. Even having students graph and post their own data is a step well aligned to the research base related to progress monitoring. Adding in goal setting for students is even better!

Of course, none of the data collection is meaningful if we do not ensure the accuracy and reliability of the data. If an oral reading fluency (ORF) measure is to be administered over one minute or a Maze measure over three minutes, then timing is important! More than one teacher has seen student data spike (or plummet) inconsistently when they have not carefully controlled the administration procedures. Without fidelity to administration, comparisons via norms become impossible as the testing conditions have changed! Finally, data is used most meaningfully when it complements instructional decision-making related to SDI. If we collect the data but do not use it in a timely manner, it cannot influence our regular lesson design. This kind of data need not be evaluative or intimidating for educators (see Knight & Faggella-Luby, 2024). Rather, we hope the data bring hope to educators by helping to connect their efforts during instructional design to specific student outcomes.

It is not uncommon for educators working with students with disabilities to despair at the limited growth students are experiencing. Ironically, failure to measure growth at all will never alter this perception, and in fact may lead to growing frustration and burnout. Yet, with assessments specifically aligned to SDI, including CBMs that measure rate and level of student growth, even minimal growth can be observed. By administering, collecting and analyzing the classroom assessment data, educators avoid the insanity of repeating the same behavior over and over, expecting a different result. Instead, they can use the data to make informed decisions about what elements of the SDI are working, and which are not. Educators become data-driven problem solvers, empowered and hopeful that they will be able to continue revising instructional conditions to maximize student progress toward annual goals.

Reflection question:

- How well are you aligning effective classroom assessments to SDI for SWD? What is one area you would like to work on? Who might be able to collaborate with you to improve this area?

A Brief Word on Assessment Adaptations

In the case of students with disabilities, assessments may also include a variety of adaptations (accommodations or modifications) as agreed upon by the IEP team. Common adaptations include extended time, alternate formats, use of assistive technology (including calculators), simplified or reduced language, breaks during testing, a quiet testing environment, modified response formats, or reduced number of test items among many others. The key aspect of assessments is that the adaptations remove any barriers to drawing conclusions with assessment data about the efficacy and efficiency of student learning outcomes or instructional interventions, accommodations or modifications. The critical component to remember when assessing student performance related to SDI is to focus on the learning objective. For example, it would not be appropriate to use a text-to-speech reader when assessing a student's reading fluency to determine their progress toward a reading fluency goal. Look to Chapter 3 for more on the specific relationship between accommodation or modifications and SDI.

Textbox 6.3. *Key Suggestions for Analyzing Classroom Assessments Related to SDI*

1. Collect and Review SDI Data Routinely

    - ☐ Schedule regular data collection (e.g., weekly, after units, quarterly).
    - ☐ Use formative and summative assessments to inform SDI.
    - ☐ Make adjustments based on trends (e.g., regroup students, adjust interventions).
    - ☐ Incorporate data analysis into SDI lesson planning to ensure continuous improvement.

2. Review the SDI Data Together

    - ☐ Hold routine team meetings to discuss student progress based on SDI.
    - ☐ Collaborate with grade-level teams, IEP teams, and administrators.
    - ☐ Share progress data with families and involve them in discussions.
    - ☐ Foster open communication and a supportive team environment for decision-making.

3. Use Multiple Data Analysis Techniques

    - ☐ Combine formal (e.g., CBM, benchmark tests) and informal (e.g., observations, work samples) assessments.
    - ☐ Analyze growth trends, including rate and level of progress.
    - ☐ Identify patterns between informal and summative data to refine practices.
    - ☐ Use targeted analysis to guide SDI interventions and instructional changes.

4. Pay Close Attention to Patterns and Trends in the SDI Data

    - ☐ Analyze both individual and class-wide data over time.
    - ☐ Identify recurring skill challenges or long-term trends.
    - ☐ Use local norming to evaluate curriculum and teaching strategies.
    - ☐ Anticipate needs based on longitudinal data to plan proactively.

Sharing Classroom Assessment Data with Key Stakeholders in SDI

Classroom assessment and analysis of data is clearly critical, providing insights concerning the effectiveness of SDI for individual students. We have provided four key suggestions for analyzing classroom assessments related to SDI in Textbox 6.3. However, it is equally critical this data is not hidden, ignored, or dismissed. Rather, we value the sharing of classroom assessment data with a variety of stakeholders, including students, families, other educators and specialists, and as a part of documentation and record keeping. The primary stakeholder for SDI-related data is the student themselves. Providing feedback to students has several benefits. First, it demonstrates the teacher-as-guide in the learning process, showing that they are aware of student progress toward specific IEP goals—goals that the student may or may not be aware of depending on their level of involvement during the IEP process. Additionally, sharing data in a constructive way involves the student in their own monitoring of progress, allowing teachers to lay a foundation for supporting individual student goal setting. Collectively, these efforts show the student how their own investment in particular learning strategies can lead to improvements in their own self-efficacy, self-advocacy, and of course, the broader construct of self-determination!

No less important, especially with younger children, is communicating with families. Transparency and ease of collaboration between families and educators is a key predictor of student success, sense of belonging, and engagement. IDEA guidelines indicate that data must be shared with the families of students with disabilities at least as frequently as their typical peers. However, in our experience working in schools and as parents of children with disabilities, more frequent and proactive communication build vital trust between educators and families. Ensuring transparency and understanding of assessment results helps families to better know their children, including areas of strength and challenge (e.g., Epstein, 2011). Moreover, routine sharing of classroom assessment data, especially formative data, helps families to support students before it is too late, when end of quarter grades are finalized. Families may even ask educators for ways they can reinforce or offer more opportunities to practice critical skills at home—a partnership that every educator would value.

As we stated previously, we are passionate about supporting educators so that they never feel alone or hopeless in the work they are doing on behalf of individuals with disabilities. Consequently, classroom data should be readily available for working with other educators, related services professionals, and staff when it comes to ensuring the appropriate implementation and efficacy of SDI. We believe assessment data shared by grade-level teams should be considered a standard operating procedure! Moreover, some schools are sharing data in grade-span teams. While sometimes this is necessary because of a lack of staff (if you only have one third-grade teacher you can hardly have a grade-level team!), it also honors the vertical progression of students from one-grade level to another. It goes without saying, but if a third-grade teacher is having a challenge with SDI for a particular student, it is in the best interest of the fourth-grade teacher who might be working with the student the following year to help problem solve now. In perhaps a more positive spin, a fourth-grade teacher might be able to rely on the collegial expertise of a third-grade teacher who had previously worked successfully with a student to help problem solve reoccurring or even new issues as they have already spent an entire year getting to know the strengths and needs of that student.

While all the above is true for any team concerned with the progress of an individual student, it is particularly relevant for potential members of IEP teams. Specifically, why not invite the previous year's teacher or the following year's teacher to the IEP meeting (maybe both!) so that as a collective group (and one that the parents will need to recognize) establish themselves as support systems for one another, the family, and ultimately the student related to their SDI. This group will also be helpful when collaborating during decision-making about standardized testing conditions, placements in the least restrictive environment, or selection of appropriate interventions to be recorded in the new IEP.

Finally, and in accord with the previous recommendations, student classroom data (rather than just report cards) should be included in formal documentation and record keeping. This is vital to ensuring compliance with IDEA and the IEP's goals but is also a more complete picture of the student learning profile. A new administrator or teacher may find these archives particularly helpful for tracking student progress over time, especially during due process hearings or other legal battles. More positively, given the high turnover of educators in some schools, if members of a team are no longer present for some of the collaboration outlined above (see also Chapter 8), these records will provide a vital window into what SDI is successful (or unsuccessful) for each student. Moreover, as since 2004 MTSS (formerly RTI) can be used as part of the disability determination, there is considerable justification to find archive space for documenting CBM and other progress monitoring data. For students with behavioral challenges that might not appear on a traditional report card, saving DBR or other behavioral data for reference by future educators working with the child should be considered best practice in SDI. We believe that once a school system finds these records to be of value a few times, they will become a regular part of the annual process and review for highly performing schools delivering highly effective SDI to highly successful students with disabilities.

Reflection question:

- How are you currently analyzing classroom assessment data? Who is involved? How is the information shared? What is one area you would like to work on? Who might be able to collaborate with you to improve this area?

Conclusion

As we noted at the beginning of this chapter, SDI in the classroom is just as much about assessment as it is about instruction as see in the cases of Jada, Nolan, and Derrick. Kubiszyn and Borich (2013) note this about the effects of assessment on classroom teachers: "regardless of how a teacher feels about the relationship of tests and assessments to instruction, it is frequently the classroom teacher who must administer and then organize and interpret state-mandated high-stakes and teacher-constructed tests and assessment data, including performance and portfolio data to curious and sometimes hostile parents and other concerned parties (p. 13)." This is why the process of SDI begins with the clear alignments of learning objectives and assessments to guide classroom assessments. Alignment, whether through diagnostic, summative, or formative data of many types, aids teacher design and evaluation of instructional strategies and intervention efficacy. Moreover, each type of measure sheds light on overall student progress toward IEP goals, ensuring that more than compliance is assured, but rather that families, educators, and other stakeholders are clear in their understanding of student learning. Together, through a variety of practical guidelines for aligning effective classroom assessments and thoughtful sharing of classroom assessment data with key stakeholders, schools are better able to design and deliver SDI or, as we have made the case, is it SDI&A?

References

Black, P., & Wiliam, D. (1998). Assessment and classroom learning. *Assessment in Education: Principles, Policy & Practice, 5*(1), 7–74. https://doi.org/10.1080/0969595980050102

Deno, S. L. (1985). Curriculum-based measurement: The emerging alternative. *Exceptional Children, 52*(3), 219–232. https://doi.org/10.1177/001440298505200303

Epstein, J. L. (2011). *School, family, and community partnerships: Preparing educators and improving schools* (2nd ed.). Routledge.

Espin, C. A., Shin, J., & Busch, T. (2000). Focusing on formative evaluation. *Current PracticeAlerts, 1* (3), 1-4.

Fuchs, L. S. (2017). Curriculum–based measurement as the emerging alternative: Three decades later. *Learning Disabilities Research & Practice, 32*(1), 5–7. https://doi.org/10.1111/ldrp.12127

Fuchs, D., & Fuchs, L. S. (2006). Introduction to response to intervention: What, why, and how valid is it? *Reading Research Quarterly, 41*(1), 93–99. https://doi.org/10.1598/RRQ.41.1.4

Fuchs, L. S., Hamlett, D. F. C. L., & Stecker, P. M. (1991). Effects of curriculum-based measurement and consultation on teacher planning and student achievement in mathematics operations. *American Educational Research Journal, 28*(3), 617–641. https://doi.org/10.3102/00028312028003617

Goran, L., Harkins Monaco, E. A., Yell, M. L., Shriner, J., & Bateman, D. (2020). Pursuing academic and functional advancement: Goals, services, and measuring progress. *TEACHING Exceptional Children, 52*(5), 333-343.

Hosp, J. L., Hosp, M. K., & Howell, K. W. (2016). *The ABCs of CBM: A practical guide to curriculum-based measurement* (2nd ed.). Guilford Press.

Knight, M. J., & Faggella-Luby, M. (2024). Data rules: Elevating teaching with objective reflection. The Association for Supervision and Curriculum Development.

Kubiszyn, T., & Borich, G. D. (2013). Educational testing and measurement: Classroom application and practice (10th ed.). Wiley.

Mager, R. F. (1997). *Preparing instructional objectives: A critical tool in the development of effective instruction* (3rd ed.). Center for Effective Performance.

Salvia, J., Ysseldyke, J. E., & Witmer, S. (2016). *Assessment in special and inclusive education* (13th ed.). Cengage Learning.

Stecker, P. M., Fuchs, D., & Fuchs, L. S. (2005). Progress monitoring as essential practice within response to intervention. *Assessment for Effective Intervention, 30*(2), 3–12. https://doi.org/10.1177/875687050802700403

Yell, M. L., Katsiyannis, A., & Collins, T. (2012). *The law and special education* (3rd ed.). Pearson.

7

Integrating Specially Designed Instruction within a School-Wide Assessment Framework

Chapter Outline

Getting the Big Picture	135
Objectives and Purposes of School-wide Assessments	137
Key Differences Between Classroom and School-wide Assessments	139
Overview of SDI and School-Wide Assessment	141
Overview of School-Wide Assessment Framework Components	144
Additional School-Wide Data Analysis Steps to Inform SDI	148
Establish Data-Informed Collaboration Among Teams	149
Analyze Trends Across Grade Levels for Curriculum Gaps and Alignment to MTSS	152
Support Teacher Professional Development	153
Build Family and Community Confidence in Data-Driven Decisions	154
School-Wide Protocols to Ensure Assessment Utility	155
Conclusion	157

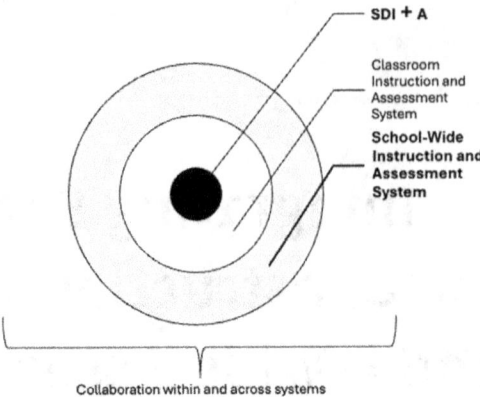

Figure 7.1 Specially Designed Instruction (SDI) + School-Wide Instruction and Assessment System.

Chapter objectives:

- Explain how school-wide assessment frameworks provide a macro-level, data-driven overview of student learning, supporting systemic decisions to improve academic and behavioral outcomes, particularly for students receiving SDI.
- Highlight key differences between classroom-based and school-wide assessments, including their scope, stakeholders, data granularity, and decision-making purposes.
- Demonstrate how SDI fits within school-wide MTSS, ensuring students with disabilities are included in universal screeners, targeted interventions, and individualized problem-solving processes.
- Show how school-wide data analysis identifies curriculum gaps, monitors intervention efficacy, supports compliance with IDEA requirements, and ensures equitable outcomes for historically marginalized groups, including students with disabilities.
- Provide strategies for data teams to analyze school-wide data collaboratively, inform professional development needs, and communicate effectively with families and community stakeholders to build confidence in data-driven decisions related to SDI.

Leadership and learning are indispensable to each other.
—John F. Kennedy

Reflection questions:

- How well does your school-wide assessment framework align with the needs of students requiring SDI? What evidence or data support this conclusion?
- How are school leaders, teachers, and related service providers in your school collaborating to analyze and use assessment data to support decisions related to SDI?
- How does your school-wide assessment framework and related data analysis promote equity for students with disabilities and ensure compliance with IDEA and other legal requirements?

Getting the Big Picture

School-wide assessment frameworks are the modern educational solution for "flying the plane while building it." Akin to the view from the cockpit, administrators and educators throughout the broader system can use comprehensive assessment frameworks to identify specific measures for examining the entire student population, small groups of targeted students not responding to core instruction, and individual students in need of SDI. Each measure can then function as a gauge on the whole-school dashboard, providing a perspective on how well student needs are being served. While classroom assessments provide insights into individual student response to instruction including rate and level of performance, a school-wide assessment framework provides an overall picture of learning throughout the school. This more holistic view supports data-driven decision-making, ensures alignment with accountability systems, and can help improve outcomes for all students, particularly students with disabilities whose data may not be clearly "visible" unless specifically part of an analysis. Whole-school approaches to assessment can also promote equity for historically marginalized populations (including students with disabilities), enhance resource allocation by signaling warning lights on the dashboard, and demonstrate compliance with IDEA requirements (e.g., NCES, 2019).

Imagine for a moment that you are in the pilot's seat. Perhaps you are a new building principal, assistant principal in charge of curriculum, special education administrator, MTSS coordinator, or department chair. Would your school-wide assessment framework provide gauges with information sensitive enough to identify and explain the following trends?

- Juan, David, Marie, and Jeri are ready to advance to level 7 in reading, but Chris and Linda are not.
- Mrs. Hashem's class has higher scores on math concepts measures than Mrs. Morrison's class.
- Donna has not responded to Tier 2 instruction in our RTI approach.

Would you have enough information to answer parent or district administrator questions like these?

- Are your students well prepared for the high stakes test next week?
- Is Billie performing at a rate and level in math that he will be ready to move on at the end of the year?
- How many students are below the 25th percentile on our universal screening test?

This chapter bridges the gap between classroom-based assessment and the broader school-wide assessment systems. While classroom assessments are essential for guiding immediate instructional decisions for individual students, school-wide assessments serve a broader purpose of shaping policy, resource allocation, and systemic interventions, ensuring consistency and equity across the school. To that end, we will explore specifics about why school-wide assessment matters and how it differs from (and leverages) classroom assessments. Our focus will then shift to how SDI fits within the model, offering examples using a MTSS assessment framework to illustrate how to ensure the dashboard has the right gauges to measure student success. As previously, we will provide specific tips on where and how to leverage assessments, as well as how to analyze the data for both individuals and groups of students.

Reflection question:

- Why is school-wide assessment important to you as a building leader? How does the data guide setting priorities regarding resource allocation and professional development?

Objectives and Purposes of School-Wide Assessments

School-wide assessments can have many objectives and purposes. We strive to illustrate that they are much more than "something to do" or worse, "something the administration has a bee in its bonnet about" from an educator perspective. In fact, there are important course corrections and investments of resources that are only possible when a macro-view of learning is available. This is why, in the words of President Kennedy, "leadership and learning are indispensable to one another." For SDI to be a priority throughout the school, from administration to paraprofessional, everyone must have a shared view of how SDI fits within the school-wide assessment framework to ensure equitable learning opportunities for all students.

While schools serve many purposes related to student development, perhaps the most consistently in focus (whether for good or bad) is monitoring student academic achievement. School-wide assessments probe skills like reading, writing, and problem-solving, and knowledge related to core subjects, all of which can include measures of SDI. From the dashboard, these data can help evaluate how well the school's curriculum is being implemented and how appropriate the curriculum is to meeting the needs of all the school's students. SDI-related data may shed light on instructional decisions such as how well practice (guided and independent), student feedback, or student groupings are impacting student outcomes across the school (e.g., Hattie, 2012). When students are not responding, whole-school data may also be helpful in judging SDI intervention efficacy to meet the needs of students with disabilities. Analysis of student performance across classrooms and grade levels can reduce the impact of independent variables like teacher effect, baseline reading achievement, student attendance, and demographic variables (e.g., SES, English language proficiency, and special education status). Monitoring overall achievement will provide insights into systemic strengths worthy of celebration (pretzel snacks for everyone!) and areas in need of improvement (dashboard warning lights) as well as provide information about individual student learning related to SDI.

When warning lights do occur, they are critical signals to the school-wide team that the school has areas for improvement that must be addressed. Perhaps specific groups of students (e.g., students with disabilities or active bilingual learners of English) are not performing well across classes with the new reading curriculum. Perhaps the math curriculum is not aligned to revised state standards. Perhaps school-wide behavior data indicates the need for social-emotional learning programs to be embedded in regular classroom instruction. Without school-wide data to confirm these trends, they might be dismissed as the results of an individual teacher's style or failure to implement the curriculum as designed (i.e., with fidelity or treatment integrity).

Reliable school-wide assessments have the added benefit of supporting compliance with IDEA (2004) regulations, safeguarding equity for students with disabilities and potentially avoiding the need for due process hearings (Yell et al., 2012). Moreover, they help ensure schools are fulfilling their obligation to provide SDI as part of a FAPE (see Chapters 2 and 3 for more). School-wide data may also demonstrate fairness in resource distribution and consistency in decision-making (e.g., see the previous scenarios), even in complex cases involving students with disabilities. Some examples might include:

- Assessment data could be used to identify students struggling with reading comprehension or mathematical reasoning skills who may have a disability requiring referral for special education evaluation.
- Behavioral data could be collected using the School-Wide Information System (SWIS) might be analyzed for a student exhibiting disruptive behaviors to identify trends in when or why the behaviors occur.
- Benchmark CBM data could guide resource allocation to ensure targeted instruction for addressing needs of students not responding to core instruction in comparison to their typically achieving peers.

When schools use appropriate and reliable assessments in these situations, they are better able to document and defend their processes and decisions transparently.

Finally, by linking SDI to the school-wide assessment framework, rather than just within the classroom, there is greater likelihood of administrator and educator buy-in. That is, we seek to illustrate SDI as a fundamental part of how schools serve all students, not as an additional or add-on component because of legal compliance. In our experience, and particularly with relation to due process hearings, if measuring impact of SDI is viewed as something more to do, it risks being devalued, dismissed, and "someone else's job" given how much educators are asked to juggle. Rather we see integration of an SDI "gauge" as critical to overall school health. When administrators are examining school-wide data and begin to ask questions like, "I see that, in general, our 7th graders are doing well on the district common formative assessments, but I am wondering if that average is inflated. How are our students with dyslexia doing on those exams? Students with other disabilities?" (see also the questions in our opening to this chapter), they are much more likely to be providing appropriate education for all students.

Key Differences Between Classroom and School-Wide Assessments

There is of course a relationship between classroom and school-wide assessments. When administered within a complementary framework together, they can create a clearer picture of student learning and system efficacy. Yet, it is important to understand that while classroom assessments focus on immediate instruction needs, school-wide data provide a more strategic overview related to macro-level goals. Below we illustrate four key differences between these two types of assessment.

Scope of Decision-Making

The most obvious difference between classroom and school-wide assessments is in the scope of decision-making. Data from classrooms is intended to inform immediate decision-making about use of targeted instructional strategies to support individual students or small groups. Some data may be for formative, in-the-moment teacher decisions about how much more practice or additional examples do students need before moving on, while exit tickets and summative data might be used to guide more reflective teacher decisions about what to teach or when reteaching of critical concepts is necessary. On the other hand, school-wide assessments guide strategic decisions, by their very nature considered over time and from multiple perspectives. This kind of data can be used to examine curriculum revisions, resource allocations, and policy changes.

Changing Stakeholder Involvement

As the scale of assessment moves toward school-wide, stakeholder involvement also changes. Within classrooms, those primarily involved are teachers, students, and families. Occasionally, classroom data is also viewed by coaches working with teachers or grade-level teams looking for trends. Yet, we contend that as soon as the lens moves to examine trends in data across environments, we have moved into school-wide assessment. As school-wide assessment begins, the stakeholder group can (and dare we say *should*) include school leaders (e.g., principals, assistant principals, curriculum directors, department chairs) in addition to teachers and related service providers. For broader accountability and transparency, school-wide data may also be used to engage community members external to the school (e.g., school board members, local government officials, employers, nonprofit organizations, workforce development agencies, or even alumni).

What's the Frequency?

While school-wide assessment can draw upon classroom assessments, the frequency and focus of classroom assessments is used differently. For example, during lessons, teachers typically conduct regular formative assessments to monitor student progress and make decisions in real time. While this data may then be provided for later school-wide review, the analysis and use occur later. More commonly, school-wide assessments (e.g., early year screening measures, benchmark assessments three-times per year, CFAs) occur less frequently, providing data for a more comprehensive review and critically across classrooms and grade levels.

Unit of Analysis

Finally, the data granularity during examination is different across these types of assessments. In classrooms, educators require more detailed insights into individual and small group performance. What is Claire's rate and level of growth in fluency this week as compared to last? Is Martin keeping his hands to himself during circle time at the same rate this week? What is Francine's rate of opportunities to respond and how accurate is she? School-wide assessments may be interested in some of this data at the aggregate level (e.g., fluency scores, office discipline referrals, opportunities to respond), but in general they offer a big-picture perspective, necessary for interpreting trends and making systemic improvements. As Diamond (2005) emphasizes, school-wide assessments help differentiate teacher support, inform curriculum decisions, and monitor intervention implementation, fostering a holistic educational approach.

Overview of SDI and School-wide Assessment

As we have suggested, a comprehensive school-wide assessment plan will result in data related to SDI throughout the framework. Most significantly, and perhaps as a sign that students with disabilities are truly receiving instruction in the least restrictive environment, students with disabilities benefiting from SDI are present at all levels within schools. Students with disabilities are part of not only screening and benchmarking assessments, but also school-wide efforts such as CFAs or SWIS data within a PBIS model of behavior management. With few exceptions, students with disabilities are also part of statewide assessments initially mandated under NCLB (2001) and continued in the last authorization as the Every Student Succeeds Act (ESSA, 2015). In fact, this latter legislation provides helpful guidance for highlighting systemic strengths and weaknesses for subgroups of students. Guidance suggests, and best practice demands, that not only is the average performance of students within a grade-level analyzed, but the performance of a historically marginalized groups such as students with disabilities or students from a variety of racial and ethnic groups should also be analyzed. The benefit of this kind of analysis with school-wide data is that if students in subgroups are doing well, there is a good chance that students in the majority are doing well. Alternatively, when students on the margins, especially those expecting SDI, are performing significantly differently from typically achieving students, this is at best a sign of unacceptable inequity within the system, and potentially an early warning sign of negative impact on other students to come.

SDI is also an important consideration in school policy related to assessment. Rather than hoping that an existing framework (likely inherited from one school leader to the next) thoughtfully includes students with disabilities in the general curriculum, it is necessary to consciously establish and maintain inclusive practices that reinforce SDI. Further, the analysis of subgroups suggested will enable schools to integrate SDI into broader school policies and improvement plans. For example, schools with significant behavior issues may find it necessary, after analyzing school-wide office discipline referral data, to begin making plans to adopt school-wide PBIS, including significant levels of support for students needing targeted intervention or SDI. Alternatively, macro-level data can also be crucial for differentiating whether a student's poor performance on a nationally normed reading assessment is a result of their disability, or within the context of the other members of the class/grade level, a systemic curriculum (or instruction) issue exists. That is, if a science of reading curriculum is not in place, or is in place but not implemented as designed, leaders might set goals related to instructional coaching or co-teaching to better ensure that both individual student and group needs are met. Finally, school policy must also ensure that assessments consider the unique needs of students with disabilities. When accommodations or modifications are mandated in IEPs, they must be made available to students during testing. Without these adaptations, assessment data may not truly reflect what students can and cannot do, thus mitigating understanding of SDI efficacy.

Once assessment data is reliable and valid and part of clear policy implementation, whether (or not) SDI is improving outcomes for students with disabilities can become a school-wide goal. The purpose of a school-wide goal is to ensure that administrators, teachers, related service providers, and other stakeholders continue to prioritize individual benefit because it is tied to systemic performance. Following the adage, "we measure what we value, and we value what we measure," if school-wide goals include enabling a child to make progress appropriate to their circumstances (*Endrew F.*, 2017) as part of the school-wide assessment plan, there will be an alignment between systemic resource allocation and instructional decision-making. This can be reinforced by connecting IEP goals to school-wide assessment practices resulting in students with disabilities being more likely to participate in and inform the interpretation of school-wide assessment data. Added value, with aligned resources, and practitioner buy-in at every level will more likely improve individual student outcomes and thus bolster overall school performance. Borrowing from another adage, "all boats rise with the tide!"

Raising SDI for consideration at the school level, especially through assessments, keeps SDI from only being a consideration during annual IEP meetings. It is easy to see how SDI can be left to the individual teacher, frequently working in isolation and without significant support for long stretches of time when SDI moves "onto the back burner" as the school year progresses bringing daily challenges and demands for attention. Yet, when SDI is part of the assessment and improvement plans, there is a reciprocal relationship: SDI can be tailored and adjusted by analyzing data trends from multifaceted school-wide assessments, with ongoing monitoring and adjustments based on results. When data indicate improvements in SDI require more resources, a new curriculum, additional or practice time, this will now be not just at the attention of the teacher, but also the administrators and other stakeholders interested in the school-wide goals. Rather than missing this data within the noise of comprehensive assessment, supporting SDI can be a focus, resulting in overall school-wide performance improving as students with disabilities improve!

Reflection question:

- How do you see SDI as a critical part of your school-wide framework? Is it an integral part or more of an additional component? What stakeholders, staff, or other administrators review this data? What does it tell you?

Overview of School-Wide Assessment Framework Components

For clarity, and because some readers may be wondering "what is a comprehensive school-wide assessment system," we provide a brief overview here. While there are many ways to do this, we have chosen to use the framework synonymous with MTSS. MTSS was chosen as a guiding framework because it is both codified in IDEA (2004) via its previous nomenclature Responsiveness to Instruction (RtI), but also because it provides a recognizable framework that integrates school-wide assessments with individual student response to instruction and is therefore very compatible with large systems and individual student IEPs. This framework makes use of universal screeners, benchmark assessments, formative and summative assessments, and other measures within a three-tiered model. Below we provide a description of the data and outcomes connected to SDI within the model for each tier.

Tier 1: Core Assessments

Like Tier 1, or universal instruction, core assessments are given to all students in a school, including students with disabilities. Typically, schools will begin the year with screening measures to identify students at-risk for academic or behavioral difficulties. Screeners typically assess a variety of skills like reading, writing, mathematics, and behavior at a macro-level. Rather than offering detailed, skill-specific data, universal screeners are broad indicators for patterns or trends that suggest closer monitoring or further evaluation with other kinds of diagnostic assessments. The value of a screening measure at the school-wide level is they provide a "quick and dirty" way to efficiently assess who is progressing as expected and who is not. Additionally, universal screeners provide a snapshot of the entire student body, allowing for broad, comparative analysis that can inform curriculum alignment, resource allocation, and use of instructional time (e.g., Jenkins et al., 2007).

In addition to universal screening measures (see Table 7.1), benchmark assessments or other periodic progress monitoring can be helpful to

Table 7.1 Example Academic and Behavioral Assessments

Academic	Behavioral
Universal Screeners	Universal Screeners
• Acadience Reading K–6 (aka DIBELS Next)	• FAST™ SAEBRS
• Exact Path Diagnostic Assessment	• BASC-3
• FastBridge	• EBS
• Iowa Assessments	• SSiS-PSG
• i-Ready® Diagnostic	• SSiS-SEL
• MAP® Growth™	• SDQ
• Star	• SRSS
Progress Monitoring Measures	Progress Monitoring Measures
• Acadience Reading K-6 (aka DIBELS Next; Oral Reading Fluency)	• DBR-SIS
• AimswebPLUS	• Momentary Time-Sampling
• Amira	• Direct Behavior Ratings
• Classworks Progress Monitoring	• Direct Observation
• i-Ready Diagnostic and Growth Monitoring	• Intervention-based Measures
• i-Ready Literacy Tasks	
• Istation	
• iSTEEP	
• Star	

For specifics and updated information, see https://www.pbis.org/ and https://intensiveintervention.org/

measure student growth over time and in comparison to national norms (e.g., Stecker et al., 2008). Typically, all students (at least those in elementary settings) are assessed at least three times per year, usually in the fall, winter, and spring. Because benchmark assessments are typically aligned to the curriculum (more on this below), data from these measures can be used to make school-level decisions about Tier 1 instructional practices at multiple points throughout the school year. Some districts will also include common formative assessments and CBMs as regular benchmark assessments as well. Such core assessments inform clear, consistent, and measurable goals and expectations for all students at each grade level. Data can be triangulated with state standards and curriculum maps to provide educator insight into what knowledge and skills to teach and when they are most appropriate. Benchmark behavioral assessments can include school climate surveys to assess overall behavioral environment and student engagement. Additionally, behavior is frequently measured using office discipline referral rates to identify trends within and across grade levels or locations in the building. Ultimately, core assessments are intended to indicate if 80 percent or more of students are attaining school-wide grade-level goals.

As suggested, school-wide core assessments can be consistently analyzed to inform SDI efficacy. For example, universal screening data can enable building or grade-level teams to identify who may require additional instruction to address specific skill areas and can be used to compare individual student performance to other groups (e.g., Molly is reading 75 cwpm but the average third-grade student at Jefferson Elementary is reading 125 cwpm). Benchmark assessments are even more helpful because they provide data about student growth over time, offering key information about effectiveness of SDI strategies and whether they need adjustment (e.g., After three months, Molly is reading 100 cwpm!) CFA or summative assessments reveal trends and patterns in achievement for students with disabilities in comparison to their nondisabled peers. Finally, combining academic and behavioral data helps inform more holistic analysis and planning.

Tier 2: Targeted Assessments

Targeted assessments are designed to assess the progress students make from Tier 2 instruction after students have demonstrated a lack of response to universal instruction. There is a higher likelihood that students with disabilities may be initially served in Tier 2 along the way to diagnosis though it is possible students with low-incidence disabilities may skip this step. There are also other students not benefiting from universal instruction. Assessment becomes more frequent as risk of not meeting school-wide goals increases for these students. Therefore, targeted assessments are typically administered at least twice-per-month to monitor student progress in response to targeted instruction or interventions. More frequent assessment allows educators to make ongoing instructional decisions based on individualized learning trajectories (rate of student progress toward goals) that can result in more enhanced learning experiences (i.e., changing the instructional intensity or dosage) or returning students to Tier 1 instruction only when areas of need have been remediated. It is critical that targeted assessments are sensitive enough to measure whether student response to instruction is accelerating their learning to meet grade-level goals or whether more intense Tier 3 supports are necessary.

Assessments in Tier 2 can be like those in Tier 1 to allow for consistent measurement and analysis. However, there are additional related academic and behavioral assessments to provide additional, more granular data to inform instructional decisions. For example, academic assessments can include bi-weekly individualized reading or math CBM measures, diagnostic assessments of phonological awareness, or group-based writing and fraction CBM measures. Behavior progress monitoring might include use of behavior rating scales or direct behavior ratings on a similar bi-weekly schedule. Alternatively, social-emotional measures might be assessed using a strengths and difficulties questionnaire, exit ticket, or student journal reflection.

Tier 3: Individual Problem-Solving Assessments

Whether students are served in Tier 3 on their way to being identified with a disability or have already been identified, the individual problem-solving associated with Tier 3 is likely synonymous with SDI. Please note, we strongly believe that aspects of SDI can be delivered in Tiers 1 and 2 because students with disabilities are served in all school settings as they access the general education curriculum as indicated by their IEPs. However, the intensive and individualized interventions of Tier 3 are directly related to the intent of SDI and almost without exception should pass the two-step test (see Chapter 4). Tier 3 assessments use individual student data to measure student response to new instructional interventions based on a lack of response to both core instruction (Tier 1) and targeted interventions (Tier 2; e.g., Fuchs & Fuchs, 2006). Because students have failed to respond to two tiers of evidence-based practices, risk of failure and disability identification have increased, making quick instructional response a priority. Therefore, in this tier, assessment of students is even more frequent with progress monitoring occurring weekly if not daily. The goal is to collect data on specific skills or strategies students are lacking to inform instructional decisions. As with Tier 2, analysis focuses on individual learner trajectory (rate and level of student success) with instruction continually evaluated so that intensity can be adjusted based on that data. Assessments should align with IEP goals and objectives for students with disabilities that will also be a part of school-wide data about acquisition of grade-level skills and strategies.

Example assessments in Tier 3 are not dissimilar to Tier 2, but become more frequent and individualized. Academic assessments target individualized progress monitoring, may include use of more diagnostic assessments, and will focus on isolated skills necessary for student success. Typically, this can look like supporting older students' phonemic awareness or phonics to develop word recognition skills necessary to meet grade-level fluency expectations. Behaviorally, goals in individualized behavior plans might be tracked with daily behavior charts or use of check-in/check-out data. Additionally, if there is a suspected need for a behavior intervention plan then a functional behavior assessment might be conducted. As noted, each assessment type aligns to the more intensive and individualized focus to meet learner needs.

Reflection question:

- How is your school implementing the components of MTSS? Does your assessment framework align? Are specific measures identified for each tier of responsiveness? Who is involved in selecting and reviewing these measures on a regular basis?

Additional School-Wide Data Analysis Steps to Inform SDI

As we noted in the introduction to this chapter, there are distinct purposes for school-wide assessment that differ from classroom assessment when it comes to informing SDI. Rather than focusing on individual students at the onset, school-wide data are about a slower, more comprehensive response, attempting to see the whole of the chessboard rather than just individual pieces like instruction. Data analysis will impact decisions about broader instructional strategies, human and financial resource allocation, professional development initiatives, and long-term strategic planning (e.g., Guskey, 2000). Therefore, responsible analysis of school-wide data can be achieved by considering the following steps as they relate to informing SDI. Moreover, we believe savvy school administrators will note that embedding these steps into their existing data analysis will have the added benefit of helping all students and educators accomplish their goals—once again demonstrating, "all boats rise with the tide."

Establish Data-Informed Collaboration Among Teams

Analysis of school-wide data is meant to be a collaborative endeavor (see Textbox 7.1). Analysis by individuals risks the data being used sparingly and only among a small group of educators (or more likely filed away after being reported "up the chain of command"). Instead, innovative leaders will establish teams within grade spans and school-wide that include multiple stakeholders. Members of the team can include school administrators (especially the ones known for getting things done), special education staff, related service providers, and general education classroom teachers.

> **Textbox 7.1.** *Establishing Data-Informed Collaboration among Teams*
>
> 1. Create Collaborative Data Teams
>   - ☐ Form teams that include administrators, general and special education teachers, and related service providers.
>   - ☐ Ensure teams meet regularly (e.g., quarterly data meetings, annual reviews).
>   - ☐ Provide access to classroom, grade-level, and school-wide data for comprehensive analysis.
>
> 2. Analyze Data to Improve SDI and Tier 1 Instruction
>   - ☐ Examine classroom and school-wide assessment data to refine SDI strategies.

- [ ] Identify patterns indicating the need for Tier 1 instructional improvements.
- [ ] Use data to determine whether curriculum adjustments are needed to prevent an over-reliance on SDI.

3. **Use Longitudinal and Grade-Level Data to Identify Curriculum Gaps**

    - [ ] Review multi-year school-wide assessment trends for systemic challenges.
    - [ ] Consider data across different student subgroups (e.g., SWD, ABLE, economically disadvantaged students).
    - [ ] Evaluate whether Tier 1 instruction is meeting student needs before increasing SDI.

4. **Align Professional Development with Data Findings**

    - [ ] Use assessment data to identify teacher learning needs.
    - [ ] Plan professional development in response to student data, not just pre-set schedules.
    - [ ] Ensure training includes evidence-based SDI strategies tailored to current student challenges.

5. **Engage Families and Communities in Data Discussions**

    - [ ] Share individual and school-wide assessment results transparently with families.
    - [ ] Use data to explain SDI decisions and intervention effectiveness.
    - [ ] Provide context for curriculum changes, demonstrating how decisions are data-driven.

6. **Ensure School-Wide Assessment Protocols Are Effective**

    - [ ] Review the frequency and purpose of assessments to avoid excessive testing.
    - [ ] Streamline data collection to focus on meaningful instructional adjustments.
    - [ ] Ensure teams analyze and use collected data to guide instructional decisions.

Teams should have access to classroom, grade-level, and school-wide assessment data during meetings to develop a broad understanding of overall school performance and how SDI may be supporting individual students. Just as the data should be collected at regular intervals, so too should data be reviewed by these teams in regular cycles (e.g., at least quarterly data meetings with significant time for an annual and reflective review). Once the data is reviewed and initial conclusions are surfaced, the information can be shared, with opportunities for alternative explanations for the trends sought during staff data meetings, as part of professional learning communities, or during school improvement planning sessions.

Sharing of data may sound familiar, but it must be carefully done and in reciprocal fashion, not just top down or as an evaluation. You may have even experienced team meetings that focus only on general class trends, leaving out discussion of how SDI strategies contribute to or need adjustment based on data. This kind of rush to use aggregate data is frequently judgmental (e.g., Ms. Lindo's students are doing well because her mean score is 5 points above Mr. Keith's) and does not meet the needs of individual learners. We prefer an example like this: at monthly grade-level meetings, teachers could bring classroom progress monitoring data to discuss how SDI supports students' level and rate of growth. As outlined by Knight and Faggella-Luby (2024), this data is likely to be more successful if it is chosen by the teacher, reliable and valid, gathered frequently and by the teacher, and tied to professional learning (more on this latter point below). The team would then discuss whether adjustments are necessary collaboratively, sharing ownership and responsibility for supporting the educators implementing the plan.

Analyzing data related to individual SDI is a helpful strategy, but the team may also notice during monthly data reviews that grade-span or grade-level data indicate the need for refinement of Tier 1 instruction. If 50–60 percent students are not responding to core instruction from a reading program, it is not possible to serve all these students with targeted Tier 2 instruction. Therefore, the team might use the data to reexamine the core curriculum for critical gaps or misalignment to student needs that could impact both students receiving SDI and those that are not. Similarly, school-wide teams analyzing data may find when reviewing quarterly trends that adjustments must be made to school improvement plans including selection and type of professional learning, reallocation of related service providers, or even need for alternative space to provide Tier 2 instruction during flexible instruction time (FIT).

Analyze Trends Across Grade Levels for Curriculum Gaps and Alignment to MTSS

There is significant utility in grade-level data analysis. Yet, the value of school-wide data, especially if it is longitudinal (i.e., similar data is collected year after year to allow for apples-to-apples comparisons), is that it can provide perspective about what is happening across multiple grade levels. With grade-span data, teams can identify curriculum areas needing improvement, leading to targeted SDI to address systemic challenges for students with disabilities. In fact, following the guidelines in ESSA, teams might analyze the data over multiple years for impact on students with disabilities, students with high poverty backgrounds, students experiencing homelessness, or historically minoritized students.

Data analysis that considers those most marginalized, like students with disabilities, provides a critical lens for judging curriculum appropriateness, implementation levels, and impact on student learning. As in the case suggested above, if 50–60 percent of students are not reading on grade level (as is the case in most of our classrooms nationally), no amount of SDI will fix the problem. SDI is reserved for meeting the individual needs of the student with disabilities to create access to the general education curriculum AFTER they have received evidence-based core instruction and targeted intervention. When more than 20 percent of students are not responding to the currently implemented curriculum, the MTSS three-tier pyramid is inverted. School-wide teams with strong building leadership will need to adjust the school improvement plan immediately, not look to special educators to increase the amount of SDI they offer.

As an example, we want to provide a vision that counters the typical narrative of building leaders unilaterally making curriculum decisions without examining trends in assessment data over time and across grade spans. This can lead to persistent learning (or opportunity) gaps in instruction for all marginalized students, but especially students with disabilities. Instead, we would like to see a building-wide team including the principal, curriculum director, and stakeholders delivering both general and special education reviewing three years of school-wide writing assessment data. They might identify persistent gaps in expository writing, especially around organization, transitions, and spelling. Educators might then reexamine the vertical alignment of the school's writing curriculum (if they have one!), noting alignment to expectations from standards at each grade level. Only then might students with disabilities be found to be behind typical achieving students and curriculum content be assigned appropriate SDI to provide underlying, as-of-yet unmastered skills. This would avoid the typically observed practice of relying solely on general education interventions from Tier 2 without individualizing supports for a student needing SDI.

Support Teacher Professional Development

When it comes to addressing the evolving needs of students, educators are the greatest resource schools have. Yes, buildings, budgets, and school boards may make schools possible, but it is the educators present with students every day, delivering SDI, that truly improve outcomes for students and make schools beacons of community success. Yet, no teacher program can prepare professionals for the changing landscape of education at a single time, especially as their careers progress. Educators are by their very nature lifelong learners, and it is a good thing because the challenges they face, and the evolving research to meet those challenges requires a dedication and commitment to studying new ways to deliver instruction. We would never trust a medical doctor practicing nineteenth-century medicine with leeches in the modern treatment of our children. Therefore, we must not expect instructional practices used in the single-room schoolhouse of the pioneers in our modern classrooms. To avoid relying on old and out of date practices, teams can use school-wide assessment data to highlight areas of student need. In cases where students need help in specific areas that teachers have no background or mastery, it is incumbent upon the team to suggest, and building leaders to listen to, how professional learning might help meet that need. Consider the example about writing instruction. Writing instruction is frequently one of the least well instructed and practiced skills in teacher preparation. Teachers may be reluctant writers themselves, unsure about passive voice, run-on sentences, or dangling modifiers in their own communication. Many do not feel confident in providing SDI for students with disabilities.

School-wide assessment data will then seamlessly guide teacher professional learning decisions, helping to inform the selection, training, integration, and implementation. Moreover, because they come from broad data analyzed by a team of educators to identify priorities for improving student outcomes, there is a higher likelihood that so-called "buy-in" will be in place by a substantial number of educators. Such a process would counter the typical narrative of building or district administrators focusing on professional development learning to improve only general teaching strategies, frequently of neither interest to general education teachers, nor of benefit to special educators. Rather, we would expect to see after reviewing school-wide assessment data in the fall, that the principal meets with the data team to make decisions about spring professional learning designed around evidence-based SDI strategies or another relevant topic. Note that this is only possible when professional development days are not pre-planned in advance for content but rather are a mix of days to be responsive to student (and educator) need.

Build Family and Community Confidence in Data-Driven Decisions

As educators, the importance of our relationship with families and the broader community cannot be underscored. Families are our primary consumer, either critics when feeling abandoned or not served, or champions when we are meeting the needs of their child. Communities are also a significant stakeholder, especially for our public schools, as both civic and economic drivers. When schools are highly touted, they help attract families and businesses to the community. Therefore, transparency is critical in the relationship between schools and family and community stakeholders. Sharing assessment outcomes and student SDI progress with families represents a best practice in supporting students with disabilities (e.g., Epstein, 2011). Moreover, they help provide the "why" surrounding decision-making about school-wide curriculum.

For example, IEP teams might share assessment results with parents during annual meetings, explaining how the data for the individual student is used to drive specific SDI strategies (e.g., improving phonological awareness interventions). This data might then be presented with the context of the entire school or community to demonstrate to parents that while your student is responding in rate and level of performance on regular CBM measures, by comparison they are still performing well below grade-level expectations and local school norms. Sharing data in this kind of transparent fashion has multiple benefits. First, it demonstrates whether the SDI decisions made during the last team meeting are benefiting the student—a primary outcome and focus of IEP meetings. Second, it helps explain to parents why these supports and engagement with related service providers are recommended to move their child toward performance closer to their typical peers. Third, it avoids a general discussion of student progress, without referencing data connected to the student or school, creating potential mistrust as families wonder on what basis decisions are made. Finally, from a compliance perspective, sharing data at two levels (student and school) provides a paper trail for due process hearings to help justify the decision-making process.

School-Wide Protocols to Ensure Assessment Utility

While not rules per se, there are certainly strong recommendations or school-wide protocols that can help to ensure assessment utility and specifically connection to SDI. Proactive administrators and data teams will routinely review not only the school-wide data but also the assessments and protocols themselves to ensure efficacy and efficiency of data collection. One of us consulted with a large urban school district in the northeast recently. When examining their school and district-wide assessments it was discovered that students were receiving some kind of formal assessment every nine days! While we have tried to establish the importance of both classroom and school-wide assessment in this book as it relates to SDI, this much assessment hardly leaves time for instruction.

Moreover, what we found was that because there was so much data, frequently assessing the same areas, no one was taking the time to analyze the data to make instructional decisions. Again, back to the Yogi Berra quote, they were, "lost but making good time." That is, they could answer a question about assessment in the affirmative—they were doing it. But was it meaningful? We think not. We provide questions to help guide data teams and administrators or annual or semi-annual (more than once per year) reviews of their school-wide assessment protocols (see Textbox 7.2).

Textbox 7.2. *Questions to Help Guide Reviews of School-Wide Assessment Protocols*

- Is the assessment aligned with the curriculum taught to students? Does the assessment also come with sufficient training and support for educators to understand how to administer it and interpret the data effectively?
- Does the assessment have adequate reliability and validity for its intended purpose? Does the data provided enable tracking student progress over time to evaluate growth (rate and level) and program effectiveness?
- Is the assessment standardized, enabling comparison of student performance to a defined set of goals? Is it normed based on a similar population to the school or at the national level?
- Does the assessment accommodate diverse learners, including students with disabilities, ABLE learners, and students from varied cultural backgrounds? Does the protocol include offering accommodations or alternative formats as part of the reliability and validity of the measure?
- Has the faculty been trained regarding the scoring rules to provide an accurate representation of students' skills and knowledge?
- Does the assessment framework sample well-defined domains of knowledge, content, and behavior, ensuring clarity on what students need to know and do to complete the items? For students whose disabilities impact behavior or functioning, does the assessment address adaptive skills, functional behaviors, or social-emotional needs?

- Does the assessment framework prioritize assessments that are efficient to administer and score, minimizing disruptions to school operations?
- Does the assessment align with broader district and state educational goals, accountability measures, and standards?

Reflection question:

- How are you currently analyzing school-wide assessment data to inform SDI? Who is involved? How is the information shared? What is one area you would like to work on? Who might be able to collaborate with you to improve this area?

Conclusion

In summary, this chapter has underscored the importance of integrating SDI into a school-wide assessment framework, moving beyond just classroom assessments. School-wide assessments using a tiered model synonymous with MTSS provide the broader context for learning of all students throughout the building, including students with disabilities. By following school-wide data analysis steps and protocols, transparency in analysis and communication with stakeholders improves. School-wide data can also be used as a warning light, indicating critical data in context for individual students and groups. For example, the combination of rate and level CBM data help explain why Juan, David, Marie, and Jeri are ready to advance to level 7 in reading, but Chris and Linda are not. CFA data can show that Mrs. Hashem's class is scoring higher on math concepts than Mrs. Morrison's class, leading to additional professional learning. Additionally, when we realize that 37 percent of students are scoring below the 25th percentile on our math universal screening assessment, data teams can suggest immediate curriculum review in response to student needs and redesign of SDI for SWD where necessary. School-wide assessments are therefore a critical tool in charting the future of academic and behavioral planning for school leaders. Moreover, when considered in combination with classroom assessments, they provide clarity in context and curriculum to support decisions and communication with families and the community about SDI.

References

Diamond, L. (2005). *Assessment-driven instruction. Perspectives, Fall 2005,* 1–4. CORE Learning.

Endrew F. v. Douglas County School District, 580 U. S. 386 (2017), 798 F.3d 1329 (10th Cir. 2015), 137 S. Ct. 988 (2017), 290 F. Supp. 3d 1175 (D. Colo. 2018).

Every Student Succeeds Act, 20 U.S.C. § 6301 et seq. (2015).

Epstein, J. L. (2011). *School, family, and community partnerships: Preparing educators and improving schools* (2nd ed.). Routledge.

Fuchs, D., & Fuchs, L. S. (2006). Introduction to response to intervention: What, why, and how valid is it? *Reading Research Quarterly, 41*(1), 93–99. https://doi.org/10.1598/RRQ.41.1.4

Guskey, T. R. (2000). *Evaluating professional development.* Corwin Press.

Hattie, J. (2012). *Visible learning for teachers: Maximizing impact on learning.* Routledge.

Individuals with Disabilities Education Improvement Act of 2004, 20 U.S.C. § 1400 et seq. (2004).

Jenkins, J. R., Hudson, R. F., & Johnson, E. S. (2007). Screening for at-risk readers in a response to intervention framework. *School Psychology Review, 36*(4), 582–600.

Knight, M. J., & Faggella-Luby, M. (2024). *Data rules: Elevating teaching with objective reflection.* The Association for Supervision and Curriculum Development.

National Center for Education Statistics. (2019). *The condition of education: Students with disabilities.* U.S. Department of Education. Retrieved from https://nces.ed.gov/

No Child Left Behind Act of 2001, 20 U.S.C. § 6301 et seq. (2002).

Stecker, P. M., Fuchs, D., & Fuchs, L. S. (2008). Progress monitoring as essential practice within response to intervention. *Rural Special Education Quarterly, 27*(4), 10–17. https://doi.org/10.1177/875687050802700403

Yell, M. L., Katsiyannis, A., & Collins, T. (2012). *The law and special education* (3rd ed.). Pearson.

8

System-Wide Collaboration and Specially Designed Instruction

Chapter Outline

Defining Collaboration	161
What Does Effective Collaboration Look Like?	164
Some Example Collaboration Settings	169
Conclusion	177

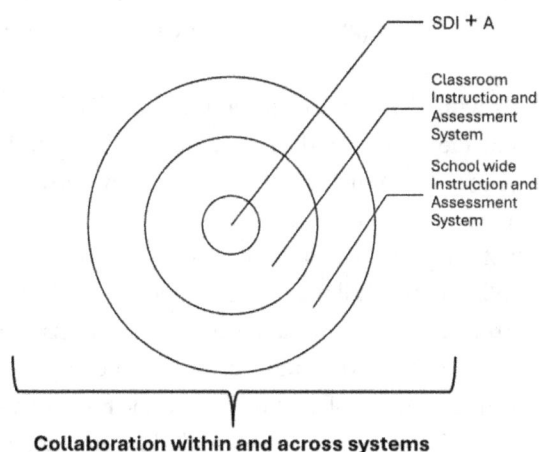

Figure 8.1 Collaboration within and across systems.

Chapter objectives:

1. Define collaboration and the critical elements of effective collaboration.
2. Describe how collaboration and incorporating the system of the school is critical to SDI.
3. Clarify the expectations for SDI as part of a three-element model in co-teaching.
4. Provide suggestions for making instruction work with SDI in co-teaching.

Coming together is a beginning. Keeping together is progress. Working together is success.

—Henry Ford

Reflection questions:

- What is effective collaboration and how is it important to SDI? How does this description compare to my school situation?
- In what ways is collaboration critical to delivering special education services and SDI?
- How do SDI and co-teaching go together? Am I seeing this in my co-taught setting? How might I make my planning for and enacting instruction in a co-taught classroom include the three elements?

The Individuals with Disabilities Education Act (IDEA) is built on the foundation of collaboration. Building an IEP and implementing it not only requires that school personnel, related service providers, and caregivers collaborate but evidence from much research indicates that collaboration improves both student and teacher outcomes (Griffiths et al., 2021). We use the term "collaboration" all the time in schools, but it is used to refer to so many things that it is unclear what the term really means. In this chapter, we will (a) define collaboration and its critical elements, (b) identify why collaboration is important to SDI, and (c) describe how collaboration can assist in delivering SDI across situations, including co-teaching.

Defining Collaboration

Collaboration is critical to how the systems of schools work to produce positive student outcomes. Research indicates that effective collaboration among groups in schools has an impact on teacher knowledge, skills, and instructional quality (Garet et al., 2001). Several studies show that in schools where collaborative relationships are strong, there is an increase in instructional quality, dramatic decreases in dropout rates, and increases in student achievement (Darling-Hammond, Ancess, & Ort, 2002; Wasley et al., 2000). Research also indicates positive collaboration between schools and families can lead to positive learning outcomes for students (Carlson & Christenson, 2005; Epstein, 2001; National Association of School Psychologists [NASP], 2012). Specifically, studies indicate that collaboration impacts completion of classwork and homework (Cox, 2005; Esler et al., 2008), attitudes toward school (Esler et al., 2008), student behavior (Blair et al., 2011; Cox, 2005) and relationships with teachers (Serpell & Mashburn, 2011).

What Is Collaboration?

Collaboration is one of those terms or ideas that everyone thinks they know but each person has a different definition and expectation for what it is. Collaboration is more than putting two teachers or families and school personnel in a room and asking them to do something together. In this chapter, we are going to use the definition of collaboration provided by Griffiths et al. (2021):

> A complex process built on trust, open communication, and mutual respect (relationship building), with all members focused on shared goals and responsibility with a common understanding (shared values), who are actively participating with a sense of shared responsibility (active engagement) and decision making. (p. 64)

Griffiths et al. (2021) go on to describe these components as building blocks. In other words, you cannot get to shared values without relationship building and effective implementation will only occur when relationship building, shared values, and active engagement are in place. Woodland et al. (2012) focused on teacher collaboration and identified a four-component cycle of teamwork that included: (a) dialogue, (b) decision-making, (c) action taking, and (d) evaluation. Dialogue means addressing disagreements and recognizing, addressing, and resolving differences, not ignoring them. Effective dialogue also includes a focus on analyzing instruction and its impact on student learning, not discussing grouping or scheduling and dividing tasks. This focus on instruction and student outcomes is linked to decision-making—what are teachers or teams going to do to impact student learning? When decisions are made, they must be enacted. Therefore, action taking is the actual implementation of decisions made—whether in instruction, delivery of services, or gathering of data. Finally, teachers (and by extension teams) must then collect data and evaluate the actions taken in order to determine whether these actions have been effective. This then begins the cycle with dialogue all over again (Woodland et al., 2012).

Clear in the definition and description of collaboration is the idea that it requires both teamwork and taskwork, or what teams do and how they do it (McEwan et al., 2017). Salas et al. (2015) state that "taskwork involves the performance of specific tasks that team members need to complete in order to achieve team goals" (p. 600). But teamwork is more about the shared behaviors, attitudes, and cognitions "that are necessary for teams to accomplish [their] tasks" (Salas et al., 2018, p. 600). In order to build effective teams that can both identify and implement SDI for students with disabilities, school personnel must commit to both the taskwork and the teamwork. In other words, they must:

1. Define collaboration and its effective implementation as a critical variable in the school's culture.
2. Work to make effective collaboration a priority by developing the collaborative skills (e.g., teamwork) of everyone in the school building.
3. Collect data, evaluate implementation, and have dialogue about performance, no matter the discomfort or difficulty.

Reflection question:

- How do you define collaboration? How does the individual's definition of collaboration impact how they are collaborative partners?

Who Is Involved in Collaboration for SDI?

It might actually be easier for us to describe who isn't involved in collaboration for SDI! Depending on student need, SDI might include general educators, special educators, related service providers, outside agencies, and others to implement. Add in families and others to plan and develop and you have a large team with diverse backgrounds, expertise, and perspectives. Just putting all of these individuals in a room and focusing on how to assist a student with disabilities does not automatically make the team work. If we define collaboration in the way we began this chapter, there is much more work and practice that needs to take place. Let's think about this in relation to the students we have discussed throughout the book. See Table 8.1 for who is collaborating for Nolan, Jonelle, and Jada.

Why Is Collaboration Important to SDI?

If the SDI for Nolan includes using below grade-level reading materials to teach and practice reading fluency in small groups and the individuals involved in implementing that SDI are a special education teacher and paraprofessional, then it would be impossible to implement SDI without their effective collaboration. If the SDI for Jonelle includes teaching, cuing, and reinforcing self-regulation strategies at school and at home and the individuals involved in implementing that SDI are a special educator, science teacher, and Jonelle's parent, then having those individuals collaborate effectively is critical to the SDI meeting her needs. If the SDI for Jada includes providing instruction and practice in a SIM self-questioning strategy in reading comprehension, delivering this instruction in a small group, and cuing its use during English/Language Arts and the individuals involved in implementing that SDI are her special education teacher

Table 8.1 Who Is Collaborating?

Student	Case	Who Is Collaborating?
Nolan	13-year-old student with Down syndrome participating in ELAR classroom	Ms. Welsch (English/language arts teacher) Mr. Dixon (special educator) Mr. Jordan (instructional assistant) Mrs. Madden (speech-language pathologist) Mr. and Mrs. Montague-Vargas Nolan
Jada	12-year-old student with learning disability in reading comprehension	Ms. Welsch (English/language arts teacher) Mr. Dixon (special educator) Mr. Justin (technology teacher) Mr. and Mrs. Ramones Jada
Jonelle	16-year-old student with ADHD	Ms. Wright (math teacher) Mr. Weinberg (science teacher) Ms. Cooper (special education teacher) Ms. Alex (school counselor) Ms. G (Jonelle's mom) Jonelle

and her English/Language Arts teacher, then having those individuals collaborate effectively is critical to the SDI meeting her needs.

Reflection question:

- Why is collaboration and a team approach so critical to students with disabilities?

What Does Effective Collaboration Look Like?

Back to our definition of collaboration with taskwork and teamwork—taskwork has been described throughout this book. It is the writing of the IEP, the evaluating student performance for instruction, the instruction for skill improvement that occurs with multiple individuals involved. We will describe those specifics in a bit more detail but this "work" in collaboration is straightforward. It is the teamwork aspect that is so often taken for granted or ignored because individuals think, "They're adults and professionals—they can get along." Unfortunately, this is just not true. Collaboration requires training, practice, and negotiation in individual and group skills, along with the general understanding that each individual on the team has something valuable to contribute and that may come from a different perspective or different area of expertise.

Individual Collaborative Skills

In order to collaborate effectively, individuals must be able to: (a) actively listen, (b) engage in perspective taking, and (c) recognize the impact of both verbal and nonverbal language. Though most adults think they are skilled at these, effective collaboration requires more intentional focus on them as we build collaborative teams.

Active listening. Active listening requires individuals to engage with their collaborative partner without distraction. Phones down. Computers closed. Face the individual speaking and (if culturally appropriate) make eye contact. Listen to complete thoughts without interrupting. Paraphrase what the individual is saying (e.g., From what you said, . . . ; I think what I'm hearing . . .). Ask questions to clarify or seek understanding (e.g., Can you clarify what you meant by . . . ? Let me make sure I understand . . .). Relate the statement or thought to the topic at hand (e.g., So, you think this data means . . .).

Perspective taking. Perspective taking means attempting to understand how another person sees data, behavioral incidents, content, whatever the discussion is about and accepting that their perspective may be different from yours. For example, there are many times when special educators hear frustration and anger from general educators about students with behavioral issues. A teacher might say, "I want him out of my room now! He disrupts my class, doesn't care about his grades, and everything I do just makes the situation worse." An ineffective response that does not acknowledge another perspective might be, "Well, if you'd just stop yelling at him . . ." Or "If you'd just ignore him . . . ." Or

"He's clearly not engaged..." Instead, trying to understand the perspective would be more helpful. For example, "Gosh, that is difficult behavior and I can understand your frustration. Let's dig a little deeper—can you tell me what that behavior looks like? When does this behavior happen? And then what happens in the classroom?...."

Verbal/nonverbal language. Again, most adults can tell you what nonverbal signals (in the majority culture) are—crossed arms often mean I'm not open to other ideas, staring at a phone or computer means I'm not listening, eye contact means I'm listening and engaged, and doodling or fidgeting means I'm uncomfortable or not engaged (for some). Confusion in interactions comes when the verbal and nonverbal do not match. For example, a team member says, "Tell me more" while at the same time answering a text on his phone. Or a teacher says to a parent, "I want to know more about your child's interests" while at the same time shifting away from the table with their chair. The connection of intentional language and corresponding nonverbal behavior is critical to making every team member feel comfortable and heard.

Critical Group Collaborative Skills

In addition to individual skill, groups, teams, and partners need to also attend to the functioning of the collective. This requires: (a) setting group norms, (b) developing a problem-solving process, and (c) dedicating time to evaluating and discussing group processes.

Setting group norms. A first step in any collaboration should be to set group norms. Norms are common understandings about ways in which members will behave in the group or partnership. How will the group recognize individuals who want to speak? Set a purpose? Include differing voices? Acknowledge different cultural norms (e.g., eye contact, speaking in opposition)? Effectively incorporate individuals at different authority levels? Set the standard to assume positive intent? Addressing all of these topics in an early meeting and then referring back to them at the beginning of each meeting is critical.

Developing a problem-solving process. All teams are going to experience a situation in which there is disagreement between members in either the topic of discussion, the outcomes, or the way the group is working. It is impossible to develop a problem-solving process when the team is trying to solve a problem. Therefore, developing a step-by-step process for how a group member can bring up a problem with the group, how that problem will be understood and handled, and how the situation can be resolved needs to be determined as group norms are being set. See a sample problem-solving process in Table 8.2.

Discussing group processes. Though there never seems to be enough time to accomplish all of the task work that is required of groups or partners, it is critical to team function to pause and discuss how the teamwork is going—are we using our agreed-upon norms? Does everyone have a voice? Are we using our problem-solving processes? Is everyone engaged? If teams just assume that everyone will be engaged, following the norms, and never have a problem, they will not work well and can get bogged down by some members not participating fully, some passive aggressive "problem-solving" behaviors, or worse—teams falling apart.

Table 8.2 Sample Problem-Solving Process

Where to start	Ask and answer the following: Is there a problem? Who owns it? Can it be solved?
Identify the source problem	Identify and define the problem (Some members of the group do not feel comfortable participating.) (Student outcomes following an intervention are not what we had hoped.)
Generate potential solutions	Generate potential solutions. All solutions should be considered. (The group reviews the norms developed at the beginning. Together, they decide if the norms need revising or if they are just not being implemented.) (Verify data from intervention. Talk with teachers who are implementing. Change the intervention.)
Evaluate potential solutions	Decide, as a group, what solution to follow.
Pick a solution	Pick a solution. Identify all of the necessary components of the solution (including what data to collect). Assign tasks. Determine how and when to follow up.
Implement a solution	Put plan into place and collect data.
Evaluate outcomes	Evaluate data and determine way forward (may have to start at the beginning of the process again)

Even if it is 5 minutes at the end of each meeting or at a specific designated time, teams must reflect on how they are working together.

Cultural Humility

Given the changing demographics of schools and school personnel, it is a sure bet that IEP meetings and other collaborative situations will require cross-cultural interactions (Murray-Garcia & Tervalon, 2017). If we define culture as shared patterns of behaviors, interactions, and understanding that are learned by socialization, then one can easily see how there may be variance among members of any collaborative team that could lead to miscommunication, confusion, and offense. Examples of differences related to collaboration may include how to greet one another, how to sit at a table, how we define and accept disability, how we behave with individuals at varying levels of authority. The list goes on. As a professional in many collaborative situations that require cross-cultural interactions, it is important to develop a mindset of interest and critical self-reflection in order to be successful. Tervalon and Murray-Garcia (1998) call this mindset cultural humility. Cultural humility is a bit of a counter argument to cultural competence in that cultural competence gives the impression that there is a certain level of mastery to be achieved in understanding cultures and, once achieved, further knowledge or exploration is not necessary (Tervalon & Murray-Garcia, 2017). In contrast, the idea of cultural humility for school personnel is that we are always learning from our colleagues, our students, and our families and we are continuously reflecting on how our own actions, language, and thinking may affect our collaborative relationships. In the words of Tervalon and Murray-Garcia (1998), cultural humility is:

> A process that requires humility as individuals continually engage in self-reflection and self-critique as lifelong learners and reflective practitioners . . . A process that requires humility in how physicians [used in original] bring into check power imbalances that exist in the dynamics of physician-patient [used in original] communication . . . and it is a process that requires humility to develop and maintain mutually respectful and dynamic partnerships with communities. (p. 188)

We need merely to substitute "school personnel" or "educators" for physicians and the idea remains the same. But the norms of behaviors and ideas are not universal for individuals who may hail from the same cultural background.

For example, from our case studies, Nolan's parents are French-speaking and originally from Mali. They are both highly educated but are learning more about Down syndrome and their child every day. In their home culture, education is not guaranteed so they feel very fortunate to have the opportunity for their children. And they feel strongly that Nolan will be a part of their community and extended family even after high school. However, Mr. and Mrs. Montague-Vargas dread school meetings because they often feel talked down to (e.g., personnel throw around numbers and words they don't understand), the long-term goals do not match their ideas of Nolan in their family, and, at the last IEP meeting, insulted because they both took two hours off of work to be at the 1:30 pm meeting and it did not start until 2 pm. School personnel wonder if they are engaged as they do not say much at the meetings. As part of their IEP discussion, it would be advantageous for Mr. Dixon or Ms. Welsch to ask questions of the parents to learn more about their hopes and dreams for Nolan, their thoughts and understanding about the US school systems, and how best to communicate with them. Trying to understand and interact with both the generalized cultural norms and unique understandings of families (and other professionals) instead of making assumptions or doing things "as they've always been done" will enhance the ability of any team to collaborate.

Reflection questions:

- Think about the groups or teams in which you have participated. Have they had these components in place? If so, how has it helped collaboration? If not, how has it hindered collaboration?
- How do your assumptions about dress, behavior, knowledge, status impact your ability to collaborate?

Some Example Collaboration Settings

As we have said from Chapter 1, schools are systems and the individuals within the system must collaborate effectively so that the system works for students with disabilities and in providing SDI. We provide a few examples below.

Collaboration in IEP Teams

In Chapters 3 and 4, we described some of the actions of the IEP team. These are critical teams—identifying student needs, creating plans for those needs, implementing those plans, and then evaluating how the plan is working. As we think about Jada, Derrick, Nolan, Jonelle, and all of the students with whom you work, we have to recognize that each student has individual and unique needs, requiring individualized plans and services. We must also think about the varied ideas of the members of the IEP team for each—teachers, related services providers, families, administrators, and the students themselves. If these groups of individuals cannot collaborate well, it is going to be impossible to see positive outcomes for these students.

It is often the seemingly "small" things that have the most impact. For example, when beginning an IEP meeting, did someone greet the parents at the door? Did everyone introduce themselves and their positions? Are all of the school personnel interspersed around the table and not all on the side opposite the family? Did a draft IEP get sent home (in the language of the family) with DRAFT clearly marked? How were the parents able to offer their ideas? Did anyone include the student? Did the teachers talk about the data they had before the meeting? Do all of the professionals know the student? See Textbox 8.1 for an example of an IEP team meeting introduction.

Textbox 8.1 *Collaborating in an IEP meeting*

Introduction of Team Members

- Introduction of all attendees
- *Thank you all for being here. I'd like to start the IEP meeting for ____ (student name). Let's begin by introducing ourselves. I'm _____. I am the case manager and special education teacher for (student name). (attendee names)____, would you please introduce yourselves.*
- Case manager/meeting lead
- Parents/caregivers

System-Wide Collaboration

- Student (if necessary)
- General education teacher
- School administrator/designee
- Other special education teacher (or notetaker, if necessary)
- Related services provider (if necessary)
- State purpose of meeting
- *The purpose of our meeting today is to review (student name)'s performance over the past year and to develop a new IEP with new goals for this upcoming year. I am hoping we can have a collaborative discussion so I am encouraging everyone to actively participate by asking questions and sharing ideas. If you need to take a break for any reason, please just let me know. Are we ready to get started?*

Present Levels of Performance

- Review interests and long-term goal ideas
- *Let's start with the present level of performance and areas of interest. When we last met (student's) interests included (state those) and the long-term goal was (state). Has anything changed in these areas? (encourage parent/student input)*
- Parent input
- Changes or updates in medical history or concerns, allergies, outside services or evaluations?
- *Are there any changes in these areas that we need to be aware of?*
- Review any **updated** testing if applicable
- Review most up-to-date state assessment scores
- Review current performance in courses/classes and performance on current IEP goals.
- *I have teacher reports for (student name)'s current grades and performance in classes. Let's start with (enter content here; read through teacher reports).*
- *From the data I've collected and from these teacher reports, it is important to note that (student name) has met (name the goals that the student has met from the current IEP). Additionally, evidence indicates that work toward these*

> goals is still in progress (name the goals that the student has not met from the current IEP).
> - *Incorporate general education teacher for information.*
> - *Incorporate related service providers for information.*
> - Ask the parents/caregivers if they have any information they would like to share about what they are seeing at home or how the student is progressing toward the current goals.
> - I would like to pause for a moment and ask you, (Mr./Mrs./Ms., etc.) _____, if you would like to share any insights or information you might have regarding (student name) progress on these goals at home.
> - What are student's strengths?
> - From the information we've shared, (student name) seems to be achieving/showing strengths in (insert areas of strength here and what evidence supports these statements)
> - What are student's needs?
> - Given these strengths, it is also apparent that (student name) requires support in (state areas). So, let's focus on developing goals related to these areas of need.

Collaboration in Co-Teaching Teams

For co-teaching teams, let's start with the end in mind. What does effective instruction (including SDI) look like in co-taught classrooms? Weiss and Rodgers (2020) propose a three-element model of instruction for effective co-teaching. See Figure 8.2.

In this model of instruction for co-teaching, every lesson should have three elements: (a) high-quality general education instruction, (b) whole or small group instruction that includes practices from special education that make the content accessible to all students, and (c) SDI. How these three elements are incorporated into instruction can vary with the six co-teaching approaches providing the option for flexible grouping in every lesson. Let's look at a few examples from our case studies.

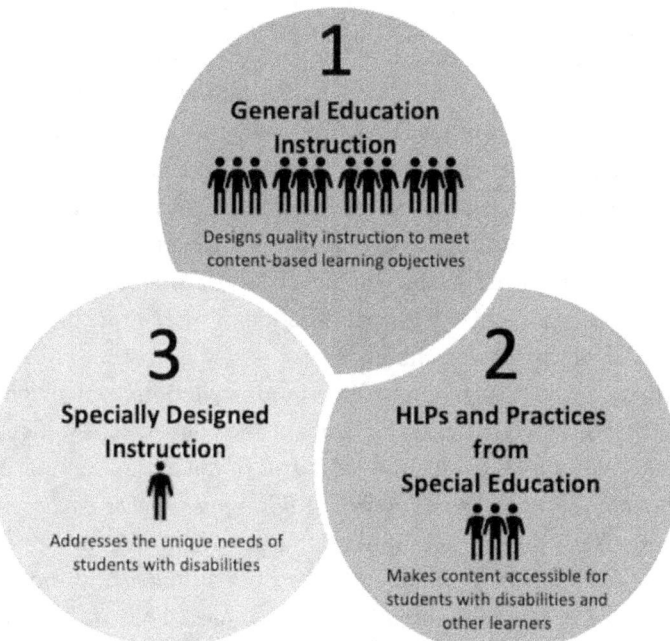

Figure 8.2 Three-element model of co-teaching.

Jada

Remember this?

> *Mr. Dixon sighed, leaned back, and ran his hand through his hair. Ms. Welsch looked at him with tired eyes and said, "I'm sorry. I thought we did everything to make it so Jada could access this material. We used small groups, graphic organizers, and guided notes. We let students choose their final projects for the unit. And you read the Midsummer Night's Dream test aloud to Jada. Everything we could think of to differentiate his experience. But she still failed it and so did several other students in the class. I thought this SDI thing would work." Mr. Dixon took a deep breath and said, "I need to learn more."*

Mr. Dixon, a special educator, and Ms. Welsch, an elementary school English/language arts teacher, are co-teaching a group of eighteen students that includes Jada, four other students with disabilities, and three English Language Learners who are below grade level in reading comprehension. As you read in Chapter 5, Mr. Dixon and Ms. Welsch are teaching *Midsummer Night's Dream*, a state-mandated text, with the goal of students making meaning from text. In the lesson, the teachers start with direct instruction in both the content of the play and in a self-questioning strategy. They then break into smaller, cooperative learning groups to practice. At the end of the lesson, it is clear to them that students are not fluent with the strategy and that the learning of the material is affected by this. Let's take this apart and look for/try to include all three elements of effective co-teaching.

Element 1: Quality general education instruction. In the vignette, it is clear that Ms. Welsch knows her content and conducts the initial part of the lesson as a whole group. The objectives of the lesson are clear to her: (a) students will make meaning from *Midsummer Night's Dream* and (b) students will use the self-questioning strategy to help them make meaning from the text. She reads aloud, cues her own thinking, and models that thinking, using a graphic organizer, as she goes about this lesson. Ms. Welsch also includes collaborative learning groups for additional independent practice of the strategy. Both of these, modeling and independent practice, are critical to student learning.

Element 2: Making content accessible to learners. Critical to students with disabilities and other students who are struggling to learn is significant practice with feedback. In this co-taught lesson, that could come in many forms. For example, after the modeling by Ms. Welsch, Mr. Dixon could complete several more examples with think aloud but also include engaging the students with questions and opportunities to respond (Archer & Hughes, 2011). These questions could be both about content and about the process of the strategy. This would allow the opportunity for immediate feedback and correction as well as allowing Ms. Welsch to collect some informal data about student understanding as she observed. Using the same graphic organizer that Ms. Welsch used, Mr. Dixon could complete the organizer at the board and/or have the students complete an organizer with him at their desks. Alternatively, if Ms. Welsch and Mr. Dixon both felt comfortable with the lesson, they could use parallel teaching to split the class into two groups and increase the opportunities to respond and to provide feedback for students in the smaller groups.

Element 3: SDI. Once Mr. Dixon and Ms. Welsch saw that students were ready for independent practice, they could do something a bit different from their original plan. They could use station teaching where they grouped the students who had grasped the strategy and the content to work in independent collaborative learning groups. The students who needed more instruction or practice from Ms. Welsch could work in a group with her. Jada and any other student with disabilities in the area of reading comprehension could work in a small group with Mr. Dixon. He would provide more direct instruction and practice opportunities in using the strategy, perhaps with different reading material before attempting to use it with *A Midsummer Night's Dream*.

Jack

Jack is a student with a disability in math who has challenges with organization and assignment completion. Mr. Reacher, a special educator, and Ms. Charlotte, a math teacher, are co-teaching geometry and Jack is in their class. Jack's SDI includes strategy instruction in assignment completion and submission, vocabulary, and multi-step math problems/proofs. Mr. Reacher and Ms. Charlotte are preparing for a unit on right triangles. The learning objectives for the first lesson are that students will be able to label all sides of a triangle and state the relationship of all angles.

Element 1: Quality general education. Ms. Charlotte begins the lesson with the whole group by asking students about the critical characteristics of triangles (three sides, three angles that add up to 180 degrees, not all sides have to be equal, longest side is opposite largest angle). Mr. Reacher writes each of these items down on the SMART board for students to copy into their math notebooks. Ms. Charlotte introduces the lesson objectives and begins to describe the characteristics of a right triangle. Mr. Reacher writes all of these items on the SMART board for students to copy. Ms. Charlotte shows several examples of triangles, thinks aloud as she determines if they are right triangles, and, if so, thinks aloud as she labels their components on the SMART board. As she finishes the fourth example, Ms. Charlotte begins to call on students to think aloud with her. Mr. Reacher labels the triangles on the SMART board.

Element 2: Making the content accessible to learners. After four or five examples, Mr. Reacher draws an example triangle on the SMART board and asks students to copy it into their math notebooks. He draws a big circle around the triangle and begins to ask students what he should think about first, second, and so on. As they tell him, he numbers the steps and lists them around the outside of the circle. When they complete the steps for the example triangle, Mr. Reacher puts another example on the SMART board and asks the students to work with their shoulder partner to complete the steps for that triangle. He and Ms. Charlotte circulate the room to evaluate student understanding. Ms. Charlotte then calls attention to the group, asks for a team volunteer to solve, and works them through the process. The teachers then split the students into groups.

Element 3: SDI. One group works independently. One group works additional practice problems with Ms. Charlotte. One group, including Jack, works with Mr. Reacher. In the small group, Mr. Reacher begins with geometry vocabulary cards that include the new words learned in that lesson. The group practices with the cards until they are able to define each one correctly. Mr. Reacher then uses the strategy graphic to work through three additional examples, asking for student responses and providing feedback. Mr. Reacher then has each student work two examples independently, with Jack repeating the directions for the group before they begin. Before the end of the session, Mr. Reacher has each student copy the homework into their assignment book.

One Note about SDI in Co-taught Classrooms

Because SDI can include adaptations to content, method, or delivery, the SDI that takes place in a co-taught classroom may include only adaptations to content (e.g., using different materials) or to delivery (e.g., small group instruction) because it is being supplemented with individualized instruction in a setting outside of the co-taught classroom. We want to be very clear that the individualized, different, and relevant instruction that is sometimes necessary for students with disabilities may not be possible in a co-taught classroom. However, the prompting, practice, and generalization of that individualized instruction may be the part of SDI that happens in the co-taught classroom. The critical piece here is that that intensive individualized instruction is taking place *somewhere* so that the student with disabilities can meet their annual goals.

Reflection question:

- How does the three-element model compare to your thinking about instruction in a co-taught classroom?

Collaboration in Planning

The lessons in these examples would not be possible without collaboration and planning between co-teachers. From its beginning, advocates of co-teaching have emphasized the necessity of common planning time and the intentional use of that time. SDI requires intentional planning for effective implementation. Let us say that again. *SDI requires intentional planning for effective implementation in a co-taught classroom (and, quite frankly, for any classroom).* A special educator cannot decide in the middle of independent practice, "Oh, this would be a great time to do a specialized reading instruction lesson with Jada!" We go back to the idea of systems—teachers working together develop systems for communicating and collaborating. These systems must support collaboration in ways such as having (and using) a common time to plan, developing norms that make that time efficient and effective, discussing and maintaining consistent and similar expectations, and supporting equal contributions. What works for one team may not work for another team so each team must carefully design their system. And that system then needs to work within the larger systems around it such as the school system (e.g., it is everyone's responsibility to work with every student), the content system (e.g., our collaborative learning team or department team will consider students with disabilities and others in our planning), and the special education system (e.g., working to help everyone understand what students with disabilities need to succeed and how that may also help others).

Conclusion

We have provided multiple examples of how collaboration is critical to school systems and the delivery of SDI. Again, this collaboration is not possible without active listening, perspective taking, cultural humility, and creative problem-solving. Too often we see schools jump to implement critical initiatives and that work falls flat because systems do not work together or individuals within the systems cannot collaborate. The provision of SDI requires collaboration across administrative, school, general education, special education, other education professionals, and family systems. If that collaboration breaks down, the students with disabilities essentially lose their opportunity for the SDI that IDEA guarantees. We cannot let that happen.

References

Archer, A. L., & Hughes, C. A. (2011). *Explicit instruction: Effective and efficient teaching.* Guilford Press

Blair, K. S., Lee, I. S., Cho, S. J., & Dunlap, G. (2011). Positive behavior support through family-school collaboration for young children with autism. *Topics in Early Childhood Special Education, 31,* 22–36.

Carlson, C., & Christenson, S. L. (2005). Evidence-based parent and family interventions in school psychology: Overview and procedures. *School Psychology Quarterly, 20*(4), 345–351.

Cox, D. D. (2005). Evidence-based interventions using home-school collaboration. *School Psychology Quarterly, 20,* 473–497.

Darling-Hammond, L., Ancess, J., & Ort, S. W. (2002). Reinventing high school: Outcomes of the coalition campus schools project. *American Educational Research Journal, 39*(3), 639–673. https://doi.org/10.3102/00028312039003639

Epstein, J. L. (2001). *School, family, and community partnerships: Preparing educators and improving schools.* Westview Press.

Esler, A., Godber, Y., & Christenson, S. L. (2008). Best practices in supporting school-family partnerships. In A. Thomas & J. Grimes (Eds.), *Best practices in school psychology V* (pp. 917–1120). National Association of School Psychologists.

Garet, M. S., Porter, A. C., Desimone, L., Birman, B. F., & Yoon, K. S. (2001). What makes professional development effective? Results from a national sample of teachers. *American Educational Research Journal, 38*(4), 915–945. https://doi.org/10.3102/00028312038004915

Griffiths, A. J., Alsip, J., Hart, S. R., Round, R. L., & Brady, J. (2021). Together we can so much: A systematic review and conceptual framework of collaboration in schools. *Canadian Journal of School Psychology, 36*(1), 59–85. https://doi.org/10.1177/08295732520915368

McEwan, D., Ruissen, G. R., Eys, M. A., Zumbo, B. D., & Beauchamp, M. R. (2017). The effectiveness of teamwork training on teamwork behaviors and team performance: A systematic review and meta-analysis of controlled interventions. *PLoS ONE, 12*(1), 1–23. https://doi.org/10.1371/journal.pone.0169604

Murray-Garcia, J., & Tervalon, M. (2017). Rethinking intercultural competence: cultural humility in internationalising higher education. In D. Deardorff & L. Arasaratnam-Smith (Eds)., *Intercultural competence in higher education: International approaches, assessment, and application* (pp. 19–31). Routledge. https://doi.org/10.4324/9781315529257

National Association of School Psychologists. (2012). *Position statement: School-family partnering to enhance learning.* https://www.nasponline.org/x26822.xml

Salas, E., Reyes, D. L., & McDaniel, S. H. (2018). The science of teamwork: Reflections, and the road ahead. *American Psychologist, 73*(4), 593–600. https://dx.doi.org/10.1037/amp.0000334

Salas, E., Shuffler, M. L., Tayer, A. L., Bedwell, W. L., & Lazzara, E. H. (2015). Understanding and improving teamwork in organizations: A scientifically based practical guide. *Human Resource Management, 54*(4), 599–622. https://doi.org/10.1002/hrm.21628

Serpell, Z. N., & Mashburn, A. J. (2011). Family-school connectedness and children's early social development. *Social Development, 21*, 21–46.

Tervalon, M., & Murray-Garcia, J. (1998). Cultural humility versus cultural competence: A critical distinction in defining physician training outcomes in multicultural education. *Journal of Health Care for the Poor and Underserved, 9*(2), 117–125. https://doi.org/10.1353/hpu.2010.0233

Wasley, P. A., Fine, M., Gladden, M. . . . Powell, L. (2000). *Small schools: Great strides. A study of new small schools in Chicago.* ERIC document ED 465 474. http://www.bnkst.edu/html/news/SmallSchools.pdf

Weiss, M. P., & Rodgers, W. (2020) Instruction in co-taught secondary classrooms: Three elements, two teachers, one unique idea. *Psychology in the Schools, 57*, 959–972. https://doi.org/10.1002/pits.22376

Woodland, R. H., & Hutton, M. S. (2012). Evaluating organizational collaborations: Suggested entry points and strategies. *American Journal of Evaluation, 33*(3), 366–383.

9
System-Wide Problem-Solving
Overcoming Challenges to Implementing Specially Designed Instruction

Chapter Outline

Challenges to Implementing Specially Designed Instruction 183
Additional Challenges 188
Conclusion 194

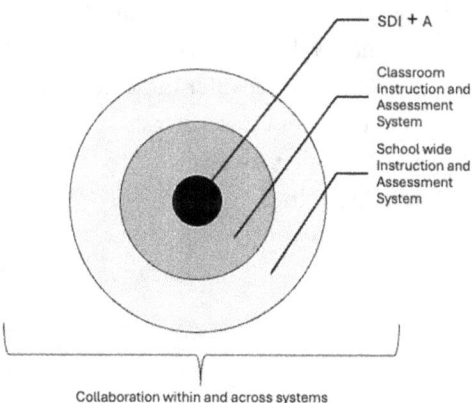

Figure 9.1 SDI as part of a school-wide system.

Chapter objectives:

1. Identify challenges to implementing SDI.
2. Propose suggestions to address these challenges.
3. Reinforce a system-wide approach to providing SDI.

> Systems thinking without systems thinkers will change nothing.
> —Derek and Laura Cabrera

Reflection questions:

- What do all educators and school personnel know about specially designed instruction in your school?
- How do all educators and school personnel in your school talk about SDI? Is it a shared responsibility?

SDI is a cornerstone of special education, ensuring students with disabilities receive individualized support to meet their unique needs as mandated by the Individuals with Disabilities Education Act (IDEA). Despite its critical role, the effective implementation of SDI is often hindered by various barriers, including procedural missteps, workforce challenges, instructional limitations, and resource shortages. This chapter explores these barriers and provides actionable recommendations to overcome them, ensuring students with disabilities can access meaningful and equitable educational opportunities. As we have described throughout the book, SDI exists within the school system. As the quote at the beginning of the chapter indicates, if we are not thinking of SDI as part of a larger school and district system, then we will face significant challenges in implementing effective SDI and meeting the needs of students with disabilities.

Challenges to Implementing Specially Designed Instruction

The implementation of SDI faces both procedural and systemic challenges, which collectively hinder the delivery of equitable and effective education for students with disabilities. Addressing these barriers is critical to meeting the legal and educational expectations outlined in the IDEA.

Procedural Challenges

Procedural challenges arise from inconsistencies in compliance, misaligned instructional strategies, and failures in the practical application of IDEA requirements. These issues often originate at the level of IEP development and can significantly impact student outcomes, as we have discussed in previous chapters of the book. For instance:

1. Poorly Articulated PLAAFP Statements (Chapters 3 and 4). PLAAFP statements are foundational to an effective IEP. However, when these statements lack specific, data-driven insights into a student's current abilities, they fail to provide a clear basis for measurable goals. This disconnect can result in vague, broad, or redundant objectives that fail to address the unique needs of the student (Yell, Bateman, & Shriner, 2022).
2. Inadequately Defined Annual Goals (Chapter 4). Goals that are overly broad, immeasurable, or disconnected from baseline data compromise the effectiveness of SDI. They hinder progress monitoring, making it difficult for educators to assess whether a student is making meaningful progress (*Endrew F. v. Douglas County School District*, 2017).
3. Misaligned Services (Chapters 3 and 4). A lack of alignment between the IEP components, such as services, accommodations, and modifications, further reduces the potential impact of SDI.

Misaligned services can lead to gaps in instructional delivery or unnecessary duplication of efforts, leaving students underserved (Sayeski, Reno, & Thoele, 2022).

The recent Supreme Court case of *Endrew F. v. Douglas County School District* highlights the critical importance of procedural fidelity in IEP development. The court's decision underscores the requirement for IEPs to be "reasonably calculated to enable a child to make progress appropriate in light of the child's circumstances" (Yell & Bateman, 2020). This sets a high bar for compliance, necessitating IEPs that are data-driven, specific, and actionable.

Addressing Procedural Challenges

To tackle procedural barriers, schools must implement practices that enhance compliance and ensure the effectiveness of SDI. Here are some examples, many of which we have discussed in the book:

1. Standardized IEP Templates. Developing standardized templates for PLAAFP statements, measurable goals, and service alignment could help educators adhere to IDEA requirements and maintain consistency across IEPs (Bateman & Cline, 2016).
2. Ongoing Professional Development. Training ALL educators on IEP development, including the use of data to inform PLAAFP and goal setting, ensures teams are equipped to create meaningful and compliant IEPs. Workshops, peer reviews, and simulations can reinforce best practices (Filderman, Austin & Toste, 2019).
3. Family Engagement. Engaging families in the IEP process fosters trust and collaboration. Parents provide valuable insights into their child's needs and strengths, contributing to more holistic and effective plans (Friend, 2015).
4. Procedural Audits. Regular audits of IEPs can identify common compliance issues and provide targeted feedback for improvement, ensuring that procedural fidelity is consistently maintained.

Reflection questions:

- What are some of the procedural challenges that you and your school face?
- Which of the suggestions provided would help overcome these challenges?

Systemic Challenges

Systemic challenges reflect broader organizational and resource issues that impede the consistent implementation of SDI. These include:

1. Lack of a Unified Framework for SDI (Chapters 1, 3, 7, and 8). Disparities in how SDI is defined and understood among educators, administrators, and families lead to inconsistent application. Without a shared vision, gaps in service delivery are inevitable (Meyer, Brandt, & Bluth, 1980).
2. Resource Constraints. Insufficient funding, inadequate staffing, and limited access to instructional materials are common systemic barriers. Resource limitations disproportionately affect under-resourced schools, exacerbating inequities in special education (Brunner & Bateman, 2020).
3. Scheduling Conflicts. Traditional school schedules often fail to accommodate the individualized needs of students with disabilities. Overlapping service times, limited availability of specialists, and rigid timetables disrupt the continuity and quality of SDI (Scruggs, Mastropieri, & McDuffie, 2007).
4. Inadequate Training and Support. A lack of ongoing professional development for both special and general educators undermines their ability to collaborate effectively and implement SDI with fidelity. This is particularly challenging in inclusive settings where co-teaching models require seamless coordination (Friend, 2015).

Addressing Systemic Challenges

To overcome systemic barriers, schools and districts must adopt strategies addressing both immediate needs and long-term goals. Again, many of these have been discussed in other chapters in the book:

1. Data-Driven Decision-Making (Chapters 6 and 7). Embedding SDI within MTSS ensures students with disabilities are included in universal screenings, targeted interventions, and individualized problem-solving processes. This approach aligns systemic practices with individual student needs (Fuchs & Fuchs, 2006).
2. Flexible Scheduling Models. Implementing block schedules, rotating service periods, or virtual support options reduces scheduling conflicts and ensures students receive uninterrupted services. Flexible models also provide more opportunities for collaborative planning (Harris, Schumaker, & Deshler, 2011).
3. Increased Resource Allocation. Prioritizing funding for staffing, professional development, and instructional materials demonstrates a commitment to improving educational outcomes for students with disabilities. Partnerships with external organizations can also supplement district resources (Diamond, 2008).
4. Collaborative Frameworks (Chapter 8). Structured co-planning sessions for general and special educators ensure alignment in instructional strategies. Administrative support for shared planning time fosters a culture of collaboration and accountability (Sayeski, Reno, & Thoele, 2022).
5. Unified Training Programs. Comprehensive training initiatives bridging general and special education perspectives help create a consistent understanding of SDI across all stakeholders. Training should include practical applications, such as using diagnostic tools like CBMs and integrating assistive technologies (Spear-Swerling, 2022). Using information across the chapters in this book for school-wide training, discussion, and understanding is one way to generate a consistent vision.

The Intersection of Procedural and Systemic Barriers

Addressing procedural and systemic barriers in isolation is insufficient; their intersection often exacerbates implementation challenges. For example, systemic issues like resource constraints amplify procedural errors by overburdening educators and reducing the time available for IEP development. Similarly, procedural failures, such as poorly defined goals, hinder the effectiveness of systemic initiatives like MTSS.

By adopting a holistic approach that integrates procedural fidelity with systemic reform, schools can create environments that support high-quality SDI implementation. This requires:

1. Leadership Advocacy. School leaders must champion SDI as a priority, allocating resources, setting clear expectations, and modeling a commitment to inclusive practices (Bateman & Cline, 2016).
2. Cross-Disciplinary Collaboration. Teams of general and special educators, related service providers, and administrators must work together to align procedural and systemic strategies (Friend, 2022).
3. Continuous Improvement. Regular evaluation of both procedural and systemic practices ensures that barriers are identified and addressed proactively. Data collected from these evaluations should inform professional development, resource allocation, and policy adjustments.

The effective implementation of SDI hinges on the ability to address both procedural and systemic barriers comprehensively. By prioritizing standardized practices, professional development, resource allocation, and collaborative frameworks, schools can empower educators to deliver high-quality, individualized support to students with disabilities. A holistic approach not only ensures compliance with IDEA but also fulfills the promise of equitable and inclusive education for all students.

Reflection questions:

1. What are some of the systemic challenges that you and your school face?
2. Which of the suggestions provided would help overcome these challenges?
3. How do you see systemic and procedural challenges intersecting in your school?

Additional Challenges

In addition to procedural and systemic challenges, there are barriers to SDI implementation that cross classrooms and beliefs.

Classroom-Level Challenges

At the classroom level, a significant challenge is the difficulty in distinguishing between SDI and general accommodations. While accommodations modify how students access the curriculum, SDI involves adapting the content, methodology, or delivery of instruction to meet individualized needs (IDEA, 2004). The conflation of these concepts often results in an over-reliance on accommodations, which, while necessary, are not sufficient for addressing the full scope of student needs (Filderman, Austin & Toste, 2019).

Another challenge is the inconsistent use of data to guide instruction. Teachers often lack training in using diagnostic and formative assessments to inform SDI, limiting their ability to respond to student progress in real time (Hallahan et al., 2023). Furthermore, time constraints and high workloads can make it difficult for teachers to engage in the iterative process of assessment, planning, and instructional adjustment that SDI requires (Scruggs, Mastropieri, & McDuffie, 2007).

Cultural and Attitudinal Barriers

Cultural resistance to collaboration and lingering misconceptions about inclusion also pose significant barriers. For example, some educators view SDI as an "add-on" rather than an integral part of teaching, perpetuating a mindset that prioritizes general instruction over individualized approaches (Friend, 2015). Additionally, misconceptions such as "one-size-fits-all" approaches to instruction and the belief that SDI is only necessary for students with severe disabilities further undermine its implementation (Bateman & Cline, 2016).

Frameworks for Addressing Challenges

Addressing these challenges requires a systemic approach that integrates SDI into school-wide frameworks while supporting classroom-level implementation through clear processes and professional development.

School-Wide Systems

Data-driven decision-making is critical for addressing systemic barriers to SDI, as we have described in multiple places in this book. By embedding SDI within MTSS, schools can ensure students with disabilities are included in universal screenings, targeted interventions, and individualized problem-solving processes (Fuchs & Fuchs, 2006). School-wide assessment frameworks provide a macro-level view of student performance, allowing administrators to identify disparities, allocate resources effectively, and align broader educational goals with the specific needs of students requiring SDI (Meyer, Brandt, & Bluth, 1980).

Policy alignment is another critical component. Schools must integrate SDI into improvement plans, professional development schedules, and resource allocation decisions, ensuring that it is treated as a priority rather than an optional add-on (Diamond, 2008). A clear policy framework ensures consistency across classrooms and grade levels, enhancing the likelihood of equitable outcomes.

Classroom Practices

In classrooms, assessment plays a pivotal role in guiding SDI. Diagnostic tools and formative assessments, such as CBM, enable teachers to monitor student progress in real time and make data-informed instructional adjustments (Harris, Schumaker, & Deshler, 2011). Teachers need ongoing professional development to effectively use these tools and distinguish SDI from accommodations and modifications. Training should focus on practical strategies for integrating SDI into daily instruction, such as using multi-sensory approaches and scaffolded techniques (Spear-Swerling, 2022).

Building Leadership and Shared Vision

As mentioned previously, effective leadership serves as the foundation for creating and sustaining a culture valuing and prioritizing SDI. School and district administrators play a pivotal role in modeling commitment to SDI by actively engaging with educators, parents, and other stakeholders. This leadership extends beyond verbal endorsements; it requires tangible actions such as allocating resources, setting clear expectations, and fostering collaboration among all members of the educational community. Administrators must advocate for SDI as a cornerstone of inclusive education, embedding it within the school's mission and vision statements to ensure alignment with broader goals.

A critical element of fostering a shared vision is building consensus around the importance of SDI for achieving meaningful outcomes for students with disabilities. Administrators can facilitate this by organizing professional learning communities (PLCs) or focus groups to collaboratively develop IEP goals that highlight the role of SDI. These efforts not only ensure compliance with IDEA mandates but also provide a platform for educators to exchange ideas and strategies for implementing SDI effectively. Highlighting the successes of students who have benefited from robust SDI practices can further galvanize support, helping stakeholders see its transformative impact firsthand (Yell et al., 2022). When leadership is transparent and inclusive in decision-making, it helps build trust, motivate educators, and create a unified approach to meeting the diverse needs of students.

Reflection questions:

1. Does your school have a shared vision?
2. How does/could a shared vision increase collaboration for SDI?

Developing Resources and Tools

Equipping teachers with practical tools and resources is essential for overcoming barriers to implementing SDI. Educators often cite lack of time, expertise, or access to materials as significant challenges. To address these concerns, schools and districts should provide comprehensive guides and templates for designing SDI-friendly lesson plans. These resources can include step-by-step instructions, real-world examples, and visual aids that simplify the process of integrating SDI into everyday instruction. Moreover, professional development sessions should focus on hands-on training, allowing teachers to practice and refine SDI techniques in a supportive environment.

Sharing examples of effective SDI practices is another key strategy for building capacity and inspiring innovation. For instance, case studies demonstrating the successful use of assistive technologies—such as text-to-speech software or adaptive communication devices—can serve as powerful teaching tools. These examples should also highlight specialized instructional techniques which are proven to support diverse learners. Additionally, districts can establish mentorship programs where experienced special educators work alongside general education teachers to model SDI implementation. Creating a centralized repository of resources, including videos, lesson plans, and research articles, ensures that educators have on-demand access to materials that can help them adapt their teaching strategies to meet individual student needs (Friend, 2022).

Collaboration among educators is another critical component of resource development. Establishing cross-disciplinary teams can foster the exchange of ideas, enabling educators to pool their expertise and develop innovative SDI strategies. Finally, districts should prioritize ongoing evaluation and feedback mechanisms to ensure the tools and resources provided are meeting teachers' needs and leading to measurable improvements in student outcomes. By investing in the development and dissemination of these supports, schools can empower teachers to deliver

SDI with confidence and effectiveness, ultimately ensuring that every student has access to an equitable and high-quality education.

Fostering Collaborative Planning

Fostering collaborative planning among educators is a cornerstone of effective SDI implementation, serving as a bridge between differing instructional practices and creating a unified approach to meeting student needs. Collaboration helps overcome cultural resistance, such as entrenched silos between general and special education staff and ensures that SDI is delivered consistently and effectively across educational settings.

At the heart of collaborative planning is the establishment of structured opportunities for general and special educators to engage in meaningful dialogue and joint problem-solving. Dedicated planning time allows teams to analyze student data, design individualized instructional strategies and align interventions with the specific needs outlined in students' IEPs. By working together to address gaps in understanding, educators can create a shared vision for instruction that reflects both the academic and functional priorities of students with disabilities. This shared planning process also fosters mutual respect and trust, which are essential for breaking down cultural barriers that may impede collaboration.

One of the most effective strategies for fostering collaborative planning is the regular review of student progress through data-driven decision-making. Collaborative data reviews provide a platform for educators to evaluate the effectiveness of SDI interventions, identify areas for adjustment, and celebrate successes. These reviews are especially critical for maintaining the "Golden Thread" of IEPs—ensuring seamless alignment between a student's present levels of performance, annual goals, and the services provided to achieve those goals. When general and special educators jointly analyze progress monitoring data, they can pinpoint discrepancies and adapt their approaches to ensure that instruction remains targeted and impactful.

Professional development plays a critical role in equipping educators with the skills needed for effective collaboration. Training sessions focused on co-teaching strategies, conflict resolution, and effective communication techniques can build capacity among educators to work together seamlessly. For instance, co-teaching models that clearly define roles and responsibilities—such as team teaching or parallel instruction—provide a framework for collaborative planning and delivery. Additionally, training in evidence-based SDI practices, such as the use of assistive technologies or evidence-based instructional strategies, ensures that all team members bring valuable expertise to the table.

Leadership support is another vital component of fostering collaboration. School leaders can create an environment conducive to collaborative planning by protecting shared planning time, providing necessary resources, and modeling a commitment to inclusive practices. Administrators who prioritize collaboration often implement policies that facilitate co-planning, such as embedding collaboration into the school schedule or providing stipends for after-hours teamwork. Leadership can also address cultural resistance by promoting a school-wide understanding of the value of SDI and the importance of shared responsibility for student success.

Technology can further enhance collaborative planning by streamlining communication and resource sharing among educators. Digital platforms that allow teachers to co-create and share lesson plans, track student progress, and access PLCs make collaboration more efficient and accessible. For example, educators can use collaborative tools to upload and analyze student data in real time, ensuring that adjustments to SDI are timely and based on the most current information.

The benefits of fostering collaborative planning extend beyond improved delivery of SDI. When educators collaborate effectively, they create a more cohesive and inclusive school culture, characterized by shared ownership of student outcomes. This collective accountability not only improves the quality of instruction but also enhances educator satisfaction and reduces burnout. Teachers feel supported and empowered when they can rely on their colleagues for ideas, resources, and encouragement.

Fostering collaborative planning is essential for the consistent and effective implementation of SDI. By creating opportunities for educators to engage in structured collaboration, supporting their efforts with professional development and technology, and addressing cultural resistance through leadership initiatives, schools can ensure that SDI becomes an integral part of instructional practices. This collaborative approach ultimately benefits all stakeholders, ensuring that students with disabilities receive the individualized support they need to thrive (Hallahan, Kauffman, & Pullen, 2023).

Reflection questions:

1. In what ways is collaboration supported across disciplines and personnel in your school?
2. How could collaboration be increased?

Conclusion

Overcoming barriers to SDI implementation requires a multi faceted approach that addresses systemic, classroom, and cultural challenges. By prioritizing leadership, collaboration, and data-driven decision-making, schools can create environments where SDI is seamlessly integrated into educational practices. This chapter underscores the importance of continuous professional learning and shared responsibility, offering actionable steps to ensure every student receives the individualized support they deserve. Educators, administrators, and policymakers must commit to advancing SDI as a foundational element of equitable and inclusive education.

Policies mandating ongoing training in SDI are instrumental in sustaining effective collaboration. Such training equips educators with the skills and strategies needed to work cohesively, including techniques for conflict resolution, communication, and joint decision-making (Yell, Bateman, & Shriner, 2022). Regular professional development sessions also provide opportunities for educators to stay updated on evidence-based practices and legal requirements, ensuring that their collaborative efforts remain effective and compliant.

Ensuring consistency between state policies and IDEA mandates is another critical factor in promoting collaborative planning. Misalignment between these frameworks can create confusion and hinder the implementation of SDI (Sayeski, Reno, & Thoele, 2022). For instance, inconsistent guidance on the roles of general and special educators in delivering SDI can lead to fragmented approaches. Clear and consistent policies provide a foundation for cohesive collaboration, enabling educators to focus on their shared goal of supporting students with disabilities.

The benefits of collaborative planning extend beyond improved student outcomes. Educators involved in collaborative efforts often report increased job satisfaction and reduced burnout, as they feel supported by their colleagues and empowered to make a meaningful impact. This sense of community fosters a positive school culture, where educators are motivated to innovate and advocate for their students.

In conclusion, collaborative planning is a cornerstone of effective SDI implementation. By fostering shared understanding, providing dedicated planning time, and aligning policies with IDEA mandates, schools can create an environment where general and special educators work together seamlessly. These efforts not only enhance the quality of instruction but also ensure that students with disabilities receive the individualized support they need to succeed.

References

Bateman, D. F., & Cline, J. (2016). *A teacher's guide to special education.* ASCD.

Brunner, R., & Bateman, D. F. (2020). Top components of special education for principals. *National Association of Elementary School Principals, Principal Magazine, 99*(3).

Diamond, R. M. (2008). Designing and assessing courses and curricula: A practical guide (3rd ed.). Jossey-Bass.

Endrew F. v. Douglas County School District, 580 U.S. ___ (2017).

Filderman, M. J., Austin, C. R., & Toste, J. R. (2019). Data-based decision making for struggling readers in the secondary grades. *Intervention in School and Clinic, 5*(1), 3–12.

Friend, M. (2015). *Inclusion: Co-teaching and collaborative practices.* Pearson.

Friend, M. (2022). Including students with special needs: A practical guide for classroom teachers (9th ed.). Pearson.

Fuchs, L. S., & Fuchs, D. (2006). Introduction to response to intervention: What, why, and how valid is it? *Reading Research Quarterly, 41*(1), 93–99.

Hallahan, D. P., Pullen, P. C., & Kauffman, J. M. (2023). *Exceptional learners: An introduction to special education* (15th ed.). Pearson.

Harris, M. L., Schumaker, J. B., & Deshler, D. D. (2011). The effects of strategic morphological analysis instruction on the vocabulary performance of secondary students with and without disabilities. *Learning Disability Quarterly, 34*(1), 17–33. doi:10.1177/073194871103400102

Individuals with Disabilities Education Improvement Act of 2004, 20 U.S.C. § 1400 et seq. (2004).

Meyer, B. J., Brandt, D., & Bluth, G. J. (1980). Use of context by disabled readers. *Journal of Reading Behavior, 12*(1), 1–10.

Sayeski, K. L., Reno, E. A., & Thoele, J. M. (2022). Specially designed instruction: Operationalizing the delivery of special education services. *Exceptionality.* https://doi.org/10.1080/09362835.2022.2158087

Scruggs, T. E., Mastropieri, M. A., & McDuffie, K. A. (2007). Co-teaching in inclusive classrooms: A metasynthesis of qualitative research. *Exceptional Children, 73*(4), 392–416.

Spear-Swerling, L. (2022). *Structured literacy and typical literacy practices: A guide for educators.* Guilford Press.

Yell, M. L., & Bateman, D. F. (2020). Endrew F. v. Douglas County School District (2017): Free appropriate public education and the U.S. Supreme Court, an update. *TEACHING Exceptional Children, 52*(5), 283–290.

Yell, M. L., Bateman, D. F., & Shriner, J. (2022). *Developing Educationally Meaningful and Legally Sound IEPs.* Rowman & Littlefield Publishing Group.

10

Future Directions and Emerging Trends in Specially Designed Instruction

Chapter Outline

Technology Integration in Specially Designed Instruction	199
Inclusion in Specially Designed Instruction	204
Equity in Special Education: Ensuring Tailored Support for All Learners	207
Research in Support of SDI	208
What Do These Ideas Look Like in Practice?	211
Future Directions: Understanding SDI as a Part of Equity-Focused Special Education Practices	213

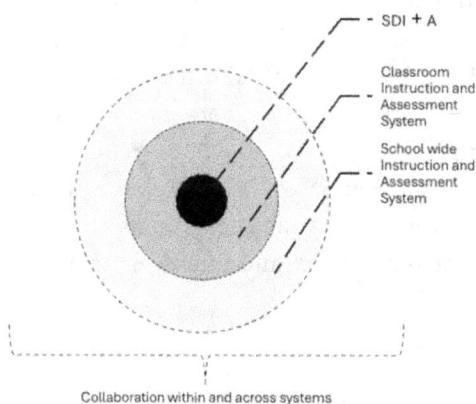

Figure 10.1 SDI as part of a school-wide system.

Chapter objectives:

- Identify key factors in the future of SDI.
- Describe how schools could incorporate these factors into their system-wide planning.
- Provide brief examples of system-wide efforts for equitable provision of SDI.

If there is no struggle, there is no progress.

—Frederick Douglass

Reflection question:

1. After reading this book, how are your ideas about SDI the same and/or different?

Education is undergoing rapid transformation, driven by technological advancements, increased diversity of student needs and abilities in classrooms, and a renewed emphasis on legally mandated equity and inclusion. These shifts underscore the need for continuous innovation in SDI to meet the diverse and evolving needs of students with disabilities. As inclusive practices expand, educators face growing demands to provide individualized, equitable, and effective instruction, making it essential to explore emerging strategies and tools that enhance student outcomes (Griffiths et al., 2020; National Center for Education Statistics, 2019). SDI, as defined by the Individuals with Disabilities Education Act (IDEA), involves adapting content, methodology, or instructional delivery to address the unique needs of students with disabilities (IDEA, 2004). While SDI has long been a foundation of special education, its future necessitates broadening its scope and effectiveness. Advancements in assistive technology, data-driven instructional practices, and interdisciplinary collaboration are reshaping SDI implementation, increasing accessibility, engagement, and learning outcomes (CAST, 2024; Fuchs, Fuchs, & Malone, 2017).

As Frederick Douglass says in the opening quote, change brings struggle, particularly in schools, where there are so many mediating factors. But without developing an intentional plan to adapt to change, students, particularly those with disabilities, will be left behind. This chapter focuses on four critical areas shaping the future of SDI: technology, inclusion, equity, and research. Technology introduces new possibilities for personalization and engagement through adaptive learning platforms and assistive devices that remove learning barriers (Diffit, 2023; DreamBox Learning, 2023). Inclusion emphasizes embedding SDI into general education classrooms, fostering collaborative practices, and reducing segregation through stronger partnerships between educators, families, and service providers (Darling-Hammond et al., 1995; Garet et al., 2001). Equity ensures all students receive appropriate support, regardless of socioeconomic background or disability status. School-wide data analysis frameworks and equity-focused strategies help educators monitor student progress and address disparities in access to specialized instruction (Diamond & Spillane2007; Wenglinsky, 2000). Finally, ongoing research related to SDI continues to identify EBPs, enhance intervention strategies, and refine assessment tools aligned with Individualized Education Programs (IEPs; IRIS Center, 2024). By examining these four areas, this chapter provides a comprehensive framework for educators, administrators, and policymakers to advance SDI in ways that align with the evolving educational landscape, ensuring all students have access to high-quality instruction (Griffiths et al., 2020; IDEA, 2004).

Technology Integration in Specially Designed Instruction

The integration of technology in education has significantly transformed instructional methods, improving accessibility and engagement for students with disabilities. From interactive whiteboards to one-to-one computing initiatives, classrooms now incorporate tools that support a wide range of learning needs (CAST, 2024). SDI increasingly benefits from artificial intelligence (AI), machine learning (ML), and adaptive learning platforms designed to personalize instruction and optimize student success (Diffit, 2023; DreamBox Learning, 2023).

Artificial Intelligence and Personalized Learning

AI-driven tools, such as Diffit™, dynamically adapt instructional materials for students with diverse abilities, ensuring content remains both accessible and appropriately challenging. These platforms analyze real-time student performance, adjusting task complexity and offering alternative content formats to match individual learning profiles. For example, AI-based reading programs simplify complex text for students with reading disabilities or offer additional vocabulary support for English learners, aligning seamlessly with SDI principles (IRIS Center, 2024).

Machine learning systems further enhance instructional delivery by detecting patterns in student data, predicting areas of difficulty, and allowing educators to intervene proactively (Fuchs, Fuchs, & Malone, 2017). Adaptive learning platforms, such as DreamBox Learning (www.dreambox.com) for mathematics and Read & Write (www.texthelp.com) for literacy, utilize data-driven insights to create individualized learning pathways, ensuring students advance at their own pace while addressing skill gaps effectively. The integration of technology into SDI fosters a data-driven approach to instruction, equipping educators with actionable insights to refine teaching strategies. Digital dashboards and analytics tools enable continuous monitoring of student progress, aligning instruction with IEP objectives and fostering a more inclusive learning environment (Fuchs, Fuchs, & Malone, 2017; IRIS Center, 2024).

Assistive Technologies in Specially Designed Instruction

Assistive technologies empower students with disabilities by addressing physical, sensory, and cognitive barriers to learning. These tools range from low-tech accommodations to sophisticated innovations designed to enhance accessibility and independence.

Physical Accessibility Supports

Students with physical disabilities benefit from adaptive equipment that promotes mobility, dexterity, and classroom engagement. Low-tech solutions, such as wheelchair-accessible desks, adjustable-height tables, and ergonomic writing tools, support student participation in learning activities. High-tech advancements, including robotic arms, powered wheelchairs, and exoskeletons, expand opportunities for students to interact with their environment and engage in hands-on learning (CAST, 2024; IDEA, 2004). All these technologies require instruction in when and how to use them, a critical component of the SDI for effective implementation of assistive technologies.

Sensory Supports for Students with Visual and Hearing Impairments

For students with visual or hearing impairments, assistive technologies such as screen readers, braille displays, and hearing aids play a crucial role in ensuring access to instructional content. Screen readers like Job Access with Speech; Freedom Scientific (JAWS; n.d.) convert digital text into spoken language, enabling students with visual impairments to engage with educational materials. Braille displays allow tactile interaction with digital content, fostering independence in literacy and comprehension. Advanced hearing aids and cochlear implants amplify sound and process auditory information, enabling students with hearing loss to access spoken communication in classroom settings (Diffit, 2023; IRIS Center, 2024). Again, all these technological supports require that educators and other specialists include instruction in how and when to use the supports as part of a student's SDI.

Cognitive and Executive Functioning Supports

Students with cognitive disabilities, including ADHD and autism spectrum disorder, benefit from technologies that enhance organization, attention, and communication. Speech-to-text software assists students with writing challenges by transcribing spoken words into text, reducing barriers to written expression. Visual schedules, digital timers, and wearable devices provide structured support for managing tasks, improving time management, and fostering self-regulation in academic settings (CAST, 2024; Fuchs, Fuchs, & Malone, 2017). As education and technologies continue to evolve, so must the implementation of SDI. The future of SDI relies on the expansion of adaptive learning platforms, assistive technologies, and data-driven practices to ensure that students with disabilities receive personalized, high-quality instruction tailored to their unique needs (Griffiths et al., 2020; IDEA, 2004). Continued collaboration among educators, researchers, policymakers, and technology developers will be essential in refining SDI methodologies and ensuring equitable access to instructional resources. With a collective commitment to innovation and accessibility, SDI on how and when to use new technologies to support their learning will be a powerful tool in advancing educational outcomes for students with disabilities, fostering their academic success and lifelong independence.

The Role of Wearable Technology in Specially Designed Instruction

Wearable technology has become an essential component in modern assistive devices, offering students with disabilities greater independence and accessibility in their learning environments. Smartwatches, for example, provide discreet alerts and prompts to help students manage time, stay on task, and regulate behaviors. Similarly, augmented reality (AR) glasses overlay visual cues onto the physical environment to enhance comprehension and engagement, making learning more interactive and personalized (Diffit, 2023; IRIS Center, 2024). The rapid evolution of wearable technology highlights its role in increasing student autonomy while reducing stigma associated with traditional assistive devices. These tools seamlessly integrate into daily routines, supporting executive functioning skills and ensuring accessibility in various learning contexts. The continued advancement of wearable assistive technology underscores the importance of maintaining an inclusive educational framework that accommodates students with diverse needs, teaches their use of these advancements, and acknowledges their place in the classroom.

Personalized Learning through Technology

One of the most significant contributions of technology to SDI is the ability to personalize instruction based on student needs. Adaptive learning platforms utilize sophisticated algorithms to tailor content delivery, ensuring that instruction aligns with individual strengths, challenges, and progress. For instance, a student struggling with reading comprehension might be provided with scaffolded texts, interactive vocabulary supports, and comprehension strategies adapted to their level, while peers engage with grade-level material (Diffit, 2023; DreamBox Learning, 2023). The flexibility of technology extends beyond content modification to delivery methods. Students with visual impairments benefit from auditory and tactile representations of information, while students with motor disabilities use voice-activated commands to navigate digital resources. This customization ensures that students can access the curriculum in ways that best suit their learning preferences and needs, making SDI more effective and inclusive (CAST, 2024; IRIS Center, 2024).

Enhancing Engagement and Participation

Technology fosters increased engagement by transforming learning into an interactive, multimodal experience. Tools such as interactive whiteboards, gamified learning applications, and virtual reality (VR) simulations offer immersive opportunities for experiential learning, making abstract concepts tangible and engaging (Fuchs, Fuchs, & Malone, 2017; Griffiths et al., 2020). For instance, VR technology enables students to explore historical events, conduct virtual science experiments, or practice real-world problem-solving skills. These applications provide authentic, hands-on learning experiences that traditional instructional methods often lack. Additionally, assistive communication devices such as augmentative and alternative communication (AAC) systems empower students with speech impairments to actively participate in discussions, collaborate with peers, and engage meaningfully in the classroom (IDEA, 2004).

Inclusion in Specially Designed Instruction

Inclusive practices ensure students with disabilities receive equitable access to meaningful learning opportunities within general education settings. The principle of LRE mandates students with disabilities be educated alongside their peers whenever appropriate, fostering academic and social development. This principle is a cornerstone of the Individuals with Disabilities Education Act (IDEA) and reflects the broader goal of maximizing inclusion while providing necessary supports (IDEA, 2004). Research consistently demonstrates that inclusive education benefits both students with disabilities and their peers. Inclusion enhances academic achievement, increases student engagement, and improves social-emotional skills for all learners. Furthermore, peers in inclusive settings develop greater empathy, collaboration skills, and an appreciation for diversity, contributing to a more positive school culture (Darling-Hammond, Ancess, & Falk, 1995; Wenglinsky, 2000).

Effective Implementation of Inclusive Practices

Throughout the book, we have emphasized ways in which special education and general education work together to achieve positive outcomes for students with disabilities. Achieving effective inclusion requires deliberate planning, collaboration, and professional development for educators. Key strategies we have suggested include:

- **Co-Teaching Models:** Special and general educators collaborate to deliver instruction that is different from that provided in a singly-taught classroom to meet diverse student need (Chapter 8; Murawski & Dieker, 2013). Successful co-teaching requires structured collaboration, shared planning time, and mutual respect between educators. When implemented effectively, it fosters an inclusive learning environment that upholds high expectations for all students (Murawski & Dieker, 2013).
- **Embedded SDI in General Education:** SDI should not be an isolated service but rather integrated into general education classrooms through accommodations, modifications, and scaffolding techniques (Chapter 5; Griffiths et al., 2020). General and special educators align lesson plans with IEP goals, ensuring that instructional activities are accessible and individualized (IRIS Center, 2024). Tools such as text-to-speech software, graphic organizers, and interactive whiteboards provide alternative ways for students to access and engage with content (CAST, 2024). Students are grouped based on learning needs rather than disability status, allowing instruction that benefits all learners. Teachers provide temporary supports, such as guided notes or visual prompts, to help students grasp complex concepts before gradually removing them as students gain independence (Fuchs, Fuchs, & Malone, 2017).
- **Collaborative Problem-Solving Teams:** Multi-disciplinary teams, including special educators, related service providers, and administrators, should regularly assess student progress and adjust interventions as needed (Chapters 6 and 7; IRIS Center, 2024).
- **Professional Development and Training:** Educators should receive training on inclusive teaching strategies, and evidence-based SDI practices to build capacity and improve outcomes for students with disabilities (CAST, 2024).

The evolution of technology and inclusive education practices has reshaped SDI, creating new opportunities for accessibility, engagement, and individualized learning in the general education classroom. By leveraging technological advancements and evidence-based instructional strategies, educators can foster equitable learning environments that empower all students to achieve their full potential. Continued research, professional development, and collaborative implementation will ensure that SDI remains a driving force in advancing accessibility and success in education (Griffiths et al., 2020; IDEA, 2004).

Despite the proven benefits of inclusion, barriers such as inadequate training, limited collaboration time, and resource constraints can hinder effective implementation. Addressing these challenges requires systemic support and evidence-based solutions (Griffiths et al., 2020; Murawski & Dieker, 2013). Many educators lack training in understanding disability characteristics, assistive technology, and behavior management strategies. Limited planning time and inconsistent communication between general and special educators can impede co-teaching effectiveness (Griffiths et al., 2020). Resistance to inclusion often stems from misconceptions about students with disabilities or concerns about increased workload (Wenglinsky, 2000). Insufficient funding, staffing, and instructional materials impact schools' ability to implement inclusive practices effectively (Darling-Hammond, Ancess, & Falk, 1995).

To address these challenges, we recommend the following which align with recommendations made throughout the book:

- Ongoing professional development to equip educators with necessary skills (CAST, 2024).
- Coaching and mentoring programs provide real-time support to refine inclusive teaching practices (Murawski & Dieker, 2013).
- Scheduled co-planning sessions facilitate alignment between general and special educators (Griffiths et al., 2020).
- Digital collaboration tools support ongoing communication and resource sharing (IRIS Center, 2024).
- Inclusion workshops and success stories can help shift educator mindsets toward embracing inclusive practices (Darling-Hammond, Ancess, & Falk, 1995).
- School cultures that celebrate diversity and promote a sense of belonging for all students (Wenglinsky, 2000).
- Funding for additional staff, assistive technology, and training ensures equitable implementation of inclusive practices (Darling-Hammond, Ancess, & Falk, 1995).
- Community partnerships and grants to supplement resources for students with disabilities (Tomlinson, 2014).
- Data monitoring enables educators to adjust strategies and ensure student progress (Fuchs, Fuchs, & Malone, 2017).

Equity in Special Education: Ensuring Tailored Support for All Learners

Equity in special education extends beyond providing equal resources—it requires tailoring instruction to meet individual student needs. Addressing systemic barriers, promoting culturally responsive practices, and ensuring fair access to services are crucial for achieving equitable outcomes (Darling-Hammond, Ancess, & Falk, 1995; Fuchs, Fuchs, & Malone, 2017).

Equality vs. Equity in SDI: Addressing Systemic Barriers

Equality assumes all students receive the same resources, while equity ensures each student has access to the support necessary for success. For example, two students with reading challenges may require different interventions: one might need phonics instruction, while another benefits from comprehension strategies. Equity-driven SDI ensures individualized support that promotes meaningful progress (Griffiths et al., 2020).

As we have discussed throughout the book, SDI is part of a broad school system that requires energy, effort, and attention to all the components. Without that intentional, sustained effort in building a culture that values equity over equality, SDI will remain an isolated and "add-on" aspect of special education services. There are several ways to address barriers to this systemic approach:

- Schools must use assessments that account for students' linguistic and cultural backgrounds to prevent misidentification (Wenglinsky, 2000).
- Professional development should focus on distinguishing between language acquisition difficulties and learning disabilities (LD) to ensure accurate special education referrals (Darling-Hammond & Bransford, 2005).
- Schools must analyze identification and service data to detect and address inequities in special education programming (Fuchs, Fuchs, & Malone, 2017).

- Schools should refine referral processes to prevent over- and under-identification of minority students in special education (Darling-Hammond, Ancess, & Falk, 1995).
- Equitable resource allocation ensures all students receive appropriate supports, regardless of district funding disparities (IRIS Center, 2024; Tomlinson, 2014).
- Increased communication between general and special educators improves instructional consistency and enhances student success (CAST, 2024). General and special education staff work together to align curriculum and integrate SDI into general education settings, ensuring seamless instructional support for students with disabilities (CAST, 2024).
- Engaging families as equal partners in the special education process fosters a shared understanding of student needs and promotes culturally responsive goal setting for IEPs. Family involvement in decision-making enhances outcomes by ensuring that instructional approaches align with students' lived experiences (Murawski & Dieker, 2013).
- Collaborating with community organizations enhances access to resources such as healthcare services, behavioral supports, and enrichment programs. For instance, partnerships with local healthcare providers ensure students receive necessary evaluations and therapies, removing barriers to learning (Darling-Hammond, Ancess, & Falk, 1995).

In addition to technology, inclusion, and equity, the outcomes for students with disabilities can only be improved using EBPs, requiring sustained lines of research and a commitment to use evidence-based and/or high-leverage practices in both SDI and general classroom instruction.

Research in Support of SDI

Research plays a crucial role in the evolution of SDI, ensuring that instructional strategies remain effective, evidence-based, and aligned with the diverse needs of students with disabilities. As the field continues to advance, several key areas of research are emerging that will shape the future of SDI, including intervention efficacy, implementation fidelity, and equity-focused practices.

The Role of EBPs and HLPs in SDI

A fundamental aspect of SDI is the use of EBPs to support student learning. Research has consistently demonstrated that interventions rooted in empirical data lead to improved academic and behavioral outcomes for students with disabilities (Fuchs, Fuchs, & Malone, 2017). The Taxonomy of Intervention Intensity, developed by Fuchs et al. (2017), provides a structured framework to determine the effectiveness of interventions within SDI, ensuring that instructional modifications are tailored to individual student needs.

Emerging research also highlights the importance of high-leverage practices (HLPs) in special education. These practices, identified by the Council for Exceptional Children (CEC) and the CEEDAR Center, focus on essential instructional strategies such as explicit instruction, scaffolded learning, and formative assessment (McLeskey et al., 2017). When integrated into SDI, HLPs enhance student engagement and promote meaningful progress toward academic and functional goals.

Implementation Science and Fidelity of SDI

While identifying effective interventions is critical, ensuring their proper implementation is equally important. Implementation science provides a framework for understanding how SDI strategies can be effectively applied in real-world educational settings. Research on implementation fidelity suggests that professional development, coaching, and administrative support are key factors in sustaining SDI practices over time (Fixsen et al., 2005).

Studies have shown that when educators receive targeted training and ongoing support, they are more likely to implement SDI strategies with fidelity, leading to better student outcomes (Cook & Odom, 2013). Moreover, the use of implementation rubrics and fidelity checklists helps educators monitor the effectiveness of SDI strategies and make necessary adjustments to improve instructional delivery.

Equity in SDI: Addressing Disparities in Special Education

Equity in SDI requires ensuring that all students, regardless of race, socioeconomic status, or disability category, receive high-quality, individualized support. Research has identified disparities in the identification and placement of students with disabilities, with historically marginalized groups often experiencing higher rates of exclusion from general education settings (Skiba et al., 2008).

To address these disparities, recent studies emphasize the need for culturally responsive SDI practices that acknowledge students' diverse backgrounds and learning experiences (Klingner, Artiles, & Barletts, 2005). This includes integrating UDL principles, leveraging assistive technologies, and utilizing culturally relevant pedagogy to make SDI more inclusive and equitable.

The Future of SDI Research: Directions and Implications

As education continues to evolve, future research in SDI must address several pressing questions, including:

- How can AI and machine learning enhance personalized learning within SDI?
- What are the most effective coaching models for supporting educators in implementing SDI with fidelity?
- How can SDI be integrated more effectively into MTSS to provide early interventions and prevent academic failure?
- What policy changes are needed to ensure equitable access to SDI across all educational settings?

By prioritizing these research areas, educators, policymakers, and researchers can work together to refine SDI practices, ensuring that all students with disabilities receive the individualized, high-quality instruction necessary for success.

What Do These Ideas Look Like in Practice?

Several school districts across the United States have successfully implemented equity-focused SDI models. These case studies illustrate strategies that have led to meaningful improvements in student outcomes and can serve as models for other districts.

Case Study 1: District A—Addressing Disproportionality in Special Education Evaluations

District A identified patterns of over-identifying Black students for emotional disturbance (ED) while under-identifying them for other disabilities, such as LD. To address these disparities, the district implemented a system-wide review of evaluation practices, including:

- **Implicit Bias Training:** All educators and evaluators received training on implicit bias and culturally responsive assessment practices.
- **Comprehensive Data Collection:** Evaluation teams incorporated input from families and community members, as well as observational data, to ensure a holistic understanding of student needs.
- **Revised Referral and Assessment Procedures:** The district emphasized multiple data sources over standardized testing alone to make eligibility determinations (Wenglinsky, 2000).

As a result, disproportionality in special education identification decreased significantly, and family satisfaction with the evaluation process improved.

Case Study 2: District B—Resource Allocation for Equity

District B, serving a high percentage of low-income students, recognized disparities in access to special education services. The district implemented a strategic resource allocation plan that prioritized schools with the greatest needs. Key initiatives included:

- **Investment in Assistive Technology:** The district provided schools with text-to-speech software, communication devices, and other tools to enhance accessibility.
- **Hiring Additional Special Education Staff:** Increased staffing ratios ensured that students received more individualized instructional support.
- **Professional Development for Educators:** Training focused on evidence-based SDI practices and culturally responsive teaching (Gay, 2018).

These efforts resulted in improved academic outcomes for students with disabilities, particularly in under-resourced schools. Additionally, teacher confidence in delivering SDI increased, and family engagement in the special education process grew.

Case Study 3: District C—Promoting Inclusion Through Co-Teaching

District C implemented a district-wide co-teaching initiative to support inclusive education and equity. Key components included:

- **Structured Co-Teaching Models:** General and special educators participated in joint planning and implemented team-teaching strategies.

- **Mentorship Program:** Experienced co-teachers mentored new teaching pairs to ensure consistent implementation of best practices.
- **Ongoing Professional Development:** Teachers engaged in workshops focused on collaboration and inclusive teaching strategies (Murawski & Dieker, 2013).

As a result, students with disabilities demonstrated increased engagement and academic achievement. Teachers reported greater job satisfaction, and families expressed confidence in the district's commitment to inclusion (CAST, 2024). Equity in special education is essential for ensuring that all students receive the individualized support they need to succeed. By addressing systemic barriers, fostering collaboration, and prioritizing equitable resource allocation, schools can create learning environments that support all learners (Darling-Hammond, Ancess, & Falk, 1995; Griffiths et al., 2020).

Future Directions: Understanding SDI as a Part of Equity-Focused Special Education Practices

As we have stated throughout the book, SDI is a right for every student with a disability who receives services through IDEA. Providing SDI, improving student outcomes, and increasing equity in special education requires a sustained commitment to continuous improvement and innovation. As part of a system-wide commitment to the delivery of SDI, there must be intention and commitment to:

- **Ensuring Access to High-Quality Instructional Resources:** Equitable funding and resource allocation must prioritize students with the greatest needs, ensuring access to assistive technology, specialized instructional support, and well-trained educators (IRIS Center, 2024).
- **Enhancing Professional Development:** Providing educators with training in evidence-based SDI practices, implicit bias, and

cultural competency ensures that all students receive high-quality instruction (Darling-Hammond, Ancess, & Falk, 1995).
- **Strengthening Cross-System Collaboration:** Partnerships between schools, families, and community organizations must be expanded to provide wraparound support for students with disabilities, addressing academic, social-emotional, and behavioral needs (CAST, 2024).

Collaboration is a cornerstone of SDI and therefore, providing equitable access to students with disabilities requires it. When educators, families, and community stakeholders work together, they create inclusive, supportive environments where all students can thrive. Case studies from districts across the country demonstrate that intentional, school- and division-wide systems focused on delivering SDI to each student with a disability to meet their needs leads to measurable improvements in student outcomes. By embracing a commitment to SDI as a system-wide venture, schools can ensure that it is accessible, effective, and transformative for students with disabilities (Griffiths et al., 2020; IDEA, 2004).

Moving forward, expanding research on effective special education practices, fostering data-driven decision-making, and strengthening professional development will be critical to sustaining progress. As schools and districts refine their approaches, collaboration will remain an essential tool for fostering fairness, inclusion, and success for all learners (Darling-Hammond, Ancess, & Falk et al., 1995; Fuchs, Fuchs, & Malone, 2017).

References

CAST. (2024). *Universal Design for Learning (UDL) guidelines.* Retrieved from https://udlguidelines.cast.org

Cook, B. G., & Odom, S. L. (2013). Evidence-based practices and implementation science in special education. *Exceptional Children, 79*(2), 135–144. https://doi.org/10.1177/001440291307900201

Darling-Hammond, L., Ancess, J., & Falk, B. (1995). *Authentic assessment in action: Studies of schools and students at work.* Teachers College Press.

Darling-Hammond, L., & Bransford, J. (Eds.). (2005). *Preparing teachers for a changing world: What teachers should learn and be able to do.* Jossey-Bass

Diamond, J. B., & Spillane, J. P. (2007). *Distributed Leadership in Practice.* Teachers College Press.

Diffit. (2023). *Personalized learning through adaptive technology: How Diffit supports diverse learners.* https://web.diffit.me/

DreamBox Learning. (2023). Personalized learning through adaptive technology: How DreamBox supports diverse learners. DreamBox Learning, Inc. https://www.dreambox.com/

Fixsen, D. L., Naoom, S. F., Blase, K. A., Friedman, R. M., & Wallace, F. (2005). *Implementation research: A synthesis of the literature.* Tampa, FL: University of South Florida, Louis de la Parte Florida Mental Health Institute.

Fuchs L. S., Fuchs D., Malone A. S. (2017). The taxonomy of intervention intensity. *TEACHING Exceptional Children, 50*(1), 35–43. https://doi.org/10.1177/0040059917703962

Freedom Scientific. (n.d.). JAWS screen reader. https://www.freedomscientific.com/products/software/jaws/

Garet, M. S., Porter, A. C., Desimone, L., Birman, B. F., & Yoon, K. S. (2001). What makes professional development effective? Results from a national sample of teachers. *American Educational Research Journal, 38*(4), 915–945. https://doi.org/10.3102/00028312038004915

Gay, G. (2018). *Culturally responsive teaching: Theory, research, and practice* (3rd ed.). Teachers College Press.

Griffiths, A. J., et al. (2020). Together we can do so much: A systematic review and conceptual framework of collaboration in schools. *Canadian Journal of School Psychology, 36*(2), 117–144. https://doi.org/10.1177/0829573520915368

Individuals with Disabilities Education Act. (2004). 20 U.S.C. §1400 et seq. Retrieved from https://sites.ed.gov/idea

IRIS Center. (2024). Evidence-based practices in Specially Designed Instruction (SDI). Retrieved from https://iris.peabody.vanderbilt.edu

Klingner, J. K., Artiles, A. J., & Barletta, L. M. (2005). English language learners who struggle with reading: Language acquisition or LD? *Journal of Learning Disabilities, 39*(2), 108–128. https://doi.org/10.1177/00222194060390020101

McLeskey, J., Barringer, M.-D., Billingsley, B., Brownell, M. T., Jackson, D., Kennedy, M., Lewis, T., Maheady, L., Rodriguez, J., Scheeler, M. C.,

Winn, J., & Ziegler, D. (2017). *High-leverage practices in special education.* Council for Exceptional Children & CEEDAR Center.

Murawski, W. W., & Dieker, L. A. (2013). *Leading the co-teaching dance: Leadership strategies to enhance team outcomes.* Council for Exceptional Children.

National Center for Education Statistics. (2019). *The condition of education 2019 (NCES 2019-144).* U.S. Department of Education. https://nces.ed.gov/pubsearch/pubsinfo.asp?pubid=2019144

Skiba, R. J., Horner, R. H., Chung, C., Rausch, M. K., May, S. L., & Tobin, T. (2008). Race is not neutral: A national investigation of African American and Latino disproportionality in school discipline. *School Psychology Review, 40*(1), 85–107.

Tomlinson, C. A. (2014). *The differentiated classroom: Responding to the needs of all learners* (2nd ed.). ASCD.

Wenglinsky, H. (2000). *How teaching matters: Bringing the classroom back into discussions of teacher quality.* Educational Testing Service.

Index

ABCD+T objective writing   108
academic achievement   37
access   7, 11, 12, 183, 192, 198, 201–3, 207, 209, 212–14
accommodation   20, 37, 46–8, 52, 65, 67, 111, 125, 142
adapting/adaptation
   adaptations   20, 54, 66–8, 176
   adapting content   25
   adapting delivery   26
   adapting methodology   26
   modify   47
administrator(s)   30, 31
advocacy   30
alternative formats   20
alternative setting   44
assessment(s)   189, 199, 209
   Benchmark   144–6
   diagnostic   104, 105
   district-wide   46
   formative   104, 112–14, 116, 119, 120, 123, 144, 145
   ongoing assessment   4
   statewide   46, 141
   summative   104, 110, 120, 123, 144, 146
assistive technology/ies (AT)   20, 23, 31
"At no cost" requirement   22
automaticity   82

behavioral intervention plan (BIP)   78, 148
building-wide team   153
buy-in   139, 154

collaboration   9, 23, 55, 149, 160–6, 168, 177, 178
collaborative process   24
compliance   23, 31, 32, 128, 136, 138, 155
content, methodology, delivery of instruction   11, 18, 25
continuum
   of evidence   87
   of research-based practice   88
   of services   45
co-teaching   172–6
culturally informed/culturally responsive/culturally sustaining practices   6, 12, 13
cultural norms   169
culture   168, 169
the curriculum   28
Curriculum-Based Measurement (CBM)   104, 113, 117, 118, 123, 125, 129, 145, 147, 155

data
   data analysis   124, 126, 149, 152
   data graphing/visualization   117
   data sharing   127
   data use   116, 124
data-based/data-driven
   data-based decisions   116, 119, 124, 135, 138, 140, 146
   data-based individualization   9, 85
   data-driven planning   9
differentiated instruction   3, 4, 12, 13
Diffit   77, 78
due process   21, 139, 155

Index

educational program 37
Embedding SDI (in General Education) 75
Endrew F. 21, 22, 38, 44, 59, 143, 184
evaluation 189
evidence-based
    evidence-based practice (EBP) 7, 8, 12, 81, 87, 89–91, 93, 103
    strategies 36
executive functioning 82, 95

families 112, 127, 154
feedback 7
    corrective 82
fidelity 124, 138
flexible grouping 4, 9
flexible instructional time 152
free appropriate public education (FAPE) 19, 22, 37, 43, 138
functional behavior assessment (FBA) 148
functional performance 37
functional skills 38
    daily life 38
    executive functioning 38
    organizational skills 38
    self-regulation 38
    vocational 38

general curriculum 19, 20, 32
    extracurricular 39
    general education curriculum/setting 40, 42, 44–7
    post-secondary transition 38, 47, 48
    "regular education" 49
general educators 80, 81, 163, 165, 187, 205
goal(s) 9, 10, 25
    IEP/annual goals 37, 39, 40, 53–5, 59, 64, 65, 67, 92, 93, 101, 102, 107, 108, 111, 114, 116–19, 124, 127, 143, 148, 176
    transition goals 39
golden thread 44, 47, 49

high leverage practices (HLP) 8, 9

implementation 187, 205, 214
inclusion 26, 28, 31, 32, 39, 44, 80, 189, 198, 199, 204, 206–9, 214
individualized Education Program (IEP) 13, 19, 38, 47, 49, 73, 77, 78, 86, 89, 107, 128, 142, 147, 160, 164
    components of the IEP 36
    IEP meeting 102, 128, 143, 155
    IEP team 44, 48, 170
Individuals with Disabilities Education Act (IDEA) 18, 21, 36, 37, 45, 47, 89, 120, 127, 136
instruction 182, 184, 186, 188, 191–4, 198, 200, 202, 204, 206–8, 210–12, 214
    appropriate instruction/education 21, 22
    direct 38
    explicit instruction 9, 19, 20, 39, 46, 48, 81, 86
    individualized instruction 5, 6, 11, 19, 32, 55, 176
    intensifying instruction 9, 10, 12, 176
    relevant 32
internal consistency 44, 45

learning management system (LMS) 124
learning objectives 103, 104, 107–9, 123, 124
least restrictive environment (LRE) 44, 45, 80, 128, 141
legal 204
    legal precedents/requirements 21, 31, 37, 39
lesson planning 123

modification(s) 37, 46–8, 52, 111, 125, 142
monitoring student achievement 137
multi-sensory approach 19, 26

multi-tiered systems of support
(MTSS)   3, 9, 10, 94, 119, 129,
136, 144, 152

needs
academic need   27, 32, 46
diverse needs   27
educational needs   36
emotional needs   27
individualized needs   37, 40, 42, 47
instructional   46
personal needs   32
social needs   27, 32
unique needs   18, 21, 24, 25, 38
vocational needs   29
wide range of needs   27

parent   181
parent input   39
placement   37, 44
planning   79
present level of academic achievement
and functional performance
(PLAAFP)   25, 37, 38, 48, 52–5,
57, 61, 64, 65, 67, 73, 76, 80, 85,
89, 92, 93, 107–9
prior written notice   24
process   186, 202
professional development/
learning   30, 31, 153
progress   22, 182, 194
de minimus   22
monitor(ing)   4, 9, 27, 37, 40, 52,
82, 85, 104, 113, 115, 116, 120,
124, 127, 144, 147, 151
reasonably calculated   22, 38, 40
substantive (standard)   22, 38
prompting   7

regulation(s)   21, 32
related service providers   66, 92, 94,
140, 142, 149, 152, 155, 160, 163,
172, 187, 205

related services   23, 42
resources   137, 140
response to intervention   9

scaffolded supports   9
school improvement   151
school policies   142
school-wide assessment
framework   135, 137, 139, 144
school-wide Positive Behavior
Interventions & Supports
(SWPBIS)   141, 142
school-wide team   138
screening measures   105
self-advocacy/self-determination   24,
92, 127
self-Questioning Strategy   38, 76
self-regulated   81
self-regulation   94, 95
services and supports   25
short-term objectives   102, 114, 116
social narratives   78
special education services/setting   37,
42, 44
special educator(s)   53, 59, 66, 68, 73,
81, 152, 154, 163–5, 173, 175,
177, 186, 187, 191, 192, 194, 195,
205, 206, 208, 212, 218
strategies   7
supplementary aids and services   37,
42, 43, 48, 52
supports for School Personnel   42, 43

transition   37, 47, 48, 52
transparency   23, 24
two-step test   50, 54, 80, 147

unique needs   11
Universal Design for Learning
(UDL)   3, 5, 12, 94
universal screeners   144

verbal think-aloud   74

About the Authors

David F. Bateman, PhD, is a principal researcher at the American Institutes for Research and professor emeritus at Shippensburg University of Pennsylvania. He is a former due process hearing officer in Pennsylvania for hundreds of hearings. He uses his knowledge of litigation related to special education to assist school districts in providing appropriate supports for students with disabilities and to prevent and recover from due process hearings. He has been a classroom teacher of students with learning disabilities, behavior disorders, intellectual disabilities, and hearing impairments, as well as a building administrator. Dr. Bateman earned a PhD in special education from the University of Kansas. Over the past twenty-eight years, he has either been a hearing officer or consultant on over 1,100 special education lawsuits. He frequently is a keynote presenter at principals and administrator conferences. He has recently co-authored the following books: *A Principal's Guide to Special Education*, *A Teacher's Guide to Special Education*, *Charting the Course: Special Education in Charter Schools*, *Special Education Leadership: Building Effective Programming in Schools*, *Current Trends and Legal Issues in Special Education*, and *A School Board Members Guide to Special Education*. He has also recently worked as the neutral fact-finder in the class action lawsuit involving the Oregon Department of Education. After the 2017 Supreme Court decision in *Endrew F. . . .*, the US Department of Education reached out to him to develop a training module for administrators on legally compliant IEPs. For more information please see SpecialEdConsultant.org.

Michael N. Faggella-Luby, PhD, is a professor of special education in the Department of Teaching & Learning Sciences at Texas Christian University. He also holds joint appointments as core faculty in the Alice Neeley Special Education Research & Service (ANSERS) Institute and the Andrews Institute for Research in Mathematics & Science Education. Dr. Faggella-Luby's research focuses on improving educational outcomes for students with learning disabilities, particularly in the areas of literacy, cognitive learning strategies, and postsecondary education. For almost two decades, Dr. Faggella-Luby's research has significantly contributed to the understanding of postsecondary education for students with disabilities, particularly through his co-authorship of the PASS Taxonomy, a pivotal framework for understanding research on disability services in higher education. Dr. Faggella-Luby has received two national awards for his research on embedded strategy instruction. Dr. Faggella-Luby is a past president of the Division for Learning Disabilities of the Council for Exceptional Children and an associate editor of the *Journal of Learning Disabilities*. His first book, *Data Rules: Evaluating Teaching with Objective Reflection*, was published by ASCD in fall 2024.

Lisa Goran, PhD, CCC-SLP, is a teaching professor at the University of Missouri, serving as the Chair of the Department of Special Education. She is a Speech-Language Pathologist who has worked in school, clinical, and private practice settings. She also is a special educator who taught students with disabilities in self-contained, resource, and co-taught general education classrooms, and served as a building-level department chair for special education in a school setting. Dr. Goran earned a PhD in special education from the University of Missouri. She is active in national- and state-level professional organizations related to speech-language pathology (ASHA; MSHA), special education (CEC: DLD, TED, CASE, DR, DEBH; MO-CASE), and teacher education (AACTE; MACTE). She recently co-authored a book, *Related Services in Special Education: Working Together as a Team*, and contributed chapters in several books including: *Advances in Special Education, Legally Compliant IEPs* and *Sexuality Education for Students with Disabilities*. She also recently co-authored an article for a special issue of *TEACHING Exceptional Children*, focusing on legally proficient IEPs.

Margaret P. Weiss, PhD, is an associate professor of special education in the Division of Special Education and disAbility Research at George Mason University. Before completing her PhD at the University of Virginia, Dr. Weiss was a special education teacher at the elementary, middle, and high school levels. She taught as a self-contained classroom teacher, a co-teacher, and department chair in North Carolina, New Hampshire, and Virginia. Dr. Weiss's main areas of research are in co-teaching and pre-service teacher preparation, and she has published this research in multiple peer-reviewed journals. With a colleague, she has developed a model of co-teaching that incorporates three elements, including specially designed instruction, and that clearly identifies the active role of the special education teacher. Dr. Weiss has served as president of the Teacher Education Division of the Council for Exceptional Children and has recently worked with administrators and teachers to improve practice in delivering SDI to students with disabilities through workshops and coaching.